EARLY PRAISE FOR *EYES WIDE OPEN*

"In *Eyes Wide Open* Mariana Caplan has given us a brilliant and clear understanding of the discernment needed for traversing the spiritual path. Spiritual seekers of all types will find this book immensely useful."

—LAMA PALDEN, founder of Sukhasiddhi Foundation

"Discrimination is one of the most important qualities needed on the spiritual journey, and yet it is most difficult to develop. Here are simple, clear guidelines to help us separate truth from falsehood, and avoid many of the pitfalls that await the traveler. This is real, grounded wisdom needed by all contemporary seekers: a book to read and re-read."

—LLEWELLYN VAUGHAN-LEE, PhD, Sufi teacher and author

"A daring, brilliant, groundbreaking look at spirituality in the modern world. With deft elegance, Caplan shows us that psychological transformation and spiritual awakening are inseparably one process. Detailing with brutal honesty the myriad spiritual pathologies we contemporary spiritual seekers engage in on a daily basis, she reveals the profound and life-changing awakenings that can occur when we expose and dismantle our neurotic, narcissistic exploitations of the great traditions."

—REGINALD A. RAY, author of *Touching Enlightenment* and *Indestructible Truth*

"Mariana Caplan is an authoritative pioneer in the study of 'the pathologies of the path,' and this book will be of interest and benefit to seekers and teachers alike. The outcome of a combination of personal experience, sheer intelligence, honesty, long years of research, and contact with original and unconventional teachers, *Eyes Wide Open* is both well-written and entertaining."

—CLAUDIO NARANJO, MD, and EdD, author of *Character and Neurosis*

PRAISE FOR THE WORK OF MARIANA CAPLAN

From *Do You Need a Guru*:
"[Mariana Caplan] unapologetically tackles the most difficult, controversial, nitty-gritty issues without hedging, flinching, or smoothing over any of the rough edges."

—JOHN WELWOOD, author of *Toward a Psychology of Awakening*

From *To Touch Is to Live*:
"An important book that brings to the forefront the fundamentals of a healthy world. We must all touch more."

—PATCH ADAMS, MD, founder of
the Gesundheit Institute, author of *House Calls*

"Highly recommended. Beautifully written. Practical advice to bring the heart into the world and the world into the heart—a formula for the peace we all long for."

—STEPHEN AND ONDREA LEVINE, authors of
Who Dies? and *Embracing the Beloved*

From *Halfway Up the Mountain*:
"Caplan's illuminating book calls into question the motives of the spiritual snake handlers of the modern age and urges seekers to pay the price of traveling the hard road to true enlightenment."

—*PUBLISHERS WEEKLY*

"*Halfway Up the Mountain* is a much-needed study of the pitfalls on the spiritual path. Helping us to recognize these distortions, she points us toward the real Truth for which we hunger. I would recommend this book to anyone who is serious about their spiritual practice."

—LLEWELLYN VAUGHAN-LEE, PhD, Sufi teacher and author

Eyes Wide Open

Mariana Caplan, PhD

Eyes Wide Open

Cultivating Discernment on the Spiritual Path

SOUNDS TRUE
BOULDER, COLORADO

Sounds True

Boulder CO 80306

Cover and book design by Dean Olson

Printed in Canada

Library of Congress Cataloging-in-Publication Data

Caplan, Mariana, 1969-

  Eyes wide open : cultivating discernment on the spiritual path / Mariana Caplan.

    p. cm.

  Includes bibliographical references.

  ISBN 978-1-59179-732-6 (pbk.)

  1. Spirituality. I. Title.

  BL624.C3455 2009

  204—dc22

                       2009011489

10 9 8 7 6 5 4 3 2 1

I offer this book to my teacher, Lee Lozowick, who taught me about spiritual discernment; to my father and mother, Herbert and Mollie Caplan, who gave me the gift of life; and to my readers, who gave me the reason to write.

It is better to travel well than to arrive.

—THE BUDDHA

Contents

Foreword

For the first time in history, large numbers of people have access to the most advanced of spiritual teachings, making it possible to become involved in spiritual practices previously available only to the select few: hermits, monastics, and saints. This is a wonderful opportunity, which has opened up a new possibility—that large numbers of people can awaken to their essential nature while at the same time living an ordinary life.

Yet at the same time, this also opens up a whole range of new pitfalls, misunderstandings, perversions, and misguided quests—which Mariana Caplan has insightfully explored and catalogued in this book. If you are interested in living and practicing the kind of integrated spirituality that she advocates, then you can certainly benefit from this guide to developing one of the most indispensable ingredients of an embodied spirituality: discernment.

Even under the best of circumstances, the path of spiritual development is not as straightforward as it might at first seem. One reason for this is that it introduces us to a higher order of truth, which is often at odds with our ordinary ways of thinking and perceiving. In Buddhism, these two levels of reality are called absolute and relative truth. Certain perspectives deriving from the absolute level—such as "nothing is real," "let go of your mind," "good and bad are but illusions," "just drop the ego and surrender"—can easily turn into instruments of self-deception, perversion, and great harm when applied in a wrong or confused way.

Encountering a spiritual teacher, teaching, or practice can open up inner riches that feel intoxicating, much like falling in love. When we fall in love, it is tempting to think, *"This is love; I've found it at last."* Yet early infatuations are but a glimpse of a much deeper, larger dimension of love that requires a journey of inner transformation to realize fully. Just as falling in love hardly qualifies us for mastering the challenges of an ongoing relationship or marriage, likewise easy glimpses of spiritual truths are a far cry from true spiritual attainment. Real, embodied spiritual development happens through a relentless process of self-confrontation that requires us to move through all our fears and resistances. This involves the purification of obstacles—all the old wounds, defenses, pretences, demands, fixations, addictions, and denials we carry with us from the past.

Yet there is now a superficial spirituality widespread in the West that offers immediate glimpses into one's essence, while requiring little else of the aspirant. It preaches a one-sided absolutism, often in the name of Advaita Vedanta, where all you need to do is to awaken in the moment to your divine nature, and all will be revealed. This is certainly appealing in a culture geared toward instant results, where people do not want to hear about how slow, arduous, and demanding the spiritual path actually is. No, let us be done with all the old spiritual practices. We don't even need practice, according to the neo-Vedantins: Practice is an effort that only postpones our awakening, because when you practice you are doing it to get somewhere. Why not save time and just wake up on the spot? It's right here, so forget about practice. Just be.

This one-sided view, as is common with so many of the pitfalls of the path, is based on a certain truth: Yes, it is true, we can recognize our ultimate nature in a brief moment at any time. Yes, it is rather easy once you know what you are looking for and how to relax into it. But no, this does not constitute a spiritual path, because it does not come to grips with the other order of reality: the relative complexities of karma, conditioning, ingrained habitual patterns, unconscious identities, psychological wounds, and self-deception of all kinds.

A simplistic formula like the neo-Vedantin admonition "Be still and just be" is like saying "Just love, and relationship, will be easy." Yes, from an ultimate perspective, the spiritual journey never needs to be made, because we are already perfect in our essence just as we are. Yet on the relative level, where we are unconsciously identified with all kinds of hidden demons, ghosts, and tyrants, the practices of the path do more than just reveal our true nature. They are also designed to help free us from these inner obstacles to truth, love, and wisdom. (To further address these obstacles, as I've argued in much of my work, dedicated psychological work can also play an important, if not indispensable, role in spiritual development.)

What then is the best way to develop the discernment necessary for sorting through the complexities of absolute and relative truth, and recognizing what to cultivate and what to refrain from on the spiritual path? According to the Eastern traditions, the essential nature of awareness is like a cosmic mirror that equally reflects and reveals the whole of phenomena—true and false, real and unreal, clear and confused—without holding onto or rejecting one side or the other. Such an all-embracing, all-inclusive awareness might at first seem the opposite of discernment. Yet Padmasambhava, the father of Tibetan Buddhism, suggests otherwise in his famous words: "My mind is as vast as the sky, and my attention to detail is as fine as a grain of sand." According to Padmasambhava, the vast mind of open, mirror-like awareness, which welcomes and allows the whole play of our experience, is also the basis for precise discrimination in the relative situations of our lives. For it is only through seeing and knowing the whole panorama of what is real and what is unreal inside us that we can recognize what to cultivate and what to refrain from. Choiceless awareness and discriminating wisdom are equally indispensable for spiritual development.

What will allow us to open up and expand the conditioned mind while sharpening the sword of discrimination is a meditative practice that can help us look deeply into the nature and process of our ongoing experience. Allying oneself with a genuine teaching, an authentic teacher, and a lineage of practice that has proven effective over many generations is also very helpful.

In the meantime, a book like this can be a start toward recognizing and avoiding many of the perversions, and misunderstandings that lead to the false starts, blind alleys, useless detours, and crash-and-burn scenarios that are so common along the spiritual journey.

—John Welwood
Mill Valley, CA
May 2009

Acknowledgments

I would like to acknowledge the many people who have helped and supported this project. First and foremost, I would like to thank my writing "angel," personal editor, and friend, Nancy Lewis, who has generously poured forth her love, attention, and discerning scrutiny in support of my writing for many years—and helped me birth this book.

There have been so many teachers, mentors, and spiritual friends whose guidance on the path and input in this book, direct or indirect, have been invaluable, including my own teacher, Lee Lozowick, of the Western Baul Tradition; Sufi sheikh Llewellyn Vaughan-Lee; John Welwood; Arnaud Desjardins; Jorge Ferrer, and Gilles Farcet. I also want to thank my posse of girlfriends around the world—Vipassana, Devi, Bhavani, Karen, Simone, Clelia, Joanne, Regina, Lesley, Kyla, Valerie, Marianne, Ute, and Ines. They are my heroines, my anchors, and the proof of my belief in the possibility of a better world.

I would like to thank my family, including my father, Herb Caplan, and brothers Joel and Nathan, who tirelessly support their eccentric daughter and sister. I thank my mother, Mollie Caplan, who passed away many years ago but who wrote in her journal when I was a baby that I would come to write books one day. Finally, I would like to thank the staff at Sounds True, particularly Kelly Notaras, Tami Simon, and

Jaime Schwalb for their diligence, respect, and vision. To all of you, my most heartfelt thanks. Your generosity abounds.

ACKNOWLEDGMENTS

Introduction

Eyes Wide Open—The Path of Discernment

*Everything we shut our eyes to, everything we run away from,
everything we deny, denigrate, or despise, serves to defeat
us in the end. What seems nasty, painful, evil, can become a
source of beauty, joy, and strength, if faced with an open mind.*

—HENRY MILLER, *Tropic of Capricorn*

I was nineteen years old and in my sophomore year of college in Ann Arbor, Michigan, when I finally learned there was such a thing as a spiritual path. Like so many young people who long for something greater, I had searched for years through whatever means were available to me—from alcohol to political activism to travel. I had begun my travels when I was fifteen, and by the time I hit college I had traveled through much of Central America and Europe, yet my thirst was not quenched—it had only increased. I was not finding the deep answers I was looking for.

The summer before my nineteenth birthday, while traveling in Central America, I met a man who had been traveling the world for twenty years—something I had dreamed of doing—and I was curious to know if he had found the answers he sought. At the end of several long days of conversation, I asked him, "Why do you travel?"

"To find freedom," he told me.

"Have you found it?" I persisted. "Does the freedom to go wherever you want and do whatever you want make you free?"

"Not really," he confessed.

When I returned to college I discovered what was then Ann Arbor's only spiritual bookstore. I clearly remember the first time I walked into the shop. My eyes darted quickly from shelf to shelf. I was dazzled and astonished by the subjects of the books: meditation, psychology, Tibetan Buddhism, Zen, Sufism, mature mysticism, shamanism, self-help, metaphysics, and more. I understood for the first time that there was a spiritual path; in fact, there were many of them. And I understood I was not alone. People throughout the world thirsted for something greater, and there were many well-trodden paths that one could follow. I was home . . . or was I?

On the one hand, I did feel I'd come home. On the other hand, I had no idea where to begin. There were hundreds of paths and thousands of books before me—how was a human being to begin this journey? Once embarked, how could one proceed with intelligence and clarity? How could I discern between this seemingly endless array of choices, how could I know what was right for me, and how could I know if I was fooling myself?

As I was to learn over the next twenty years, these questions do not necessarily get any easier to answer. Instead, they ripen into increasing degrees of subtlety. As my commitment to the spiritual path deepened, it became increasingly critical that I learn to see clearly, with my eyes wide open, so I could move through the journey of life with passion, creativity, and meaning—in a way that makes a difference. Spiritual discernment, called *viveka khyātir* in Sanskrit, is said to be the "crowning wisdom" on the spiritual path.

The *Yoga Sūtras of Patañjali* say that the cultivation of discernment is so powerful that it has the capacity to destroy ignorance and address the very source of suffering. According to *Merriam-Webster's Collegiate Dictionary,* to discern is "to recognize or identify as separate and distinct." Discrimination, its synonym, "stresses the power to distinguish and select what is true or appropriate or excellent." Those who possess spiritual discernment have learned this skill in relationship to spiritual matters, and they can consistently make intelligent, balanced, and excellent choices in their lives and in relationship to their spiritual development. Their eyes are wide open, and they see clearly.

Viveka khyātir is believed to be such a powerful tool that it has the capacity to pierce all levels of the physical, psychological, energetic, and subtle bodies of the human being. In *Light on the Yoga Sūtras of Patañjali,* B. K. S. Iyengar explains that through this unbroken flow of discriminating awareness, the spiritual practitioner:

> *conquers his body, controls his energy, retrains the movements of the mind, and develops sound judgment, from which he acts rightly and becomes luminous. From this luminosity he develops total awareness of the very core of his being, achieves supreme knowledge, and surrenders his self to the Supreme Soul.*[1]

This book is an attempt to go deep into the labyrinth of the spiritual path, to consider the possibility of a truly integrated, embodied, psychospiritual transformation. Together, we will explore how to meet the inevitable roadblocks we will encounter on the spiritual path, so we might live bold, intelligent, radiant lives of spiritual transformation. We will learn how investigating and evaluating different practices, paths, and teachers can help us make intelligent spiritual choices. And we will learn to distinguish between truth and falsity, between passion that binds us and passion that frees us.

When we were young children beginning to become curious about the big questions of life—such as death, how we got here, and the challenge of human emotion—few of us had a parent who sat us down and lovingly said, in essence:

> *You have come into a great mystery of immense joys and vast sorrows. You yourself are an expression of that great mystery. There are so many ways in which people learn to understand themselves and life, but what is most important is that you grow up and learn how to make your own choices—and that you make bright and radiant choices that will fulfill you and contribute to the world. I want to help you learn to make wise decisions in your life, particularly with respect to your spiritual journey. When you are old enough, I will introduce you to different spiritual and religious paths and practices. Meanwhile, while you are young, I will help you learn to navigate the emotional challenges that come with being human.*

Most of us never received such a wise and mature introduction to the immense challenges, privileges, and possibilities of the life we entered into. The adults in our lives didn't teach us how to make wise spiritual choices because, with rare exceptions, they didn't know how to do it themselves. Our schools didn't teach us how to manage our emotions because most teachers didn't know how to manage their own. In high school, there was no class offered that taught us how to understand our spiritual choices because there was no collective acknowledgement or appreciation of the value of educating the soul and spirit. If we have been fortunate enough to learn these things, we have either learned them on our own or have had the rare fortune to be guided by wise and mature elders.

Developing discernment doesn't prevent us from making mistakes, but it does help us learn life's lessons more clearly and quickly, turn challenges into opportunities, and avoid unnecessary obstacles. Discernment teaches us to live well, and when we die, we can do so feeling *I have lived a good life. I have gained as much self-awareness as I was capable of, and I have fulfilled a purpose on earth*. We can know that our lives have not been in vain, that we have touched—and have been profoundly touched by—life.

One of my mentors, the sociologist and bestselling author Joseph Chilton Pearce, says that when he wants to learn about a subject, he writes a book on it. He then waits to get his readers' feedback about his mistaken viewpoints, as well as the personal stories the book elicits. In 1999, I published my fourth book, *Halfway Up the Mountain: The Error of Premature Claims to Enlightenment*. Frankly, I was surprised by the widespread positive response to the book. I could not have imagined that people would be willing and eager to read more than five hundred pages of information about how we deceive ourselves and are deceived in the name of spiritual life. My next book, published in 2002, was titled *Do You Need a Guru? Understanding the Student-Teacher Relationship in an Era of False Prophets,* and it directly addressed the intricate challenges and complexities of the student-teacher relationship in contemporary Western culture.

Since these two books were published, I have met and received letters from hundreds of individuals who have dedicated their lives to the spiritual path. They have inevitably encountered self-deception and disillusionment—whether with themselves and their own tendencies toward egoic confusion, or with their spiritual teachers and communities. Opening my e-mail inbox, I routinely encounter moving stories of human beings who long for happiness, meaning, fulfillment, and truth, and who are boldly willing to face the obstacles to that truth no matter how much it hurts. They are warriors of the spirit—fellow travelers on the spiritual path who are committed to creating a better world and using their lives as an opportunity to understand themselves in endlessly deepening ways. No matter what they have been through, they have not given up their optimism or their desire to grow spiritually. They see that disillusionment itself has awakened them to deeper levels of truth, and they have learned that discernment is a necessary skill to cultivate on the spiritual path.

Since I wrote those two books, some of my perceptions have changed, and others have not. What has not changed is my perception of the pervasive self-delusion, confusion, superficiality, and materialism that permeate much of contemporary Western spirituality, especially the New Age variety. I have allowed my heart to be broken many times over by the hundreds of stories of disillusionment and betrayal I have heard: stories about betrayal by a teacher, about spiritual scandal, and about people discovering the depth of their own psychological wounding and the ways in which they have hurt others through their own spiritual confusion. I have also watched my own life unfold, and I continue to discover ever subtler layers of blindness that obscure clarity in many important aspects of my life. I have seen that, in the name of spirituality, I continue to deceive myself at increasingly refined levels. I see this tendency in myself as well as in the lives of spiritual teachers, psychotherapists, seekers, and practitioners. Life on the spiritual path in no way exempts us from human error, and it ideally teaches us to be more accountable for our confusion and mistakes.

The defining distinction between this book and the previous two is that in this one the finger is pointed not outward, but wholly toward ourselves. This book is not about gurus and spiritual teachers, it's about you and me—though "you and me" includes those very same gurus and spiritual teachers, because absolutely no one is exempt from the pitfalls and trappings that are part and parcel of the spiritual journey. This book is about taking full responsibility for the whole of our lives, including our intrinsic radiance and our greatest spiritual potential—as well as our confusion and undeveloped knowledge.

Self-deception unfolds with increasing subtlety as we move from our false selves toward the more authentic, truer aspects of our experience. The slipperiness of the spiritual path cannot be underestimated; its pitfalls are as numerous as the steps that can be taken, and all of us fall into them. Still, the more we know about the road, the more able we are to avoid its potholes.

The Italian psychiatrist and founder of psychosynthesis, Roberto Assagioli, suggests that a complete psychotherapy would not only treat psychopathology but also foster spiritual awakening, and then deal intelligently with the difficulties and new levels of challenge that such an awakening brings. As we unearth new levels of our consciousness, we inevitably also uncover that which is unwhole and unhealed within us at personal, familial, cultural, and historical levels. This is not a problem to be feared or a wrong to be righted, but a necessary and healthy aspect of spiritual unfolding that must be met with increasingly potent and effective discernment.

Several years ago, I went to visit the Buddhist teacher Jack Kornfield. "I have a question for you," he said. "Are *you* halfway up the mountain?" He was not the first to have posed this question to me over the years, and my internal response has always been the same: I am so much *less* than halfway up the mountain! It would be wildly presumptuous to claim to be even halfway up, much less to claim any type of "arrival." I have come to understand that the possibilities of spiritual unfolding are literally endless, and the mountain of spiritual possibility does not have a summit.

I believe that most of us live our lives playing in the foothills of the metaphorical spiritual mountain. Regardless of whether we have been labeled "spiritual teachers," have had hundreds of spiritual epiphanies, or have been sincere spiritual practitioners for thirty years, we are all still learning to tie our shoelaces and step carefully. Sometimes we get high enough on the "mountain" to have some view, but we also trip and fall continually. The path is infinite, and human integration is an awesome and laborious task. There are a few extraordinary masters and saints—some of whom are mentioned in this book—who have seen and learned to abide in a truly great vision. But the rest of us are left with the humble task of deep and lifelong self-study and the creation of spiritual alliances so that together we can learn how to walk this path with diligence and passion.

For a human being who hungers for truth, what is most beautiful is that which is most truthful. If the road to truth means having to learn what is untrue and to face unconsciousness and obstacles within ourselves, the lover of truth gladly accepts this challenge. Each time we expose and face that which is untrue, we are that much closer to what is true.

This book is intended to support seekers and serious spiritual practitioners from all traditions. Through my personal and professional research I have had the privilege of meeting and spending extended periods of time with many individuals whom I consider to be the world's greatest spiritual teachers, psychologists, yogis, healers, and religious leaders. Many of the quotes you will read here are from personal interviews and conversations with these individuals. The teachings included in this book come from research, experiments, and experiences with many different spiritual traditions and paths, including Sufism, yogic traditions, Tantric Buddhism, Judaism, Hinduism, Taoism, Fourth Way traditions, Shamanism, and the Diamond Approach, as well as the Western Baul tradition under the guidance of my teacher, Lee Lozowick. I have also immersed myself deeply in Western psychological traditions—both traditional approaches and cutting-edge body-centered psychotherapies. My deep wish is that this book will be relevant to people from all religious and spiritual traditions as well as from many psychological schools, and that the gaps in my knowledge of certain religious traditions will not eclipse the relevance of the basic principles of spiritual discernment considered here.

A book about discernment is one of questions rather than answers. It attempts to address some of the most challenging questions on the spiritual path from a variety of perspectives, so we can learn how to ask the right questions at the right times and to discriminate truth from falsity. We are called to "live the questions," in the words of poet Rainer Maria Rilke, so that we may "gradually, without noticing it, live along some distant day into the answer."[2]

～

"May you be born in interesting times," says a purported Chinese expression. Whether this is to be interpreted as a blessing or a curse, we have indeed been born into "interesting" times. The planet's resources are disappearing, and the fate of the earth itself is in question. There is widespread crime, poverty, and ignorance. Religions are breaking down, and many young people are choosing not to follow their parents' religions. We are born in a time in which there is little or no education about the body, emotions, or spirit. When the renowned Buddhist teacher and peace activist Sister Chân Không came to America for the first time, after having helped countless orphans in the Vietnam War, she exclaimed that nothing she had seen in her years of work with orphans neared the poverty of spirit and spiritual alienation she found in Western culture. Those who have walked the spiritual path in cultures throughout the world over many centuries have not been exempt from scandal, disillusionment, and the very challenges that being human brings to the path, but different cultural conditions and historical eras do bring with them distinct challenges.

According to Sufi sheikh Llewellyn Vaughan-Lee, one of the unique characteristics of our era is that "we have forgotten that we have forgotten": not only have we lost touch with our deeper spiritual nature, but often we do not even know that this is the case. How can we remember who we really are and discern how we need to grow if we do not even know that we have forgotten something?

The psychologist Abraham Maslow wrote, "Certainly it seems more and more clear that what we call 'normal' in psychology is really a psychopathology of the average, so undramatic and so widely spread that we don't even notice it ordinarily." We are living in confused times when we are so misguided in our values that we do not even realize how imbalanced we have become.

Still another aspect of the "interesting times" we are living in has to do with the mass importation of non-Western techniques into Western culture. The new and important vistas these spiritual possibilities offer us also bring with them their own set of challenges. Each mystical tradition arises from a particular cultural context that includes family and social structures, language, and relationship to the earth. The Western psyche is markedly different from either the Eastern or indigenous psyche, and not all aspects of a given Eastern or shamanic tradition will be applicable to the Western psyche. In the case of tantra, yoga, and many popular shamanic practices, the greater spiritual context is frequently "lost in translation" during the importation process.

It is important to recognize that most contemporary spiritual traditions simply were not designed to penetrate the cellular, psychological wounding caused by the type of trauma that is so prevalent in Western culture that arises from broken homes, disconnection from our bodies and nature, and alienation from authentic sources of spiritual wisdom. Any attempt to transplant Eastern-based and indigenous spiritual technologies—as transcultural and objective as their wisdom appears to be—must take into consideration the sometimes radically different psychological, cultural, and historical circumstances in which those technologies arose and were appropriate.

Llewellyn Vaughan-Lee says of the interesting times we are living in:

> *There is a veil that humanity has created that distorts everything. Even if you look inward, everything is distorted. There is nothing you can do about it. It's like a hall of mirrors. If you say anything, it becomes something else. Human beings have created this veil, and people do spiritual practice in this veil, and they make spiritual paths in it.*[3]

The presence of veils is not in itself a problem; rather, it is a challenge that needs to be addressed by cultivating discernment and becoming conscious of the complexity and the variables involved in this process. Interesting times require creative solutions. If the veils that obstruct our clarity are many, the cultivation of discernment is that much more important. This book addresses many of the distinct challenges that we as spiritual seekers and practitioners in the Western world face during these interesting times, and it considers the subtle distinctions we must make to navigate the possibilities and potholes of the spiritual path more effectively.

Chapter 1, "What Is Spirituality Anyway?" begins with an overview of the contemporary Western spiritual supermarket and considers basic issues such as why there is such a prevalence of spiritual scandals today and whether enlightenment is really the point of the spiritual path at all. Chapter 2, "Spiritually Transmitted Disease," catalogs many of the common traps the contemporary spiritual seeker is likely to encounter along his or her journey, while Chapter 3, "The Posture of the Mind," considers the attitudes we must cultivate in order to travel the spiritual path with discernment.

Chapters 4 and 5, "The Psychology of Ego" and "Spiritual Materialism and Spiritual Bypassing," offer an inquiry into the relationship between ego, psychology, and karma—and the traps that arise when our development in these areas is uneven, confused, and out of balance.

The following chapters explore the value of discernment as a transformational tool that helps us turn crises, as well as all other aspects of life, into opportunities for spiritual development. Chapter 6, "The Healing Crisis," reveals how the

journey of descent, which most people who commit themselves to the spiritual path eventually encounter, leads them
to the capacity to discern and penetrate broader and deeper
aspects and dimensions of their experience. Chapter 7, "The
Tantric Principle," considers how the careful application of
discernment can literally turn internal and external poisons
into medicine and ordinary experience into the extraordinary.
Chapter 8, "Pandora's Secret: Demystifying the Shadow,"
further illustrates how the application of discernment to our
shadow selves reveals a radiant possibility for potent and integrated spiritual transformation.

Chapters 9 and 10, "The Body as Bodhi Tree: The
Imperative of Embodiment" and "The Union of Psychology
and Spirituality," explore the living integration between psychology and spirituality and how we assimilate and express
this integration through the body.

A book on discernment would not be complete without
considering its application to the student-teacher relationship,
which is one of the most difficult aspects of spiritual life to navigate with clarity. Chapter 11, "The Question of the Teacher,"
attempts a balanced view of the unique spiritual benefits of
working with a teacher as well as the psychological challenges
this relationship presents to both student and teacher. Finally,
in Chapter 12, "Om Mani Padme Grow Up!" we close our
consideration of discernment by reflecting on what it means
to grow up—both psychologically and spiritually—and move
toward authentic spiritual maturity.

When I was twenty-two and just beginning to explore topics in
spirituality more deeply, I went to a seminar taught by Buddhist
teachers and writers Stephen and Ondrea Levine. They were

heroes of mine, dedicating their lives to self-knowledge, consciousness, and service to humanity. Throughout the weekend I drank in with great thirst the wisdom they had clearly earned through intense and uncompromised lives of spiritual practice, ceaseless study and experimentation, and hard-won humility. Toward the end of the weekend, a woman raised her hand and lamented that, whereas Stephen and Ondrea had become such model practitioners, she herself was too screwed up from her past to ever achieve such depth and wisdom.

Stephen looked at the young woman with such tenderness, and then, to our great surprise, he shared the story of the harrowing pasts he and Ondrea had each lived. By the time they met, he said, they were both in rehab—one of them for alcohol abuse, the other for drug addiction. One spent afternoons hitting their head on a rock; the other suffered deep psychotic states. Then Stephen looked straight out into the audience, as if speaking to each of us individually, and said, "Look. It's pretty simple: Buddha and Jesus were Joe and Mike down the street. The only difference between them and you is that they made a powerful decision about their lives and stuck to it. You've got to believe me. If we could come this far, *anybody* can."

"I teach what I need to learn," said T. Krishnamacharya, the forefather of modern yoga. I offer this consideration of spiritual discernment so that I, and all of us, can move toward greater spiritual clarity in our lives. May the fruits of our shared study and inquiry make even a small contribution to the decrease of suffering and the increase of peace on the planet.

Chapter 1

~

What Is
Spirituality
Anyway?

There is no question that there is an unseen world.
The problem is how far is it from midtown
and how late is it open?
—WOODY ALLEN, *Without Feathers*

When I was nineteen years old and on an airplane to Mexico City to apprentice with a renowned Aztec shaman—fancying myself an up-and-coming neo-Carlos Castaneda—I wrote in my diary, "I am confident that if I practice really hard, learn all the rituals, and do everything the shaman suggests, I will be enlightened within three years."

In addition to exposing me to powerful Aztec rituals and introducing me to exceptional people, my shaman, Kuiz, turned out to be an alcoholic who repeatedly and aggressively attempted to extract sexual favors from me as the price for his teachings. When I demonstrated my unwillingness to pay in the commerce of sex, he tried to coerce me into giving him the remaining three hundred dollars I had saved for the rest of my summer in Mexico. Needless to say, I learned more about spiritual "endarkenment" than spiritual enlightenment on that trip, and that was only the beginning.

Kuiz was my first formal spiritual teacher. Fortunately, I did not give up on teachers after that shocking disillusionment, nor did I give up after disappointment with the next one—or the one after that. I went on to study with transpersonal psychologists, self-proclaimed goddesses and witches, Jews, Buddhists, Hindus, and Native Americans. Even at a young age and with little experience, I knew that the human psyche and spirit were vast and complex and that one needed a profound and rare quality of guidance to learn to navigate the labyrinth of the inner world and become a person of knowledge and wisdom.

Although I did not have a term for it, I somehow understood that I must learn what I later came to understand as the need to cultivate spiritual discernment. I learned that there were well-developed teachings and methodologies to guide one along the spiritual path. But as a young person with a hungry heart, I didn't yet have a road map that would lead me to the elusive destination where I wanted to arrive but had no name for. I had no instruction manual to help me understand how to "do" my life. *Enlightenment* was a term that was tossed about freely in my circles, but what it was, who could help me find it, where it was best to look for it, who and what should be avoided along the way, and what subtle traps lay within me all remained utter mysteries. Discernment was something that would be discovered by trial and error.

It is now two decades after that first trip to Mexico, and I eventually found a spiritual teacher of integrity whom I have studied with most of my adult life. Through as many errors as I have had trials, I have learned something about discernment and how to make distinctions among various paths, practices, teachers, and internal processes. Whereas each human journey is unique—and no one can walk the path for another or guard others from making their own mistakes and learning their own lessons—we can learn how to cultivate discernment. In so doing, we learn to make increasingly intelligent and effective choices for ourselves and minimize unnecessary detours and suffering caused by a lack of education and awareness. The "sword of discernment," depicted in many spiritual traditions, is our greatest protection on the spiritual path.

As contemporary spiritual movements continue to evolve in Western culture, there is an increasing number of spiritual schools and approaches that focus on different aspects of spiritual integration. Drawing on the wisdom of many traditions and practices, this book offers an integral model of transformation applicable to practitioners of all religions and spiritual traditions—a model that specifically takes into account the challenging times we are living in, the subtleties involved in working with the egoic mind and Western psychology, and the imperative of integrating our transformation on all levels.

In the course of this book we will consider a wide variety of processes, perspectives, and principles that most people who engage a spiritual path over a long period of time are likely to encounter. Regardless of the tradition in which they practice, sincere spiritual aspirants will face challenges such as self-deception, breakdown and healing crises, and disillusionment with the dream of enlightenment and the teachers who proclaim to be enlightened. The immense task of navigating the complexity of working with the psyche and ego alone requires a fine-tuned capacity for discernment.

"Keen perception and judgment," "the quality of being able to grasp and comprehend what is obscure," "the trait of judging wisely and objectively" are a few of the ways in which discernment is defined by world dictionaries. Our task as spiritual practitioners is to learn to see with clarity, to keep our eyes wide open, to distinguish truth from untruth, and to bring to the light of awareness that which is unconscious within us.

In these times, navigating the spiritual path with clarity and wise judgment can be a daunting task, and every human journey comes with its own unique needs. The spiritual supermarket is brightly lit and packed with an overwhelming quantity of merchandise. Making choices that are healthy, nourishing, and economical at any point on one's journey can be challenging. Even those who have been engaging spiritual practice for many years will inevitably be faced with the challenge of discerning which of the plethora of practices and teachers available is the most effective option to deepen their practice at a given stage of their lives.

To initiate our consideration of discernment as an essential tool on the spiritual path, we begin with a survey of the state of contemporary spirituality in the Western world. How have spirituality and enlightenment changed from a search of the soul to big business? What propaganda about spirituality and enlightenment are we being sold in the spiritual marketplace? Why have so many great gurus risen to fame and then catapulted into scandal, leaving once-devout aspirants disillusioned by the spiritual path and opting for ordinary lives? Why has the Dalai Lama captivated the world, and why is Buddhism such an attractive and popular path? What *is* enlightenment anyway? And what is it that we really want?

Nothing is so hungry as the human heart. A craving and longing for spiritual as well as human fulfillment stirs so deeply within us that most of us do not dare acknowledge its presence for fear it will consume us. We sense a volcano of stored potentiality stirring beneath the surface of our own consciousness. We sense that universes exist within us. We intuit our own subterranean existence. We are dying to be born: to release the unharnessed potential within us, to transcend our limitations, to discover an intimacy within ourselves that we have tasted through our life experience or intuited through dreams. This longing lives in the very fiber of our cells.

Unable to even name this hunger, most of us simply suppress it and go on about our predictable, mechanical lives. As my friend Zak, a Bollywood film producer, once told me, "I do not dare to ask the first question of myself, because I know that it would open the door to thousands—millions—more questions, and I'm afraid it would destroy my life as I know it."

And it might. But for many of us there comes a point at which we cannot deny this hunger. Our personal suffering is too great. Our minds torment us; our lives are not working out as we imagined, or they're working out on a mundane level, but we still have not found the deeper joy we sense is possible. Our conscience gnaws at us, and we can no longer deny the need to know what our yet unlived potential consists of. And so we go in search of some form of guidance or practice that will help us feed our hungry hearts, and we find ourselves on what is loosely referred to as "the spiritual path."

For others of us, it seems that the path reaches toward us, inserts itself into our lives. We are just going about our ordinary lives when some person, book, or experience arrives in the midst of it and rocks our world, speaking to us too loudly to deny. It comes as a great revelation yet feels so intimately familiar. The spiritual path is often like that. Something seemingly "new" arrives in our lives, and yet we sense that it has always been with us.

Whether we were searching knowingly or not, finding the spiritual path is often a time of great celebration in the human heart. It comes as a private and intimate rite of passage: *I have been found.* Often it brings with it illuminating experiences or insights. The path seems easy and obvious. All we must do is study, understand, quiet the mind, and do some practices, and in time, enduring peace of mind and self-knowledge will be ours.

"And God is amused you once tried to be a saint," writes the Persian mystic Hafiz. If we are fortunate, the initial insight of spiritual life, the great spiritual honeymoon, will last as long as the honeymoon phase of a great romance: months, perhaps years. Eventually, a commitment is made between one's limited self and one's limitless self, or between oneself and God, or Truth, and then the profound work of the path begins.

The Spiritual Marketplace

When we initially become interested in the spiritual path, we are wise to heed the caution, "Buyer beware," as authentic spirituality is often co-opted and manipulated into a commodity that is bought and sold in the marketplace. Spirituality is not only a path to liberation, truth, and compassion; it is also big business. Spirituality has mixed with capitalist culture to such a degree that there now exists a literal "economy of spirit," which is surprisingly easy to mistake for genuine spirituality.

In his article "Yogis Behaving Badly," journalist Paul Keegan writes that in 2002 there were an estimated 18 million practitioners of modern yoga in the United States, and the market for healthy, environmentally friendly products was estimated to be about $230 billion. Yoga mats can be purchased at Kmart and Wal-Mart and even in many supermarkets and roadside service stations—perhaps for those who wish to practice yoga *āsanas* in their cars? Many large spiritual retreat centers offering classes in everything from conscious divorce to mindful knitting are working with multimillion-dollar budgets. Plastic buddhas can be won out of gumball machines, and in Sedona, Arizona, savvy marketers have professed to have actually bottled the special spiritual vortex energies that are said to be found there. As a result of the East-West encounter and trends in globalization, aided by the consumerism that characterizes American culture and its increasing impact on the rest of the world, a plethora of spiritual movements has sprung up and is spreading throughout the world as quickly as McDonald's and Starbucks.

If you are not aware of how vast the scope of the spiritual marketplace really is, go to a large mind-body-spirit conference or a New Age expo and allow yourself to be shocked, titillated, appalled, and allured by the thousands of surprising and not-so-surprising products you will find there. There are enormous markets for goddess-ware, "spiritual" clothing, and meditation and yoga paraphernalia, including Zen alarm clocks, crystal pyramids to place on your head to activate your chakras, and plastic contraptions to help you spread your toes for your yoga practice. The list is endless, and then there is the spiritual book market, which is oversaturated with everything from spiritually oriented romance and mystery novels to self-help books that promise to teach you everything from how to become a shaman to how to have spiritual sex.

Spiritual "tourism" has also become big business—not only the kind that takes you to Maui to study dolphin tantra or to the Brazilian rainforest to do shamanic rituals, but the more common and less easily recognized form of whirlwind tours through different paths, teachers, workshops, and practices. It has become rather hip to be spiritual, and we would serve ourselves well to be clear about whether our interest in spirituality is due to its being a socially "in" hobby or whether it results from a deeper hunger—not because one approach is better or more noble than the other, but because it will help us to accurately orient ourselves as we enter the spiritual marketplace.

As is wise when we shop for anything of value and import in our lives, becoming a discerning consumer is essential when it comes to spirituality. Just because a charismatic guru skillfully uses the language of enlightenment to sell himself and his teaching doesn't mean the product or service he offers is genuine or of high quality. Fast-food franchises sell "food," but the nutritional and health benefits they offer are far from what the consumer gets from free-range poultry, grass-fed beef, and organic fruits and vegetables. We need to be as knowledgeable and discerning when we enter the spiritual marketplace as when we enter the supermarket. The spiritual equivalent of fast food is slickly marketed and readily available—ranging from weekend seminars that promise lifelong transformation to so-called "enlightened" masters who readily declare tens, or even hundreds, of their students enlightened at the first sign of spiritual insight and experience.

Not all spiritual paths, practices, and teachers offer the same quality of spiritual instruction. Particular practices and processes may be helpful at certain times in your journey—they may even to introduce you to the fact that there *is* a journey—but it is important over time to learn to make clear distinctions between the variety of paths, practices, and teachers available. It is also important to scrutinize your own motivation to engage with spiritual subjects. If we hope to discover the real wealth spiritual practice has to offer, we must first learn to discern the rhinestones from the diamonds in the literature, paths, practices, and teachers who are vying for our attention. "Fool's gold exists," says Rumi, "because there is real gold."

The Rise and Fall of Great Gurus and Great Students

As a result of my research, the kinds of books I write, and a counseling practice that often attracts individuals who have been disillusioned by spiritual life in one form or another, I have found myself privy to an uncommon body of spiritual data— what we might call the "underbelly of enlightenment." This is the kind of spiritual gossip that would make any serious aspirant to the path quiver. If taken seriously, it reveals that absolutely no one, including teachers and ourselves, is exempt from the pitfalls one inevitably encounters on the spiritual path.

I have heard harrowing tales of how some of the most admired, "enlightened" teachers of our time have abandoned their children in their pursuit of spirituality; how they have used spiritual practice to avoid human connection and to mistreat their intimate partners, often justifying their behavior with spiritual terminology and concepts. Scandals about sex, money, and power pervade the contemporary spiritual scene like a lewd virus that spreads undetected until it has caused irreparable damage.

Nearly every time I give a public presentation, somebody approaches me and begins, "I've got a story the likes of which you have never heard . . ." and then proceeds to tell me a relatively common story about how "X" teacher, a self-professed celibate, slept with countless students, claiming they were receiving a "tantric initiation"; or how he cheated on his wife and had sexual relationships with the young women and/or men in the community; or how he or she forbade women in the community to have children, telling them it would cause too much attachment or that it was impossible to raise a healthy child before one was enlightened oneself. People download stories of how self-proclaimed enlightened teachers manipulated their students into giving them large sums of money or how teachers' narcissism ran rampant and they ended up lying, cheating, and abusing their students and loved ones on a physical, psychological/emotional, or spiritual level.

All I need do is open my e-mail inbox to find more stories of spiritual scandal than I want to know about. It is no wonder that so many people have a reaction to the term *spirituality* that is characterized by a string of curse words rather than a feeling of love and compassion. As Theravadan Buddhist teacher Jack Kornfield is fond of saying, "If you want to know how enlightened somebody is, ask their husband/wife."

Understanding the multifaceted causes of scandal and disillusionment with regard to spiritual teachers is a highly complex topic that was addressed thoroughly in my previous book, *Do You Need a Guru? Understanding the Student-Teacher Relationship in an Era of False Prophets*. I provide a brief consideration here as a baseline for understanding what is involved in creating an empowered, nonscandalous path of spiritual learning and growth in your own life.

First, it is important to acknowledge the pervasiveness of scandalous behavior on the spiritual path. While life-threatening instances of abuse do occur, they are the exception. Most of the infringements are milder—and therefore less visible—including psychological, financial, and sexual coercion. Even more common is the phenomenon of spiritual mediocrity, which occurs when unprepared individuals prematurely place themselves, or are placed in, positions of power they are not equipped to handle. Under such circumstances, subtle manipulation or organizational dysfunction is instituted within a spiritual group, often rationalized with spiritual, or dharmic, terminology. Whereas it would be nice to believe that the label "spiritual" represents a commitment to impeccable integrity, it is not surprising that in a modern world whose gods are money, power, and fame, simply labeling a teacher or path "spiritual" doesn't exempt them from the same corruption that occurs in every other aspect of life. Thom Birch, a prominent teacher on the yoga conference circuit before he opted out of the yoga business, exclaimed, "Many of these people are the biggest thieves, bullies, and sex addicts—all of it under this veil of spirituality."[1] In some ways, spiritual corruption is among the most insidious forms of fraud because it is often justified using the language of truth.

Second, it is worthwhile to consider what behavior actually constitutes being out of integrity. Does a spiritual teacher having a sexual or romantic relationship with one of his or her students constitute outright spiritual abuse? Or is it the element of secrecy or contradiction (such as self-professed celibacy) that constitutes the abuse? Does it depend upon the circumstances surrounding the inception of the relationship and the degree of maturity involved? And if it does contain an element of questionable motivation, does that discount the teacher's wisdom and capacity to transmit knowledge? Does the request to tithe 10 percent of one's income or donate an inheritance to a spiritual organization qualify as financial coercion, or does it become so only after one has become disillusioned with a particular path or teacher? Similar questions could be asked with respect to all types of spiritual manipulation, and I am convinced there are no easy, across-the-board answers, as each situation comprises a unique set of variables. Some spiritual institutions have attempted to create formal charters of ethics to minimize spiritual abuses, but such movements can also have a stifling effect on teachers whose job it is to support the practitioner to personally access the wild, unbounded mystery of creation, and can sometimes create safety at the expense of creativity and freedom among practitioners.

I suggest that the primary source of the problematic behaviors we find in spiritual communities exists within each one of us. To really *know* this can shift our perspective from one of victimization to one of self-responsibility. The term *mutual complicity,* which I introduced in *Halfway Up the Mountain,* refers to the principle that a teacher and student, or group of students, are cooperating—even if largely unconsciously—to allow a circumstance of corruption to emerge between them. It takes two to tango on the dance floor, and it takes two or more to create a system of corruption in a spiritual school. Mutual complicity is essentially spiritual codependence.

When spiritual corruption is present, it suggests that in addition to the conscious purpose of the student and teacher's alliance—spiritual enlightenment, awakening, serving God, or some other goal—there are also unconscious needs and agreements in place. These may involve the teacher's need to feel powerful, in control, special, needed, or loved, while the student might unconsciously need to be saved, protected, cared for, or absolved of the need to grow up and take personal responsibility for his or her own behaviors. Regardless of the details, corruption arises from mutual unconsciousness within the teacher-student relationship.

Although it is true that a teacher is in a position of great power and influence, most of the people he or she influences are—or should be—adults. As we further explore the subject of psychology in this book, we will come to appreciate how frequently our spiritual aspirations are confused with unmet childhood needs and wishes; thus, we often find ourselves in spiritual circumstances that replay unresolved circumstances of our early lives. As Carl Jung taught, "When an inner situation is not made conscious, it appears outside as fate."

I know this principle to be true from my own life. In my seven years of seeking a spiritual teacher before finally meeting him, I found myself in a number of circumstances with male spiritual teachers who reflected conflicted aspects of my relationship with my father that I had not yet worked through. The pain in these situations is real, and the abuses such individuals perpetrate are unconscionable on their part and devastating to their students. Although we cannot stop another from enacting violence, we *can* become conscious of our own tendencies to place ourselves in potentially violent situations. One of the greatest tragedies occurs when individuals with a passion for truth give up on the spiritual path because they cannot recover from the disillusionment they have experienced with a spiritual teacher, or even from their own naïve participation in a less than optimal situation. Their soul loses the opportunity for profound growth in this lifetime, primarily due to psychological circumstances that they could have overcome.

Again, let us remember that none of us is beyond falling into the traps of spiritual confusion and misunderstanding. Most of us haven't been given enough power, authority, and fame to fully appreciate the subtlety and pull of their temptations. We cannot know how we would behave if placed in the same position. Most of us have not penetrated the subtleties of dharmic wisdom deeply enough to fully appreciate the degree to which the still-unconscious aspects of ego can co-opt truth, creating a sterling-silver layer of armor flawlessly justified in the language of truth itself. As the philosopher Robert McDermott once told me, "I am not interested in a scandal that is more than seven years old. If I am not big enough to allow other people to change, I shouldn't consider myself a spiritual person."

To approach spiritual paths and practices with intelligent skepticism is advisable. Intelligent scrutiny is required for two reasons: because spiritual organizations, teachers, and communities operating at a high level of integrity across all levels are the exception, and because our attraction to spiritual paths and practices usually results from a combination of the soul's authentic need combined with our own inevitable psychological needs and blind spots. Yet, to discount the possibility of authentic spirituality simply because fraudulent, or "rhinestone," spirituality exists is as nonsensical as discounting the possibility of discovering love simply because we have had some bad relationships. One of the primary purposes of this book is to offer support in learning how to sort through the great morass of our spiritual and psychological concepts, experiences, and subtle egoic mechanisms, so we can make powerful, intelligent spiritual choices in our lives.

Enlightenment Is Beside the Point

If you go to my teacher's website, you will find this sentence: "If you're looking for enlightenment, look somewhere else."

Another teacher, Claudio Naranjo, a Chilean-born mystic, writer, and educator, experienced a great insight into enlightenment in 1971. A spiritual school sprung up around him, and he lived in a state of transparency, heightened inspiration, and clarity that lasted nearly three years—until it went away, replaced by a dark night of the soul that went on for more than a decade. After four more decades of spiritual integration, he reflected upon how his perception of "enlightenment" had shifted to include the totality of human experience, which includes both light and dark:

> *You can use the light of an experience to see your dark-*
> *ness. The experience is being lost only to the extent that it*
> *is being reinvested in yourself. The light you receive mixes*
> *with your own darkness, and then it is not light anymore,*
> *but neither is the darkness so dark anymore. Your being*
> *is transformed.*[2]

"One does not become enlightened by imagining figures of light, but by making the darkness conscious," said Carl Jung. I, personally, can no longer relate to the idea of enlightenment, and it is not simply because I am not enlightened. Like most die-hard spiritual aspirants, I, too, once had a grandiose idea about my spiritual potential. Like so many others, I shared that secret fantasy of having a special access to enlightenment. This is common, particularly in the early years of our spiritual life when we tend to be captivated by dramatic insights and stunning experiences. The voice of grandiosity says something like, "Other people don't know it, but *I* am just a little more special than everyone else. *I* have a special 'in' with God." The pervasiveness of this fantasy is a kind of collective secret life among spiritual seekers.

I remember the precise moment when my personal enlightenment bubble was burst. I was a young twenty-four-year-old seeker traveling in India and had just met my teacher Lee and his master, a great saint named Yogi Ramsuratkumar. I received lots of personal attention from the saint, was given special treatment, and experienced ecstatic moments of God-intoxication that are not uncommon when one first awakens to one's inner nature. Though I would not have admitted it aloud, I was convinced that I was special. Then one day my friend Michael, who was living in India and had been a student of Lee's for twenty years, said to me, "I bet you believe that you have not only a special, but an extra-special, relationship with the Divine. I bet you secretly believe you have an access the rest of us don't have, that you have a greater chance at enlightenment than everyone else. You know, Mariana," he said, "almost every serious seeker feels that way."

What embarrassment! And what a gift. I knew he was right, for at that very time I had gotten to know another young couple who did not have the good fortune to have their bubble burst. The guy was English, about thirty, and had had a big enlightenment experience that lasted for three months and prompted him to go to India to connect with the great enlightenment traditions. He had found an Australian girlfriend who became his first disciple, and they were traveling around looking for more disciples. When I told him I couldn't continue to spend time with them because I was uncomfortable with him continually placing himself in the role of teacher, the pair attempted to put a black magic spell on me so I would suffer for my betrayal of them.

It was also during that period when a great teacher named H. W. L. Poonja, commonly known as Poonjaji, was alive and giving teachings in Lucknow, India. He was clearly a greatly illumined man according to the accounts of all who met him, yet one of the tragedies of Poonjaji's teaching ministry is that he either told, inferred, or allowed hundreds of individuals to believe they were fully enlightened simply because they'd had one, or many, powerful experiences of awakening. These "enlightened" teachers then proceeded to enlighten their own students in a similar way, and thus was born what is known as the "neo-Advaita," or "satsang" movement in Western culture—a co-option of the Sanskrit term *satsang,* which simply refers to "being together in truth." To assume that such temporary experiences of perceiving emptiness and enlightenment are the end of the path is a grave error, one that is often propagated by teachers in this movement and results in hundreds of thousands of earnest seekers migrating around the world, going from teacher to teacher getting "hits" of spiritual truth that they naïvely mistake for enlightenment. Traditional Indian Advaita-Vedanta, from which this approach arose, involves decades of study and practice under the guidance of a qualified teacher and has little to do with the "enlightenment" that is proclaimed in much of the present-day neo-Advaita movement.

Although later in his teaching career Poonjaji claimed that he had merely sent out ministers who had mistaken themselves for kings, this late proclamation was not sufficient to remedy the avalanche of premature claims to enlightenment that had been set in motion. A parallel phenomenon began to arise around the same time with the students of a small number of other Indian teachers. Some of these seemed to be outright scandalous, while others were simply naïve to the egoic tendency, particularly in Western culture, to unconsciously misuse spiritual experiences to escape from dealing with the laborious, vulnerable process of coming to terms with all levels of our human experience. (See Chapter 5 for more on spiritual bypassing.) Whereas there are notable exceptions to the rule—both in terms of teachers and students in the satsang movement[3]—I believe that this is one of the most confused spiritual movements in the history of contemporary Western spirituality.

Not long after the publication of *Halfway Up the Mountain,* I received a call from a man who asked if he could meet me for lunch to talk about my book. As I sat across the table from this man, he proceeded to tell me that he had become enlightened a few years before but that he couldn't get anybody to see it—and not only that, he had lost his best friend and a number of other close friends who told him they could no longer relate to him in his enlightened state. He was concerned about his friends' state of suffering and was asking my counsel regarding how to get others to see his enlightenment. Choking on my Thai food, I suggested to him that it is usually more appropriate to assume the function of a spiritual teacher when other people ask you to, or when your own teacher (whom he did not have) suggests you do so, rather than to set up your own shop. Through my travels and research I have met literally hundreds of people who claim to be enlightened and hundreds more who believe they are but would not dare say so.

As we will see, it is not that difficult to have profound spiritual insights and experiences that match the definitions of what many texts suggest enlightenment to be. However, we will also see that, rather than marking the end of the spiritual journey, these insights and experiences are a point of initiation. While they do mark a powerful moment in our spiritual development, they are closer to the beginning of the path than the end.

Most Western practitioners of spirituality are not aware that the term *samādhi*—often used to describe a state of one-pointedness and concentration in which the consciousness of the experiencing subject becomes one with the experienced object—actually has many distinct levels. The preliminary ones are not uncommon, and the more advanced levels are so rare that few human beings, even those who are highly developed, will ever experience them. *The Yoga Sūtras of Patañjali*, a text more than two-thousand-years old on the science of spiritual development through the path of yoga, which I refer to throughout this book, describes these levels.

Vitarka, the first level, refers to an intellectual grasp of knowledge or truth derived from deliberate thinking and study. We experience this level of samādhi when we study spiritual texts and receive a great "Aha!" or profound level of intellectual comprehension. The next level, *vicāra,* involves a more subtle understanding attained as a result of personal investigation, where the mind becomes stilled and a depth and acuteness of perception are revealed. Many people who have engaged an extensive process of meditation and/or inquiry have experienced this level of samādhi, and many of those who believe themselves to be enlightened are at this level of development. Next is *ānanda,* or bliss, another powerful state of realization that is often mistaken for enlightenment and is fairly common among those who deeply engage the paths of yoga, meditation, or inquiry. This is followed by *asmitā,* in which the individual dwells in his or her true Self. Not only do these preliminary states have subtle levels of development contained within them, but there exist still further levels of samādhi, known as *asamprajnātā sāmadhi* and *nirbīja samādhi,* where consciousness merges into a mindless, beginningless, and endless state of being.[4] It is not difficult to understand how spiritual aspirants, and even spiritual teachers, can find themselves experiencing and even integrating one or more of the lower levels of samādhi, unaware of the possibilities and subtle distinctions of further spiritual development. The result is the presumption that they have reached the goal of the path, while in fact they are just beginning.

Rather than holding on to an imagined concept of enlightenment as a product that can be attained, it may be more helpful to consider spiritual awakening as an endless process of progressively deeper levels of integration. If we can effectively revision our ideas of enlightenment in this manner, we can be spared the experience of falling into many otherwise unavoidable traps on the spiritual path, several of which will be considered in the next chapter. Although it may initially be very disappointing to realize we are not as wise as we secretly thought, or as near to an imagined goal of spiritual life as we hoped we were, we also become more humble and more real when we let go of the goal-focused outlook.

What if enlightenment were less about fireworks and eternal bliss and more about dissipating the illusions we have about what life itself is? About becoming more authentic, compassionate, and real—and stopping our pretending? About letting the protective layers of our personality structure crumble? About becoming progressively more effective agents of transformation and of the alleviation of suffering in the world, beginning with ourselves? In my years of practicing, interviewing, and researching spirituality, I have come to believe that although different paths have different goals, an authentic and integrated spiritual path should make us more real and human, not less.

My spiritual heroes are not the usual holy people. A lot of so-called holy people I know, both teachers and students, lack depth, dimension, and texture. The energy invested in keeping the darkness at bay somehow distorts the quality of their light. Like Claudio Naranjo, who came to understand that his great illumination had been sacrificed in order to integrate that which was still "dark," or unconscious, within him, I believe that we, too, must be willing to suffer our own darkness if we truly aspire to know the deeper spiritual potentialities that exist within us.

What Do You Really Want?

"What is the difference between an egg sandwich and a ham sandwich?" asked Sufi sheikh Llewellyn Vaughan-Lee, before quickly providing the answer. "In the egg sandwich, the chicken is *involved;* in the ham sandwich, the pig is *committed.*"

To ask this question of ourselves—"Am I committed, or am I just involved?"—and give an honest answer helps us to make intelligent choices about which paths and practices are best suited for the spiritual development we seek. The problem arises when we profess one thing and live out another, because we confuse ourselves and others, and we limit our growth.

If only we could say honestly and without shame, "I engage spirituality as a hobby," or "I want a spiritual practice that will give me some peace of mind but without any commitment or discipline," or "I'd like to keep spirituality as my mistress but maintain comfort and security as my spouse," or "I want to be seen as a spiritual man or woman because that will make me more sexy." If only we could simply admit, "I'm a New Ager," "I'm a fashionable Buddhist," "I'm an imitation Hindu," "I'm a wannabe guru," or "I'm a bliss chick." Or perhaps we could use more simple, straightforward language, such as "I'm a serious spiritual aspirant," "I'm a seeker of moderate interest," or "I'm a part-time, casual spiritual tourist." It is not *wrong* to have such an approach to spiritual development. We grow from where we are, and if we pretend to be somewhere we are not and try to move forward, we are likely to travel in a very crooked line and become more confused than necessary.

I think it is fair to assume that almost everyone has a deep desire to be happy, to find meaning, to suffer less. And certain approaches to spiritual teachings and practices, as well as intelligent approaches to psychological growth, can help us toward that end. For example, my friend Karen is an excellent therapist, a fantastic mother and wife, and a loyal friend who honors the presence of spirit and respects the earth. She once told me about a powerful experience she had on a solo vision quest, during which she was temporarily broken open to vast visions of consciousness, both light and dark, and shown what was required to understand these domains of awareness. She made a conscious decision that in this lifetime she didn't want to make her life about the realization of these levels of consciousness. Instead, she wanted to live an honest, loving, and balanced life, respectful of the earth and her community. I have great respect for a choice like this because it is conscious and honest.

For many of us, however, a choice such as the one Karen made is not an option. An unrelenting need from within pounds at the doors of our conscience demanding that we go deeper. All the great masters who have dared stretch their consciousness to its furthest capacities say that the entirety of the path is traveled along a razor's edge, and it is a road of no return. They say that the price of truth is greater than we could ever imagine upon entering the path, far beyond what most of us would consider paying.

In Patañjali's *Yoga Sūtras* it is explained that there are three basic types of spiritual seekers—mild, medium, and intense—and that within each of these categories are three subcategories: mildly-mild, medium-mild, intensely-mild; mildly-medium, medium-medium, intensely-medium; mildly-intense, medium-intense, and intensely-intense.[5] In other words, there are roughly nine levels of spiritual seekers, and to situate ourselves correctly on this spectrum is not an easy thing. Why? Because our ideas about ourselves are often inaccurate, and what we would like to believe about ourselves is different from what is true of us. On the spiritual-seeker scale, most of us evaluate ourselves far higher than we actually are.

I once went to traffic school for a speeding ticket. The instructor asked us to evaluate the level of our driving capacities on a scale from 0 to 10, 0 being a poor driver and 10 signifying an excellent driver. On average, those of us in the class rated ourselves at least three levels above what research had shown was an average score for all drivers, much less those in traffic school.

I believe that our involvement in spiritual life is a lot like that. It is a natural tendency to think of ourselves as intensely-intense spiritual practitioners, or at least mildly-intense, not only because of an egoic tendency to overestimate our degree of knowledge and wisdom but because most of us in the West have no reference for what authentic spiritual attainment is and the sacrifices it involves. I believe, for example, that Ramana Maharshi, Mother Teresa, the Dalai Lama, J. Krishnamurti, and U. G. Krishnamurti were intensely-intense practitioners. So are two female Tibetan Buddhist spiritual teachers I know: Tenzin Palmo, who did a twelve-year solo retreat in a cave in the Himalayas before she undertook the job of creating a woman's monastery in India; and Robina Courtin, who teaches Tibetan Buddhism to prisoners on death row. My own teacher, Lee Lozowick, who has lived among his students and is available to them almost all day every day—and who has served his own guru ceaselessly without a day of vacation in more than thirty years—is clearly an intense spiritual practitioner. Understanding and appreciating the lives of such individuals tends to cast a more accurate light upon our own degree of spiritual achievement.

When we are willing to be where we are rather than where we wish we were, there is great possibility for growth and for attracting the help we need to deepen the intensity of our aspiration. Our degree of commitment to ourselves and to our spiritual potentialities can grow and change throughout our lives. Many of us simply have no idea what is possible in terms of spiritual development. One aspect of the fruition of spiritual practice is the understanding of how vast and even endless the possibilities of spiritual development are. For how can we aspire to something we don't even know exists?

As I suggested in the introduction, every one of us is on the spiritual path, whether we know it or not—and most of us do not. The fact of our incarnation implies that we are on a great journey. Whether that journey is just one of becoming conscious, whether we have been disillusioned countless times by ourselves, paths, and teachers but are still hanging in there, or whether we are deeply committed to our practice, the question, "What do I want?" still applies.

Many of the great Vedic texts begin with the term *atha*. From the subtle language of Sanskrit, atha is frequently translated into English as "now." But atha really suggests that every *now* in which we find ourselves is a moment that has never existed before and will never exist again, and that in this moment we begin again. Even if we have been searching, meditating, and engaging spiritual practice for years or decades, we choose in each moment to begin again. We open ourselves once again to infinite possibility, and we courageously, and as consciously as possible, step into the unknown.

The Need for an Integral Spirituality

Regardless of whether we aspire to uncompromised truth or are simply coming to spiritual life to learn to suffer less, the harrowing circumstances of the world we live in, which clearly seem to be intensifying, require us to develop a

Western model of spirituality that addresses all levels of our experience. Our spiritual path and practices must support us in being part of the solution to the immense challenges humanity faces—not part of the problem. This is not a time for monks on mountaintops. It is a time to pursue our spiritual work with depth, focus, and efficiency and bring whatever morsels of wisdom we discover to all of our structures and systems—families, schools, politics, and policy—in order to transform these structures and infuse life force and integrity back into a suffering earth and cultures that are increasingly void of spirit. Insight and awakening must be actualized externally.

This is not a new idea. Sri Aurobindo, an Indian mystic and revolutionary, coined the term *integral yoga,* which refers to "not only realization of unity in the Self, but of unity in the infinite diversity of activities, worlds and creatures."[6] Philosopher Ken Wilber's integral theory advocates a model of transformation that is inclusive, balanced, and comprehensive. The Russian mystic G. I. Gurdjieff offered a method of transformational work, often referred to as the Fourth Way, that integrated the paths of the *fakir,* who approaches self-mastery through the body; the monk, who approaches it through faith; and the yogi, who approaches it through knowledge and the mind. Most of the genuine tantric traditions aspire to integrate enlightened wisdom into the body.

We must understand that in these times we cannot afford to aspire to enlightenment, or even to acquire wisdom, for ourselves alone. We must do so for the good of all beings and the healing of the earth and all of its inhabitants. Insight must be integrated into action, and the harmony we wish to see on the earth must simultaneously be cultivated in our own bodies and our own lives.

Chapter 2

~⌒

Spiritually Transmitted Disease

Be careful where you are headed
or you may end up where you are going.
—LAO TZU

S everal years ago, I spent a summer living and working in South Africa. Upon my arrival I was instantly confronted by the visceral reality that I was in the country with the highest murder rate in the world, where rape was common and more than half the population was HIV-positive—men and women, gays and straights alike. I eventually learned more statistics on sexually transmitted disease. For example, more than nineteen million new cases of sexually transmitted disease are reported each year in the United States alone.[1] One in five Americans is infected with genital herpes.[2] Worldwide, the statistics are far worse.

As we begin to understand the challenges Western practitioners face and the importance of approaching the path with our eyes wide open, we need to get very specific in our self-inquiry about the obstacles that get in our way. The "spiritually transmitted diseases" surveyed in this chapter offer an overview of some of the most common ones we must learn to carefully discern.

As I have come to know hundreds of spiritual teachers and thousands of spiritual practitioners through my work and travels, I have been struck by the way in which our spiritual views, perspectives, and experiences become similarly "infected" by "conceptual contaminants"—comprising a confused and immature relationship to complex spiritual principles—that are as invisible, yet as insidious as sexually transmitted disease. Bodily fluids are the infecting agent for sexually transmitted diseases, whereas concepts, perceptions, and egoic confusion are a few of the primary agents through which spiritually transmitted diseases are contracted. Due to their invisibility, these spiritual contaminants are extremely challenging to detect.

Spiritually transmitted diseases, not unlike those that are sexually transmitted, can become so highly contagious that they infect entire groups and subcultures. Because spiritual diseases are diseases of ego, and therefore subtle, they can go undetected for years in ourselves and in our communities. That which is invisible is by its nature hard to detect, and nothing is as invisible as the human ego, where spiritually transmitted diseases reside. In spiritually transmitted disease, the ego mixes with our spiritual yearnings and insights, and little by little—so slowly that it usually escapes our notice—a variety of spiritual "dis-eases" begin to eat away at us, silently, like parasites. If left untended, they can corrupt our clear sight and effective growth on the path.

The goal of this chapter is to bring awareness to the existence of spiritually transmitted disease. How common is it?

What are the different diseases? How do we diagnose it in ourselves? How can we identify it in others? How do we protect ourselves from contracting such a disease? Many of us have learned to practice safe sex, or at least to be aware of the risks of not practicing it. If we take responsibility for educating ourselves about spiritually transmitted diseases, we protect ourselves against being unknown carriers, bring awareness of these STDs into our communities, and become discerning students and practitioners of spirituality.

The Inevitability of Spiritually Transmitted Disease

Most of us who are deeply involved in the spiritual journey will find ourselves in various states of spiritual dis-ease throughout our lives. As sincere as our intentions are, and as deep as our spiritual insights may be, most of us are living out of balance in some way—an inevitable consequence of living in a time and culture that is itself out of balance and in a state of dis-ease. Given that most aspects of our lives—politics, the environment, our relationships with nature and the natural rhythms of life—are out of balance and anywhere from mildly to severely diseased, why would we assume our spiritual lives to be otherwise?

One very common confused belief among those on the spiritual path is that someone who has been involved in spiritual life for ten, thirty, or fifty years—whether as teacher or student—is by virtue of longevity exempt from the same psychological and karmic forces that everyone else must face throughout life. Spiritual development is a *long* process, far slower than most of us would like to believe. It often takes decades for practitioners to grow into mature understanding, if they ever do. The domain of that which is unknown is vast, even for the wise ones, and everyone labors against massive obstacles to consciousness. For those who dedicate their lives to transformation, the chance of contracting a spiritual disease is as likely as catching the flu.

Also, there exists a force within the universe, and within each of us, that the Russian mystic G. I. Gurdjieff identified as the "denying force." Gurdjieff said there is a great battle—the battle between Yes and No—that rages within every human being. Throughout our lives on the spiritual path, the Yes moves toward consciousness, clarity, and radiance, while the No attempts to thwart Yes's efforts at every turn. This denying force takes on endless guises, both externally in our lives through sabotaging behaviors and internally in our minds as confused spiritual knowledge. This is an important force within us that we need to be aware of, and discerning about, as we move through our lives on the spiritual path.

The Spread of Spiritually Transmitted Disease: Culture, Teacher, and Ego

Regardless of what label we put on that which resists spiritual growth, there are three primary mediums of transmission: (1) through cultural influences, (2) from the teacher to the student, and (3) from within one's own ego structure: an "assault on oneself."

Cultural diseases of the spirit are so subtle and pervasive that often we don't even know we have been infected by them until we find ourselves spiritually ill from their influence. An example is the way that Judeo-Christian beliefs have permeated the Western psyche. The fundamentally sinful nature of mankind, its polarization of flesh and spirit, and its negation of women and dismissal of feminine wisdom have insinuated themselves into the collective Western psyche so effectively that even our most radical spiritual movements contain subtle Judeo-Christian underpinnings.

Spiritually transmitted diseases are also passed on from teachers to their students. Many spiritual teachers, even if not outright corrupt, are immature in their knowledge and unintegrated in their psychological development—and they are teaching at a level beyond their understanding. A weak teacher may unintentionally pass on a variety of spiritual diseases to his or her students. Some of these simply inhibit the students' growth, while others have a devastating effect.

Finally, the diseases generated by one's own ego are the subtlest, most difficult to detect, and therefore hardest to protect oneself from. In this type of disease, the ego co-opts the insights and perspectives of the greater Self. This level of spiritual disease assumes a literally endless array of expressions and degrees of subtlety.

Anyone can fall prey to spiritually transmitted diseases, and there is no known antidote. Most do not operate in isolation but in relationship with other diseases. When our spiritual immune system is weak, which is inevitable in a culture in which spiritual discernment is not taught, we are likely to be infected with one or more of these at any given time.

As with diagnosing physical or psychological disease, identifying spiritual disease has its pitfalls. While we should become aware of the diseases we have been infected with so we can deal with them and restore ourselves to spiritual health, we need to be careful that in identifying and categorizing them we don't fall prey to imposing rigid labels and categories on ourselves and others. Spiritual dis-ease is not "bad"; it is simply a broken thread in the greater fabric of our deeper possibilities and potentials. Labels are useful only to the degree that they help us isolate and become aware of specific problems. Becoming overidentified with our own spiritual disease, or entranced by analyzing those of others, is simply another level of spiritual disease.

Ten Spiritually Transmitted Diseases

The following categorizations are not intended to be definitive but are offered as a tool for becoming aware of some of the most common spiritually transmitted diseases.

1. Fast-Food Spirituality

Mix spirituality with a culture that celebrates speed, multitasking, and instant gratification and the result is likely to be fast-food spirituality. *Super Size Me,* a documentary focused on the McDonald's enterprise, revealed the painful reality of fast-food culture, a mentality that extends far beyond its restaurants. Many of the most popular spiritual books, movements, and teachers promise a lot and demand very little of their adherents. Popular books such as *The Lazy Man's Guide to Enlightenment* suggest that it is possible to become enlightened without effort. One can go to an "enlightenment intensive" and get enlightened in one weekend. Fast-food spirituality is a product of the common and understandable fantasy that relief from the suffering of our human condition can be quick and easy. One thing is clear, however: spiritual transformation cannot be had in a quick fix. For some people, a highly franchised enterprise like Bikram Yoga or a small glimpse of nonduality discovered at a weekend intensive will provide an important doorway into spirituality and their interior world, but it is important not to confuse these temporary "highs" and "glows" with a process of transformation that, once committed to, is an ongoing and ever-deepening process.

2. Faux Spirituality

Faux spirituality is the tendency to talk, dress, and act as we imagine a spiritual person would. It is a kind of imitation spirituality that mimics spiritual realization in the way that leopard-skin fabric imitates the genuine skin of a leopard. This disease is most likely to be found in New Age culture. It manifests when the ego appropriates spiritual truths and assumes that elevated states of consciousness can be accessed by externally emulating what it imagines an enlightened person looks and acts like. Not unlike make-believe games in which a child pretends to be a firefighter using the garden hose or puts on her mother's high heels and makeup to attend a make-believe gala, adult human beings don spiritual garments and imitate the behaviors they see in people they believe to be spiritual. They attend spiritual events and assume they have accessed the perennial wisdom taught by mystics throughout all time—without being willing to do the actual work required to initiate a profound and authentic process of internal transformation.

3. Confused Motivations

This pervasive disease has its roots in confusion about our motivations for seeking spiritual growth. Although our desire to grow is genuine and pure, it often gets mixed with lesser motivations, including the wish to be loved, the desire to belong, the need to fill our internal emptiness, the belief that the spiritual path will remove our suffering, and spiritual ambition—the wish to be special, to be better than, to be "the one."[3]

Although confusion is inevitable when we first embark on the spiritual path, if our spiritual practice does not eventually reveal the unconscious forces working to co-opt our spiritual health, these forces result in disease. We may succumb to the need to cater to our psychological needs for acceptance,

meaning, and specialness and miss out on the deeper possibilities that spiritual life offers. Or our expectations are not
met and, rather than understanding this perceived failure as
an aspect of the path, we blame God, our teacher, or the path
and become disillusioned with spiritual development itself.

4. Identifying with Spiritual Experiences

"A religious awakening which does not awaken the sleeper to
love has roused him in vain," said American Quaker writer
Jessamyn West. Whereas mystical and nondual experiences
may have profound impacts on us—perhaps the greatest of
which is to initiate us into a lifelong commitment to the spiritual path and a life of service—it is clear that, for most people,
accessing nondual states of consciousness is not the same as
integrating them. In this disease, the ego identifies with our
spiritual experience and takes it as its own, and we begin to
believe that we are embodying insights that have arisen within
us at certain times. This is a disease of ego inflation. In most
cases, it does not last indefinitely, although it tends to endure
for longer periods of time in those who believe themselves to
be enlightened and/or who function as spiritual teachers.

At times one can become so overidentified with spiritual
experience as to literally get lost in it. The twentieth-century
Indian saint Meher Baba undertook the task of seeking out
masts, dedicated spiritual practitioners stuck in high states
of spiritual intoxication, and helping them integrate their
knowledge, so they could become more highly functional
human beings.

"Satori sudden enlightenment is a wonderfully slippery
concept," writes Hungarian author Arthur Koestler.[4] For
most of us, mystical experiences fade in spite of every effort to
cling to and sustain them. Combine this with the humbling

realities of the body, disease, and human relationships, and eventually we discover that mystical experiences are, in essence, simply experiences.

5. The Spiritualized Ego

This disease occurs when the very structure of the egoic personality becomes deeply embedded with spiritual concepts and ideas. The result is an egoic structure that is, in the words of Llewellyn Vaughan-Lee, "bulletproof." When the ego becomes spiritualized, we are invulnerable to help, new input, or constructive feedback. We become impenetrable human beings and are stunted in our spiritual growth, all in the name of spirituality. The spiritualized ego manifests at both subtle and extreme degrees, an example being what I have come to call "Zen boyfriends" and "Zen girlfriends," who skillfully misuse spiritual concepts, ideals, and practices to avoid authenticity and vulnerability in romantic relationships.[5]

6. Mass Production of Spiritual Teachers

There are a number of current trendy spiritual traditions that produce people who believe themselves to be at a level of spiritual enlightenment, or mastery, that is far beyond their actual level. Both the Western and Eastern worlds are overpopulated with mediocre teachers who instruct sincere spiritual aspirants at a less than optimal level. This disease functions like a spiritual conveyor belt: put on this glow, get that insight, and—bam!—you're enlightened and ready to enlighten others in similar fashion.

The problem is not that such teachers instruct but that they represent themselves as having achieved spiritual mastery. This premature assumption doesn't just thwart these teachers' own continued evolution; it creates a highly limited concept of spiritual development among their students. T. K. V. Desikachar advises: "At no stage on the yoga path should we think we have become masters. Rather, we should know that the feeling of being a little better today than yesterday exists just as much as the hope we will be a little better in the future."[6]

7. Spiritual Pride

Spiritual pride arises when the practitioner, through years of labored effort, has actually attained a certain level of wisdom and uses that attainment to justify shutting down to further experience. It is indeed tempting to hoard spiritual achievement and try to rest in it rather than being willing to continually open oneself to deeper knowledge. Prideful spiritual practitioners must find the courage and integrity to expose themselves to individuals who can and will push and test them.

Tibetan Buddhist master Chögyam Trungpa Rinpoche said that spiritual pride is one of the most difficult obstacles to overcome. He believed it to be widely found among spiritual teachers who thwart their own continued growth by believing they have reached the end of the spiritual path, and among longtime spiritual practitioners who have become smug and arrogant about their knowledge—especially in relation to newer and younger students on the path.

A feeling of "spiritual superiority" is another symptom of this spiritually transmitted disease. It manifests as a subtle feeling that "I am better, more wise, and above others because I am spiritual." Mental symptoms include a feeling of "I am in the know"—I really understand ego, consciousness, spirituality. Physical expressions of it are a sense of aloofness, offering knowing looks of approval when others are exploring spiritual topics, and the need to assert one's own (superior) spiritual knowledge in conversation.

8. Group Mind

Also described as groupthink, cultic mentality, or ashram disease, group mind is an insidious virus that contains many elements of traditional codependence. A spiritual group makes subtle and unconscious agreements regarding the correct ways to think, talk, dress, and act. Shared intentions with respect to practice and protocol become invisible, and institutionalized agreements homogenize the group, offering a level of psychological safety that has little to do with the shared task of spiritual development. Individuals and groups infected with "group mind" reject individuals, attitudes, and circumstances that do not conform to the often unwritten rules of the group. There is no group, no matter how developed, that does not embody some aspect of unhealthy cultic dynamics as part of its structure—and the denial of such dynamics, or lack of awareness of them, is one of the most common indicators of this disease.

Cultism and groupthink are inevitable consequences of human psychology. In some groups, the consequences are not dangerous, whereas in others they are deadly: recall the mass suicides of Jonestown and Heaven's Gate. Within spiritual groups, individuals will play out unconscious roles and dynamics that resemble their roles in their families of origin. In the absence of awareness of this dynamic, a spiritual group can become a collective replica of the individuals' dysfunctional families and of the same codependence they live out in their other relationships. They receive the comfort of a sense of belonging and the gratification of identifying with a group and/or a charismatic leader, but at what cost? To what degree is their greater spiritual possibility and human integrity compromised?

It is important for us as individuals to recognize to what degree we are at the unconscious behest of the collective group mind. Likewise, groups should be consciously aware of the unhealthy psychological dynamics the group or community is expressing. To see this and to refine our relationship to it makes for a more thriving spiritual practice and community.

9. *The Chosen-People Complex*

Related to the disease of group mind but with an added aspect of spiritual pride, the chosen people complex is pervasive among spiritual groups. It is the belief that "Our group is more spiritually evolved, powerful, enlightened, and simply put, *better* than any other group." This is followed closely by "Our teacher is the *greatest* teacher who exists" and accompanying beliefs such as "There has never been a spiritual group such as ours (in the evolution of humanity)" or "Our work is more important or valuable to the salvation of humanity than that of any other group."

It is often a profound and unconscious psychological disposition of powerlessness, of unlove, and of not mattering that prompts teachers and students to believe that their path is the greatest one, rather than simply the right one for them. There is an important distinction between the recognition that one has found the right path, teacher, or community for oneself, and having found *The One*. It is the difference between saying, "My wife/husband is the best partner in the world for me" versus "My wife/husband is the best person there is."

It is also common for people to bolster their own sense of psychological worth by believing that their association with a powerful and perhaps enlightened teacher somehow makes them more powerful or enlightened themselves, a phenomenon also known as "the cult of personality." It is much like when parents overidentify with their children's beauty or accomplishments, as if those qualities or actions were a reflection of themselves and not of the child.

10. Survival of Ego Based on the Illusion of Separation

One of the most subtle and pervasive spiritually transmitted diseases—one that affects the vast majority of the world population of spiritual aspirants—is the belief that spirituality is about *me: I* am studying, doing practices, service, and whatever other efforts *I* might make so that *I* can feel better, be happier, or become a better person.

The essential fallacy in this approach is the assumption of "me." The "I" that almost all human beings identify with is a psychological construct, created for survival, and we have become so attached to it that we believe it to be who we are (a point that will be clarified in Chapter 4, "The Psychology of Ego"). Mystics of all traditions have confirmed that "God is One" and "Thou art That." All human beings intuitively know this, and many have tasted this truth for themselves; yet the belief that we are separate persists throughout life.

This fundamental misunderstanding of our own true identity, which is the core problem all spiritual aspirants face, is the foundational base of all spiritually transmitted diseases. This unshakable conviction that "I am who I believe myself to be"—which tends to be equally strong among those who understand this concept intellectually and those who do not—is so virulent that it taints every aspect of our spiritual practice, from service to meditation to ritual. Most of us spend our entire lives on the path with this spiritual dis-ease embedded in our consciousness. It infects teachers, students, religious movements, and all

spiritual traditions. It is perhaps the most difficult spiritually transmitted disease to eradicate.

The Deadly Virus: "I Have Arrived"

There is one disease I have set apart to bring special attention
to, as it is so potent that it has the capacity to be deadly to
our spiritual evolution. This is the belief that "I have arrived"
at the final goal of the spiritual path. Our spiritual progress
ends at the point where this belief becomes crystallized in
our psyche; for the moment we begin to believe that we have
reached the end of the path, further growth ceases—and if we
are not going forward, we are going backward.

The disease of believing one has arrived—also known as the
premature claim to enlightenment, Zen sickness, or the mes-
sianic complex—is the most well-documented in spiritual and
religious traditions. In *The Heart of Yoga,* T. K. V. Desikachar
explains: "The most dangerous of all obstacles occurs when
we think we know everything. We imagine we have seen the
truth and have reached the zenith, when in reality we have
simply experienced a period of calm that makes us say: 'This
is what I have been looking for! I've found it at last! I've made
it!' But the feeling of having reached the top rung on the lad-
der is only illusion."[7]

The tragedy of this disease is its capacity to infect others
in a way that seriously damages their love of truth. Powerful,
popular charismatic spiritual teachers who really do have profound insight—but have lost their humility and appreciation
for what they do not know—have caused great damage by
teaching their students half-baked truths and practices. Cases
like these, which often result in feelings of betrayal when the
"truths" are revealed to be false, are hard to heal. Many sincere
spiritual aspirants who have suffered the effects of someone

carrying the "I Have Arrived" virus never recover sufficiently to trust the spiritual path or another teacher throughout the remainder of their lives.

A less appreciated aspect of this spiritually transmitted disease manifests in the mini-messiah within each of us. It's easy to imagine a charismatic leader such as Jim Jones convincing his followers to drink suicidal Kool-Aid or a New Age tantric messiah professing to teach his or her students how to unite with God through sex (usually with himself). It is more challenging to find the miniature messiah within ourselves. It is that small voice that tells us, against all evidence and even against the clarity of our own awareness, that we really know what is going on, that we are somehow more wise than all others, that our judgment is objective judgment, that our perspective is accurate and true. If we are honest, most of us would have to admit that we have experienced at least an occasional moment of presumed messiahship. Can we be that honest?

Spiritually Transmitted Disease Prevention

The greatest protection we have against contracting spiritually transmitted disease is the capacity for spiritual discernment, known in Sanskrit as *viveka khyātir,* or "the crown of wisdom." The term *viveka* refers to the capacity to discern between the real and the unreal, and *khyātir* is an outlook of knowledge or consciousness. Thus, those who have developed spiritual discernment have developed their consciousness to the extent that they possess a capacity to consistently make intelligent and balanced choices in relationship to their own spiritual development. And they have a base of knowledge that keeps them continuously alert to egoic self-deception and subtle pitfalls on the path. Viveka khyātir is, in effect, the true spiritual condom that offers effective (though not foolproof) protection against the contraction of common spiritually transmitted diseases.

We should not assume that we have such spiritual discernment, for it is something that is cultivated rather than inherent. Most spiritual paths, particularly in Western culture, are more likely to advertise techniques to help the practitioner have spiritual experiences or relieve suffering than to focus attention on cultivating skills that lift the seemingly infinite veils of self-deception we encounter on our journey. Very few paths offer thorough training regarding the obstacles we encounter on the path to self-development.

"Ruthless self-honesty" is the way Lee Lozowick refers to the process of developing spiritual discernment. In many cases we have the capacity to see our spiritual impediments clearly but we lack the willingness to do so. We would rather maintain the comfort of our dis-ease than change in the ways necessary to heal ourselves. Fortunately, many spiritually transmitted diseases are detectable early and are curable, and there are ways to be tested for them—if we have the courage to subject ourselves to such tests, and if we are more interested in spiritual truth than fiction.

Testing for Spiritually Transmitted Disease

"Truth is not afraid of questions," said the renown Indian master Paramahansa Yogananda, best known for his book *The Autobiography of a Yogi*. If our spiritual insight and knowledge are authentic, we should be willing to have them tested.

Who, even among teachers, is so pure and stainless that they are beyond subtle and unconscious egoic drives that taint their perspective? I am convinced that spiritually transmitted disease is just as common among those who engage the spiritual path as sexually transmitted disease is among those who engage in sexual relationships. Yet many people have been tested for sexually transmitted disease, but few of us take responsibility for being checked for spiritually transmitted disease. What are these tests, and how can we take advantage of them and what they offer us?

Test 1: Life Experience

Life itself presents many tests for detecting the presence of spiritually transmitted disease, yet even if we suspect that we are being tested in some fashion, we are often unable to read the results accurately. Such tests may come in the form of receiving power, money, and opportunities for sexual seduction. Countless spiritual teachers, both Eastern and Western, have been tested in this way. Celibate yogis, swamis, rinpoches, and tulkus have come from the East to teach and quickly found themselves sleeping with attractive young students while still professing celibacy. Many contemporary spiritual figures ask exorbitant sums of money for their teachings and demonstrate dubious investments with the money they have received. Power dynamics are often more subtle, but they are equally pervasive—misusing power to extract agreement, adoration, and favors. Of course, this happens all the time among politicians, movie stars, and ordinary people, yet we want to think that because we identify ourselves, or someone else, as "spiritual," we or they will be immune to such afflictions. This is not so.

Life also tests us through shocks: betrayal in a relationship, divorce, severe illness, accidents, and death. My own experience of chronic illness was a powerful reality check that gave me a very clear perspective on where my spiritual strengths are and where my weaknesses remain. In circumstances where the body is so weak, or the psyche is so shocked, that we do not have the energy to maintain our persona—or even to maintain the internal and external practices we use to keep our weaknesses at bay—we get to see how deeply our practices, beliefs, and faith have penetrated us and where we remain stuck in fear, doubt, victimization, and lack of faith. I know of a number of Buddhist teachers who have fallen into deep depressions as a result of divorce or marital conflicts.

There is no spiritual law that says a teacher cannot become depressed, contract illnesses that totally deconstruct his or her identity and worldview, pass through crises of faith, or even become psychotic for a time—as in the case of Carl Jung, who intentionally provoked a state of psychosis within himself in order to become more deeply familiar with his unconscious. Such circumstances provide us with a powerful reality check and the chance to see ourselves in a different way from that to which we are accustomed.

Life's tests can also be affirming. Several years ago, Arnaud Desjardins, a great master of Advaita-Vedanta in France, found himself on a stretcher being rushed to the hospital as his lungs filled with fluid. A student with him heard Desjardins quietly repeating, "oui, oui, oui," or "yes, yes, yes," practicing even in the face of imminent death. He was saying "yes" to life—to *all* of life—one of the primary practices he teaches in his spiritual school. Although Desjardins is revered throughout France as a great master, he said upon his recovery that only then, in his late seventies, was he finally convinced that he was a true disciple of the path and that he possessed a practice solid enough to stand up to death itself.

Test 2: A Teacher's Observations

Another level of testing comes through being evaluated by one's teachers. History is littered with tales of self-proclaimed prophets, but spiritual lineages have always been designed with a built-in system of checks and balances—the teacher, community of practitioners, and the teachings—to assist practitioners in avoiding the countless traps they will encounter on the path and to help them get out of those traps should they fall.

A competent teacher will point out spiritual disease to his or her students and will help them heal should they become infected; this is the very job of such physicians of the soul. The question is, "Will we listen?" I had a very close friend, a student of my teacher for more than twenty years, who was itching to do public teaching work. He was well known in the community as having a weakness with women and a tendency to seduce them in highly inappropriate circumstances. At his insistence, my teacher allowed him to do some public work, and not surprisingly, his "teaching" quickly became mixed with his dating and sex life. At that point, my teacher suggested he stop teaching for some time, and my friend chose to leave the community and teach on his own.

Test 3: Feedback from Peers

On one of my first trips to Europe with my teacher, I shared a room with one of his most senior students, a woman in her fifties who had more than thirty years of experience on the path. At the end of the week she sat down on my bed and said to me, "We have just spent a week together living in close proximity. Please tell me what you have seen in my practice and behavior that I am blind to and not able to see in myself."

I was instantly disarmed. She was a very senior practitioner coming to me, a new, twenty-six-year-old student, asking me for my observations. I told her what I had seen, and the vulnerability of the circumstance prompted me to ask her to tell me what blind spots she had seen in me. The thoughts she shared with me that day have stayed with me for many years.

No matter what our level of practice, the honest feedback of peers is an invaluable reality check—if we are willing to ask for it and receive it. We tend to see others with far more clarity than we see ourselves, and if we are willing to be vulnerable, our peers can often tell us precisely where we are blinded on our path.

A group of teachers known as *acharyas,* appointed by Chögyam Trungpa Rinpoche to carry on his work after his death, schedule routine meetings to give and receive feedback from their peers, particularly in relationship to their blind spots. In my experience and research, I have found that many contemporary spiritual traditions have a system for peer observations. The majority of teachers, however, work in isolation at the top of their hierarchy, and even those who have peers are rarely willing to use them as a mirror.

Still, we must be cautious with respect to which peers we receive feedback from. Many people in spiritual circles have an unconscious codependent agreement with their peers to affirm each other at the cost of being truthful, and many other people are simply afraid or do not have the skills to communicate truthfully and lovingly to their peers. Still, in order to maintain spiritual health and prevent disease, we must look for those who see us clearly and take their input seriously.

Admitting Our Errors
Every one of us on the spiritual path will err, whether as a new practitioner of meditation or a famous teacher. We will manifest spiritual disease and pass it on to others, spreading our confused knowledge and ignorance to those who know less than we do.

Once, when I was a zealous young practitioner on the path, I went to a talk by a very famous teacher. I asked a question about how to confront the great "No" within me that manifested itself as resistance to spiritual practice. He asked for an example, and I told him that I'd had two cups of coffee that day, which felt like an escape from reality and a breach in my commitment not to use intoxicants to alter my state of mind.

Amid the roar of laughter in the room—for at that time his students ran the local café where I had sinfully indulged in my two cups of coffee—his response pierced me deeply and has remained with me to this day. "Listen, honey," he said, "you are just beginning this path, and it is a long road ahead. You are going to make mistakes on this path, and you are going to make *big* mistakes. Save your energy for the big mistakes you are going to make and what you will have to do to remedy those."

Now, fifteen years later, I see quite clearly that both I and the teachers I respect continue to make mistakes, many of them on a large scale. The very same teacher who taught that I must save myself for the big mistakes went on to make very big mistakes himself, yet he has been unable to acknowledge and take responsibility for them. This is unfortunate, because admission creates an opening. In my experience, people can be tremendously resilient and forgiving. When approached with the humility of true remorse and heartbreak and with the admission of human error, hearts open and karma is undone. Deep spiritual wounds and diseases of resentment, guilt, anger, and even betrayal can be lifted from the body and spirit through simple but genuine gestures of remorse.

A colleague of mine was a very close student of Yogi Amrit Desai. In fact, she was one of those who sued him for his sex scandals (to which she had been subject), and she won the lawsuit. They remained in contact with each other and eventually did therapy together, which allowed them to explore the unconscious dynamic they had enacted and to express remorse and forgiveness. Many years later she returned to him as his student, and they now have a mature, thriving, adult relationship as guru and disciple. Change is possible. Forgiveness is possible.

We all make errors. One of the greatest we can make is to believe that we do not make errors. If we understand this, we can accept it when we err, apologize and make amends as needed, and continue our process of deepening on the spiritual path.

A critical part of learning discernment on the spiritual path is discovering the pervasive illnesses of ego and self-deception that are in all of us. That is when we need a sense of humor and the support of real spiritual friends. As we face our obstacles to spiritual growth, there are times when it is easy to fall into a sense of despair and self-diminishment and lose our confidence on the path. We must keep the faith, in ourselves and in others, in order to really make a difference in this world.

For those of us who share a lifelong commitment to the spiritual path, the bad news is often the good news, for it is the very process of learning to see what we could not see before that marks the awakening of our consciousness and a deepening discovery of discernment. When we can truly appreciate that we are unconscious because this is the very condition of being human, rather than because we have done something wrong, we become increasingly interested in the endless road to becoming ever more conscious. We know that our capacity to bring healing to ourselves, those we love, and our world is directly proportionate to our degree of awareness.

Chapter 3

The Posture of the Mind

Ninety-nine percent of all work on self is attitudinal.
—E. J. GOLD

It is ten o'clock on a December evening in 1999, and I am standing in the pouring rain outside the YMCA dormitory annex in Chennai, India, draped in a soaking-wet white Indian sari, with three other women, all my teacher's students. Forty of us have been with him on a five-week pilgrimage throughout southern India, traveling Indian style, meaning that any Western concept of physical comfort has long since been dashed on the rocks of the reality.

Having lived in India previously and made many subsequent trips, I am acutely aware of the distinctions among the variety of dwellings that pass as hotels and hostels in this country, and my senses immediately tell me that the abode we are to sleep in this night does not approach even the low end of acceptable lodgings. At this point on the pilgrimage, our exhaustion is severe and our morale fragile. So, before placing the key in the lock, I turn to one of the women, a former nun and the most pious of our group. "Please, Regina," I implore, "give us some words of wisdom before we enter!"

Regina stretches her six-foot-four-inch stature into an even greater regal height, inhales intentionally, and quotes Swami Papa Ramdas, a twentieth-century south Indian sage: "The whole universe is the work of God's art. To anything that we see, we do not give any particular importance as different from the rest of the world. But we see the whole universe equally as the manifestation of God, everything a beautiful manifestation."

Fortified by her words, we open the door and are not surprised by what we see: a floor slick with some unidentified liquid, two rusty bed frames, and four "mattresses" which feel, when we poke at them, as though they're filled with pebbles. On the bathroom floor there is excrement—most likely human. Rats and cockroaches scurry about, and a ceiling fan dangles by a rope in such a way that not only the blades of the fan move but the whole apparatus circles our room like a helicopter gone awry in a storm. But we have just been told that we have the possibility to see the whole universe equally, as a beautiful manifestation of God, and this is our intent. So we take the few cleaning supplies available and begin to sing and work together. We use shampoo for soap and scrub the toilet and floors, remove the various creatures, burn incense, hang silk scarves. We go to sleep uncomfortable—for no amount of positive attitude will take the rocks out of the bed—but with a sense of love in our hearts and communion among ourselves as women. That evening remains the most memorable event of that trip—more memorable than the ancient temples, sacred rituals, and sumptuous meals we experienced. Through the act of changing our minds we transformed a nightmare into a livable place full of support and communion.

Developing a healthy mental posture as described in this chapter is both the prerequisite for developing discernment on the spiritual path and a fruition of our labors. It cannot be overstated how essential the cultivation of attitude is to having a successful journey on the spiritual path. We cannot swim in the waters of the unconscious if we are not prepared with the right equipment—in this case, appropriate attitudes—and it is through diligent cultivation and keen discernment that these attitudes are developed and strengthened. This chapter outlines twelve attitudes that can strengthen our discernment and help us travel the spiritual path with greater clarity and less confusion. When our mind's posture is unaligned and imbalanced, our "spiritual immunity" is weakened, and we are prone to many forms of egoic confusion, including the spiritually transmitted diseases discussed in Chapter 2.

Webster's New World Medical Dictionary defines posture as "the attitude of the body" and "the carriage of the body as a whole." Like the body, the mind, too, has a posture, which is expressed through our overall attitude and disposition. Whereas it is clear that we must intentionally take care of our bodies—giving them healthy food and exercise and healing them when they are ill—we tend to give little attention to the cultivation of a healthy mental posture.

Attitude is one of the most significant expressions of the mind's posture. Our attitude largely comprises beliefs and viewpoints that have constellated into our worldview and is the result of conditioning, the origins of which extend far beneath our conscious awareness. To understand how the mind's posture becomes constellated through conditioning, consider the body's posture. If we closely study someone's physical carriage, we see how the body's posture expresses physical and emotional challenges that person experienced throughout his or her life.

Similarly, the human mind also contracts into a particular posture as a result of our upbringing and life experience.

The physical body reflects the mind's posture on a more gross, manifest level. "Good health begins in your consciousness," wrote T. Krishnamacharya, and thus cultivating a healthy mental posture is critical to the overall balance of mind and body necessary for spiritual practice, or *sadhana,* as well as for a high-quality life and general sense of well-being.

It's All about Attitude

"Everything can be taken from a man but . . . the last of the human freedoms—to choose one's attitude in any given set of circumstances, to choose one's own way," wrote Viktor Frankl, renowned author and Holocaust survivor, in *Man's Search for Meaning.* If an individual enduring torture in the Auschwitz concentration camp and living at the threshold of death can recognize the freedom to choose his attitude, it is fair to assume that all of us have this liberty, regardless of circumstance.

It is easy to assume that attitude is a gift of God, that we are either born with a good attitude or not. It is true that some very few human beings have been placed on this earth with an inherently good attitude. Perhaps these rare individuals were parented "just so" or were born with an atypical disposition such that they are naturally joyful, optimistic, friendly, and easy to be with. These people, however, are the true minority. The rest of us have to cultivate our attitudes and work diligently with our minds, because attitude is something that is earned, not given. Once we decide to take responsibility for our own attitude—for its continued development, maintenance, and growth—we have begun a process of internal work.

According to yogic philosophy, our attitude must be assiduously cultivated. The possession of a healthy attitude is a hard-won, prized possession that results from consistent efforts. The mind is continually expanding and contracting throughout the day, mostly beneath our conscious radar. As extensive meditation practice reveals, when the mind is contracted, it automatically produces thoughts and feelings that are an expression of that contraction. If the mind is left unattended, we experience ourselves as the victims of our thoughts, which are largely informed through our conditioning.

Ayurvedic doctor and author Robert Svoboda has suggested that nearly 90 percent of our thoughts today are the same as we had yesterday. We believe that we are thinking our thoughts, but in reality our thoughts think us. The Latin root of the word *posture* is *ponere,* which means "to put or place." It is through the intentional placement of our attention on our attitude that we are able to cultivate a healthy posture of mind.

Patañjali offers a recipe for attitudes necessary for success on the yogic path, often referred to as the "yoga vitamins." *"sraddhā vīrya smrti samādhiprajñā pūrvakah itaresām,"* He teaches that "practice must be pursued with trust, confidence, vigor, keen memory, and power of absorption to break spiritual complacency."[1] We must cultivate faith on the basis of what we have experienced and intuited and what has been offered to us by trusted spiritual texts and authorities. We must become confident and warriorlike, using our power of perseverance to sustain our efforts and cut through obstacles. We are called to constantly remember what we are doing and why we are doing it, and to remain absorbed in our task, unmoved in the face of distractions that tempt us away from our deeper purpose. In this way, says Patañjali, the deep knowledge that lies within us is revealed.

Cultivating attitude takes time, patience, inner attention, and great discipline. Unfortunately, many of us are simply too lazy or disinterested to make the intensive efforts required. We prefer, as Henry David Thoreau wrote, to "lead lives of quiet desperation," living vicariously through the images and people we see on television and the Internet. A healthy attitude requires a willingness to meet the emptiness, sorrow, and fear within, all of which insist that we do not choose our own well-being.

The first step toward cultivating a healthy attitude is to become aware of the unhealthy aspects of our present attitude. We must ask ourselves clearly, directly, and honestly, "What do I value, and is who I am an expression of those values? And if not, why not?" Once we place our conscious attention on our attitude, it begins to change. The first changes come quickly, deeper changes more slowly.

To change our attitude deeply enough that it will last a lifetime is not an easy—or quick—task, but what is more worth doing? Most of us are unaware that we can consciously choose our values and attitudes, and if we are not choosing them, they are choosing us. We must be clear about the attitude we wish to embody, and then consciously, intentionally, and systematically do what is necessary to develop and nurture it.

Twelve Attitudes for a Discerning Journey on the Spiritual Path

1. Sincerity of Intention

At the core of all accomplishment lies intention—the seed of creativity that is cultivated through subsequent effort. Nothing can happen without clear, strong, and sincere intention. To transform one's mind—to radically surrender control of one's limited self and allow something greater to be discovered—is one of the most difficult and frightening things a human being can do. And it is the ultimate requirement of any authentic spiritual path.

Not to be confused with the popularized concept of intention as "thinking your way into a new car," true intention is a type of clear seeing. We can find examples of the power of intention when we examine the lives of exceptional people. For example, the successful Missionaries of Charity began as an inner calling of a young Catholic nun from Albania named Agnes Gonxha Bojaxhiu, whom we now know as Mother Teresa. When the young woman was appealing to her superiors to start the Missionaries of Charity, she wrote that she knew she was no one special, yet she had a vision and a sincerity of intention behind her vision that she believed could bring it to fruition.

As human beings, we are both insignificant and possessed of immeasurable capacity. The sincerity of our intention itself can carry us as nothing else can. With strong intention we are saying to Life, "I understand that I am messed up, confused, and arrogant, but I am also sincere and good, and I want the wisdom that you offer." We must be clear that intention alone does not mean that we will "get" or "achieve" anything we intend or desire, which is sometimes implied in New Age philosophies and approaches. Life is neither that linear nor predictable, and a discerning approach that cultivates sincerity of intention includes the recognition that we are living in a complex universe that does not comply to all of our wishes. The sincerity of our intention is our offering to the spiritual path, and that intention needs to include a willingness to grow from whatever life provides us.

2. Compassion

When I was a new student, an older student who had been with my teacher for several years asked him, "Will my spiritual life be successful if I can just learn to be kind, generous, and compassionate?" I felt sorry for this man, for I was off to become enlightened, and he was simply learning to be kind, generous, and compassionate. It took me many years to appreciate what a challenge it is to be a consistently kind person—to learn that being truly generous with our time, energy, resources, and love is the exception to the norm and that true compassion is a very high state of being, rarely achieved.

Many of us like to think of ourselves as compassionate people, but we tend to vastly underestimate how rare and precious real compassion—the act of consistently placing others above oneself—is. During my yoga instructor training, there was a very beautiful woman in my class who, though very capable of the physical postures, was psychologically wounded to the point of psychosis. She was full of repressed rage, vampiric in energy, and so self-obsessed that she literally did not know how to be still and listen to others. Her default behavior was to talk incessantly, and she had learned to dress her psychosis in the drag of yogic concepts and philosophy. Her psychosis carried a banner that said, "Unity. Peace. Enlightenment." One day she came into class very concerned and frustrated because other people couldn't be as compassionate as she was. Why, she wondered aloud, couldn't other people love each other in all circumstances the way she did?

This student's overestimation of her compassion is a dramatic case, but in many ways it reflects the built-in human tendency toward self-centeredness, even if our "self" includes our children, family, and close friends. True compassion is earned through practice, experience, devotion, love, and heartbreak. It cannot be imitated or role-played. Mahatma Gandhi demonstrated compassion when he was assassinated. After the bullet hit him, but before he died, he prayed for his assassin. Those who have truly forgiven another person who has profoundly hurt or betrayed them have tasted compassion. We all experience powerful moments of compassion when our hearts open and we feel genuine love for all people or selfless care for a stranger in need. To express this compassion with unwavering consistency, regardless of circumstance, is a rare human achievement but an attitude worth striving for.

3. Vulnerability and Openness

Vulnerability is a good thing. Many people, especially men, shrink when they hear this word because it connotes being weak, undefended, and overexposed. But vulnerability is in fact a sign of great inner strength. "The soft overcomes the hard," says the *Tao Te Ching*. We allow ourselves to be touched by life in all its beauty and pain, to be transparent rather than guarded, and to let others in. Vulnerability carries with it a sense of rawness and genuineness that allows for authentic intimacy with others and with life.

To be open is to be vulnerable to life, to continuously look within oneself and out to the world, without guarding ourselves from feeling. Love, according to author John Welwood, is a combination of openness and warmth. Openness is the heart's gesture of vulnerability. When we are open we are present and available. From the perspective of transformation, nothing can happen until we decide that we wish to open. Once that decision is made, we have begun a journey of conscious evolution that has no end.

4. Patience

"Lord, grant me patience, but hurry!" read the framed plaque I had in my kitchen for years. Impatient by nature, I have learned little by little that my impatience does not make the

al process, or anything else for that matter,
quickly.

n't open if I yell at it and say, 'Bloom,'" notes
_yst and author Marion Woodman. The spiritual
path, or any journey of self-knowledge, takes a long, long
time. Many of the greatest teachers I have met say that the
changes we hope for when we enter the spiritual path might
not be seen for twenty or thirty years—and that the fruits
of spiritual practice may be so different from what we initially expect that we may not even notice them when they
do emerge. We should not be surprised if we see few changes
in decades of practice. Certain things do change, of course,
but transformation is slow, and it is easy to feel impatient—
even defeated—when the suffering that brought us to the
path does not disappear, and the enlightenment we planned
for fails to appear. For those who aspire to authentic spiritual
wisdom, there is no quick fix, and those who believe there is
will eventually have to make peace with the fact that spiritual
integration requires a lifetime of work. The path is going to
take its own sweet time.

5. *Equanimity*

Equanimity is the capacity to remain emotionally steady
regardless of circumstances. There is a wonderful story about
the eighteenth-century Zen master Ryokan, who, after the
theft of all of his very few possessions, sat down and wrote:
"The thief left it behind: the moon at my window."

Most people are tossed about by circumstances and lack
a center to sustain them. We live on the roller coaster of life
and, depending on our emotional disposition, we manifest
this externally in lives of high drama, self-hatred, depression,
or illness.

"Be that which nothing can take root in," says Lee Lozowick. We must gradually learn not to take all of life personally, either as a reward when things go our way or as a punishment when they do not. We are each, in our own way, primarily self-centered and self-oriented, and as a result we tend to think that everything is happening *to* us, rather than that things happen because the world operates in larger ways we cannot perceive. Equanimity is not cultivated easily and is a result of gradually learning to manage our minds.

6. *Responsiveness*

When I asked Tibetan Buddhist teacher Reggie Ray what his definition of enlightenment was, he said one word: "responsiveness." It took time for me to appreciate that the great, sought-after state of enlightenment could be defined as the capacity to respond appropriately to every circumstance, both internally and externally—but I think he is right.

The spiritual path is a one-way road full of potholes, challenges, and both pleasant and unpleasant surprises—particularly as we attempt to navigate the dark, murky, and unruly waters of the psyche. Our own journey is unique and highly unpredictable, and if we do not cultivate flexibility and willingness to respond to changing circumstances, we will get stuck.

An attitude of responsiveness requires discernment. Whereas routine can be very useful, habits can calcify into rigidity. Even spiritual practices can become an excuse for staying contracted and secure in the name of spiritual discipline or obedience. We must monitor our minds to be sure our practices are teaching us to be more flexible, not justifying our rigidity. For example, we might become so attached to our meditation practice that we cannot function sanely if we miss a day, or we become so insistent on eating healthy or organic food that when we visit our parents we are unwilling to eat what they provide.

"Response depends entirely upon circumstance," Lee Lozowick says. There is no cookie-cutter correct response to any circumstance, not even a spiritual one. Being resonant and responsive in a given moment is fully dependent upon all of the surrounding circumstances, seen and unseen, conscious and unconscious. Every circumstance and every moment is unique.

7. Passion

Translations of spiritual texts from many traditions warn us that we must tame our passions, and many people imagine that spiritually advanced people are very quiet and soft-spoken, and that they do not like wine, sex, music, or beauty. That is not my experience.

Passion is a complex and misunderstood subject, one that I repeatedly consider throughout this book. The misunderstandings are largely due to the conditioning we have received from Judeo-Christian brainwashing and from Eastern texts written for monks and nuns. Both traditions tend to equate passion with concepts of sin and sex, suggesting that passion is dark and dirty and linking it to temptation and mankind's fallen nature. On the contrary, great passion is required to meet the challenges of a lifetime commitment to the path; spiritual life should make us *more* passionate, not less.

Many of the world's great monks and nuns—people such as Thomas Merton, Swami Vivekananda, Teresa of Ávila, and Thich Nhat Hahn—were driven by great passion, in some cases erotic passion. The greatest spiritual teachers and practitioners I have met possess a tremendous capacity to engage life deeply, to extract its nectar, and to move effectively and with great love through life's labyrinth. For example, in addition to running three ashrams and living an austere lifestyle for months or years at a time, Lee Lozowick can also be found selling art, enjoying fine food, supervising artistic and theatrical projects, and singing on stage—dreadlocked and tattooed—to thousands of people on his band's annual European tours.

The Sanskrit term *tapas* (not to be confused with delicious Spanish appetizers) refers to the "fire of transformation" or "essential energy." Tapas is an internal fire that must be stoked until it begins to consume us, eventually burning away all obstacles separating us from who we really are. It is the act of learning to breathe and endure the burning-hot fires of transformation. Spiritual life is not always pleasant. Often, in fact, it is not, but it is our deep internal passion and conviction—as well as the joy we find in life—that sustain us through its challenges.

8. Relaxation

A few years into my apprenticeship with my spiritual teacher, he called me into his office and asked if I wanted some feedback. When I said I did, he told me, "If you want to move as quickly and effectively along the spiritual path as you say you do, you need to relax, relax, relax. Do you understand? Relax. Relax. Chill out and relax. I mean, you need to relax!"

In car accidents, your chances of getting seriously hurt are significantly lessened if your muscles are not tense. At fifteen I was in an almost-fatal car accident. My life was saved only because I was asleep in the backseat when it happened. My bones and muscles were relaxed enough to endure being smashed against the doors, roof, and floor of the car. The capacity to relax under stress, which is most often learned rather than innate, is a vital attitude to be cultivated on the path.

Spiritual life is a fine balance between effort and surrender. *"Prayata saithilya ananta samāpattibhyām.* Relax the tension brought forth by your efforts!" My yoga teacher, Bhavani, would quote Patañjali during intensive yoga practices when we were biting our tongues and our eyes were rolling back in our heads. In spite of what the fast-food spiritual teachers of our time claim, spiritual practice requires tremendous effort, and effort brings with it a certain amount of tension. We must learn to relax that tension, so we might open to the grace, depth, and energetic subtleties that are the result of practice.

9. Contentment

"Good day, sir," a student says to his master in a famous Zen story. "Is there such a thing as a day that is not good?" responds his master. For most of us, there are definitely bad days! Contentment, known as *santosha* in Sanskrit, must be diligently cultivated. Happiness in the way most of us consider it is largely dependent upon circumstances. If things go the way I want them to, and people are nice to me, and I get a great new pair of jeans, I'm happy. If things do not go as I wish they would, and my child won't listen to me, and my partner doesn't want to have sex with me, and I discover I have a cancer, I'm unhappy. This is an understandable response. We seek pleasure and avoid pain, and to the degree we are able to accomplish this goal, we imagine ourselves to be happy. But this kind of happiness is a very tenuous state— and it is the only kind most of us know. Our happiness lasts as long as the pleasurable stimulus or circumstance out of which it arose continues to exist.

Contentment, on the other hand, is noncircumstantial and is not emotionally based. It is an inner state of being that flourishes in the presence of receptivity, flexibility, and openness to meet whatever life brings—one of the fruitions of learning to keenly discern within the contents of one's own mind. We learn to gracefully receive what life gives us, rather than demand that life should always give us what we want. Such contentment is a mood of gratitude. It is a way of saying "thank you" even when life does not give us what we think we want. French spiritual master Arnaud Desjardins tells of a time earlier in his life when he was beginning to learn to master his emotions. When a difficult emotion arose, he would say, "Bring it on!" He was committed to developing contentment and equanimity, its sister, in the face of all apparent obstacles.

10. A Sense of Humor

"To listen to some devout people, one would imagine that God never laughs," wrote Indian philosopher Ghose Aurobindo.

Author Angeles Arrien tells a wonderful story about when she was a very serious young woman on the spiritual path and her teacher gave her a mantra. She went home and began to practice reciting the sacred syllables she had been given. *Sansah humah, sansah humah, sansah humah, sansah humah,* she repeated again and again, until suddenly it clicked. "Sense of humor!" Her teacher was telling her to lighten up and not take her spiritual process so deadly seriously.

The documentary *Sunseed* shows the renowned Japanese Zen master Suzuki Roshi—who was perhaps more influential in bringing Zen Buddhism to the West than any other person—playing with a yo-yo, talking about the sacrifice required on the spiritual path, and laughing as if it was the funniest thing he had ever thought about.

The south Indian saint Yogi Ramsuratkumar had a raging sense of humor. One time he asked me to lead Sanskrit chanting in front of more than a hundred of his disciples, and as soon as I started he began to wave his arms wildly, like a bird flapping its wings, making silly gestures and sounds next to me until I began to laugh so hard tears rolled down my face and I doubled over to the point that I could no longer chant. The more I laughed, the sillier he became—while his Indian devotees were becoming very angry with me for my sacrilegious behavior. It was important to him that we not only chant sacred syllables but that we laugh unreservedly and experience joy.

A sense of humor is necessary to make the trials of transformation bearable, and it is also a valuable transformational tool. When we are laughing, our defenses are down, and we are receptive and permeable to the inflow of grace, transmission, and energy. Humor, joy, and the capacity to make fun of ourselves are essential on the spiritual path. We must learn to laugh at ourselves, at the path, at ego. The divine play is beautiful, difficult, and absurd. When we can laugh at it, and ourselves, we find greater ease in the face of the transformational fires.

11. Wonder and Openness to Magic

In *Alice's Adevntures in Wonderland,* the queen says to Alice, "Sometimes I've believed as many as six impossible things before breakfast." We must strive to cultivate a sense of wonder and an openness to magic as we proceed along the spiritual path.

Magic is constantly present in the world, but most of us have shut down our perception of it. We all knew magic when we were children, and we often touch magic when we are falling in love, in the presence of great beings, during sacred rituals, or in nature. Yet learning to experience wonder and openness to the ordinary magic of daily life is an attitude that is cultivated. It comes through paying attention to detail, valuing small things, and appreciating the flickering moment of time that is our lives. It is not easy to open to magic and wonder, but opening precedes perception. A friend of mine who is a student of shamanism said, "From an ordinary perspective, seeing is believing. From a shamanic perspective, believing is seeing."

12. Humility

"Knowledge has become just one more commodity of commerce, the fuel we burn on the information superhighway," writes Robert Svoboda in *The Greatness of Saturn*. Many of us know a great deal about a lot of things, but few of us know ourselves. Not only do we *not* know ourselves, but we believe that we *do* know ourselves, so we do not even realize that we do not know. Distinct from the imitation humility that is so commonly pedaled in spiritual scenes, the true recognition that "I know that I do not know" allows us to stay open to the learning that the life process continually makes available to us.

We have to admit that we do not know what is going on. We have not intentionally deceived ourselves, nor have we been deceived. We simply do not know ourselves, and we must accept this fact before we can begin to discover who we truly are. In this simple recognition and admission begins the great journey to understand the mechanism of egoic functioning, to discover how our psyche functions and how to work with our emotions, and to gradually perceive the karmic and greater cosmic laws and learn how to function intelligently within their realm. Even what we believe to be knowable is a result of our mental conditioning and is limited by our current knowledge. The terrain of knowable reality extends far beyond our current knowledge.

"So let me get this clear," I said, as I walked up to my teacher's desk many years ago. "You're telling me that I absolutely cannot trust myself because the mind is conditioned, confused, and full of lies and self-deceit, and at the same time, I must trust myself implicitly because there is nothing else I can trust."

"Exactly," he said.

We cannot trust ourselves, and yet we *must* trust ourselves. The mind is full of self-deceit. This deception is so pervasive within our collective human understanding that we scarcely notice it is there. The mind lies and confuses. There are many "I"s within us, a subject we will explore in Chapter 4; some of them know the truth about ourselves and life and others do not.

It is a sign of discernment and human maturity to begin to make distinctions between what we know and what we don't. We gradually discover what it is possible to know and what we may never come to know, and we learn to place our attention skillfully. In this way, we build genuine confidence in ourselves just as we are, no more and no less, and we become more interested in what we don't know than in what we do.

Author Gilles Farcet says we tend to think of enlightenment as a state of all-knowing, but perhaps it is a condition of all-unknowing. Rather than placing all of our attention on trying to know everything, which is often a defense against the frightening vulnerability of our human condition, let us strive to *not* know and let the barriers erected by our spiritual arrogance and superiority be worn down until we become permeable to the wisdom of life itself.

Not everyone is capable of cultivating and expressing all twelve of these attitudes. Even the great teachers are human and prone to moments of faithlessness and even desperation. However, much as the overall health of the body is a result of attending to and nourishing its various components, our overall attitude improves as we attend to certain aspects of our mental posture. It is the sincerity of our attention combined with intelligent and discerning efforts that is responsible for an overall healthy posture of the mind.

The Necessity for Self-Study

> *In order to see, he must* learn *to see; this is the first initiation of man into self-knowledge. First of all, he has to know what he must look at. When he knows, he must make efforts, keep his attention, look constantly with persistence. Only through maintaining his attention and not forgetting to look, one day, perhaps, he will be able to see. If he sees one time he can see a second time, and if that continues he will no longer be able not to see. This is the state to be looked for; it is the aim of our observation; it is from there that the true wish will be born, the irresistible wish to become: from cold we shall become warm, vibrant; we shall be touched by our reality.*

> —JEANNE DE SALZMANN, *"First Initiation"*[2]

"I don't think I want to know what is inside myself," a childhood friend who was accompanying me to a dinner with a renowned psychologist told me. "I'm happy enough as it is, and if I knew what was inside of me I might not be anymore."

Most people do not know themselves very well, and like my friend, many people do not really *want* to know themselves, though few are honest enough to admit it. It is as if we would like to experience the imagined fruits of spiritual life—radiance, wisdom, compassion, understanding, clarity—yet we are unaware of, or even wary of, making the required effort. Although the attitudes just mentioned seem natural and healthy, available to everyone, in fact they are hard-won fruits of the path that are cultivated through intensive self-examination, contemplation, and practice.

Self-study, or *svādyāya* in Sanskrit, refers to a long and profound process of soul-searching by which a person tries to understand his or her own nature. It begins with the study of books and teachings through which we grasp concepts, progresses into gaining insights into our own psychology (often with the help of teachers, therapists, and mentors), and eventually comes down to the soul—to the nature of mind itself. To gain knowledge of oneself is perhaps the most important and most difficult thing we human beings are called to do, and it is indispensable in cultivating the attitudes required to navigate the spiritual path with discernment and clarity.

Authentic spiritual development cannot begin until we deeply comprehend that we do not really know how to see ourselves. Development can only begin from where we are, and if we believe that we are more knowledgeable than we actually are or that we know ourselves more deeply than we do, the initial lessons of the path will be to reveal to us how little we actually know. The invisible must be made visible before we can do anything about it, and the simple act of beginning to see ourselves *is* doing something about it. How is it that we live within these bodies and minds for decades and yet do not know what they are made of and how they function? Why are we so afraid of what is inside of us that we are willing to endure profound psychological suffering, physical illness, and even death and war between nations rather than see ourselves and understand our condition? Understanding the forces within us that sabotage our self-knowledge will gradually help us to undermine this self-destructive dynamic.

To begin with, the ego is designed to prevent us from seeing ourselves. Our current personality, or ego, is largely a conditioned survival structure that was formed in childhood to make sense of and cope with the vulnerable situation we found ourselves in. The ego is conditioned to believe that *it* is who *we* are. Because the ego does not know that it is a fabricated construct, any attempt to dismantle it is perceived as a death threat; therefore, as one aspect of ourselves moves toward self-knowledge, another unconscious aspect attempts to thwart its efforts at every turn. If we cannot outgrow the ego, what was once a valuable protective mechanism in childhood becomes the greatest obstacle to our development.

Next, we do not know how to see ourselves without judging ourselves, often harshly. We judge our thoughts, feelings, actions, motivations, and even our judgments, failing to see the underlying mechanism that supports the mind's house of cards. The function of judgment is to impede seeing. When we judge, we do not see. If someone else were to voice judgment of us as we judge ourselves, we would probably write them out of our lives—yet we constantly speak this language of judgment to ourselves.

Many of us are afraid to honestly see ourselves—to look deeply, without buffers, at our own self-deception and lies. We are unwilling because we feel so bad about ourselves, so essentially unlovable, and we are so full of self-criticism that we fear we'll crack under the vision of ourselves as we actually are. Full of self-hatred, self-doubt, and existential insecurity, most people operate only on the surface of their life experience. We prefer fiction to truth, and many of us lose the opportunity to know who we truly are. But just as the person we fear we are is a lie, the person we think we are is also a lie. We are neither. We are something different, and greater, than either of these. What that is can only be discovered in an authentic way through a long, dedicated process of soul-searching.

Once we have begun soul-searching, however, we enter a one-way street, one with many twists and turns on the long journey to self-knowledge. *Neti, neti,* or "Not this, not this," is the great process of purification by which we gradually discover what is ultimately real by seeing the endless levels of internal and external delusion and falsity that cover what is essential. According to the *Brihadaranyaka Upanishad*, we are able to distinguish what we are in those moments when we disidentify from the objects of our perceptions. Paradoxically, we discover who we are by seeing who we are not.

I think of a friend of mine who lives in Kauai, Hawaii, nature's paradise. He is thirty-eight, very handsome, a successful health-care practitioner, a gifted artist, and passionate about learning. Yet he suffers overwhelming internal tribulations in the same way many human beings suffer—the challenge of emotions, of digesting a difficult childhood, of finding deeper purpose and meaning. Living in paradise or not, our task is the same. While in Bodh Gaya, India, I heard His Holiness Gyalwang Karmapa speak to a group of thousands of monks assembled there. He told the group that a great part of the spiritual path is simply coming to terms with the challenge of emotion. There is no ultimate escape, and the realization of this is very good news. If we do not do something about our situation, nobody will. The recognition of this is the dawning of self-responsibility.

When we finally admit that there are things about ourselves we cannot see, there arises a possibility to begin to take responsibility for our lives and, in so doing, to open ourselves to more understanding, more heartbreak, more challenge, more expansion, and a greater ability to serve humanity in progressively deeper ways. Although we may have felt we were looking inward in years past—and we were to the degree that we were capable at the time—we turn more deeply inward than we ever have before. We let go of our previous knowledge and allow ourselves to be rebuilt into something greater.

"For me," said French Zen teacher Jacques Castermanne in an interview I conducted with him, "spiritual experience is to see differently. It is not to see something else. I might see this flower every day, and all of a sudden I can see it differently. I am taken aback. And for that I have to be attentive, taking care of the act of seeing."

Cultivating a healthy and flexible posture of mind helps prepare us to understand and learn to work with the deeper processes that underlie our egoic functioning. The next chapter, "The Psychology of Ego," dives directly into the complexity of ego itself and its relationship to psychology, karma, and projection.

Chapter 4

~~

The Psychology of Ego

I am not my fault.
—WES NISKER

L ook. There is no reason to keep wearing that costume. No one here is impressed," said radical spiritual master E. J. Gold to the intimate group of spiritual students assembled about him in his dining room. We had just arrived before daybreak at his center in Grass Valley, California, for a day of private teachings about the complexity of the egoic structure. Highly skilled spiritual teachers possess the capacity to share teachings that represent a certain aspect of reality and to momentarily transmit the *experience* of truth itself. In that moment, it was painstakingly evident to those assembled that the "costume" Gold referred to is none other that the totality of who we assume ourselves to be, including all the concepts, conditioning, and identifications that make up the perception of "myself." In that moment of recognition, it was as if all pretension dissipated, and we were left vulnerable and raw to the moment before us.

Ego: that shell of constructs and conditioning Shakespeare described as a "tale told by an idiot, full of sound and fury, signifying nothing." It is easy to assume that we know what ego means. We assume that we can, and do, accurately assess the size, shape, and health of our own, or someone else's, egoic structure. We don't often recognize that we are dealing with the single most complex and subtle apparatus of the human machine. We imagine that the complexity of the human psyche can be reduced to a few mommy-daddy issues that can be transcended through a course of therapy, or that the principle of karma can be reduced to the equivalent of a parlor game in which we interpret favorable events as "good karma" and unpleasant consequences as "bad karma."

Mystics and visionaries of the world's greatest traditions have investigated the intricacies of the ego for thousands of years, and now both pop psychology and many new spiritual movements have reduced these complexities to quick formulas and aphorisms that are bought and sold in the modern spiritual marketplace. Yet when we oversimplify these vast and important principles and prematurely assume we have understood and even mastered them, we easily fool ourselves, and we do not represent these principles clearly to others. We miss out on deeper possibilities.

This chapter begins an exploration into the complex, challenging, highly interrelated, and often misunderstood principles of ego, psychology, and karma. In order to cultivate spiritual discernment in our own lives, it is critical that we commit ourselves to an ongoing and even lifelong investigation into the nature of the egoic mechanism and the processes that inform it. Learning to work with and make distinctions with respect to ego, psychology, and karma is perhaps the most important and challenging task we are faced with on the spiritual path. The deeper fruits of spiritual understanding, such as wisdom and compassion, increase in relationship to the depth of practical understanding we have in relationship to these vast topics.

Our exploration into the topics of ego, psychology, and karma include a wide variety of other accompanying questions, such as: What is this ego that we so readily and facilely talk about? How does it function? Is our task on the spiritual path to destroy it or to work with it? How does projection work, and can we learn to withdraw the psychological projections we place onto others and onto life? What is the relationship between karma and psychology, and can we work with our karma through deep psychological inquiry? Although this chapter provides only an initial inquiry into these vastly complex, infinite topics, each morsel of understanding we are able to digest increases our capacity for discernment.

Perspectives on Ego

We talk about ego as if there were a collective agreement about what it is, how it functions, and how to keep it in check, yet no one seems to know where it is or what it is made of. When I ask my university students where the ego is, most say it is in their heads, and when I ask which part of the head, they say the mind. But no scientist has ever located a physical ego—why is that? Why are people afraid of having an ego that is too big but not one that is too small? Can we really claim to have a grasp on how the ego functions in our own lives, or should we always be investigating still deeper? Many spiritual traditions tell us that we must get rid of the ego, but how can we do that if we cannot even find it—and are we sure we would want to be rid of it, even if we could?

Ego is perhaps the most poorly understood concept in Western spirituality. We create endless presumptions, assumptions, generalizations, prejudices, and misunderstandings in relationship to ego, precisely because it is so complex and slippery. Since ego is intelligent, slick, and committed to avoiding being exposed, it's not surprising that we still know so little about it, in spite of all the attention it receives from psychologists and spiritual teachers.

To be able to discern with relationship to ego, psychology, and karma is a great help on the spiritual path. As we learn to understand our experience in a larger context, we can make wiser and more effective choices. It is important to remember that even if we *think* we understand ego, it is an elusive process that will constantly attempt to evade our understanding; thus we must be willing to explore the question of ego again and again.

The Multiple "I"s

"Who are you?" said the Caterpillar.

This was not an encouraging opening for a conversation. Alice replied, rather shyly, "I—I hardly know, Sir, just at present—at least I know who I was when I got up this morning, but I think I must have changed several times since then."

—LEWIS CARROLL, *Alice's Adventures in Wonderland*

Russian mystic G. I. Gurdjieff taught that human beings tend to imagine themselves as a seamless, continuous experience, but in reality we are made up of many small "I"s that arise in our consciousness, one after the other, each capturing our attention and convincing us that *it* is who *we* are. We do not notice that these "I"s are continually rotating within us, often arising as a conditioned response to our internal and external environments. This is why, for example, a businessman may be strong and confident while presenting at a meeting, but whimpering and fearful when his controlling mother calls him on the phone. At other moments he may be overwhelmed with depression, feel intensely sexual, and so on. Every human being has multiple personalities, and the egoic personality structure identifies with each of them as they arise.

One of the critical errors we make is to believe that we are the subpersonalities that arise within us. Some of us may have a relatively healthy, likeable, functional set of subpersonalities, while others have a more challenging set. Until we know how our ego functions and can choose whether or not it dominates our experience, we are not free human beings.

While we are endlessly caught up in and carried along by the unruly stream of our thought patterns, identities, ideas, and opinions, assuming always that they are "our own" new and original thoughts and perceptions, we are, according to Gurdjieff and other mystics, a machine. This machine comprises countless unconscious programs that endlessly and mechanically repeat themselves throughout our lives. To become conscious is to learn to observe this repetition and know intimately the stories we tell ourselves, which obscure the radiant and objective creativity in our lives.

We work to develop our being such that there is one "I" among the multiple "I"s within us that is steadier and more authentic than the others—a part of ourselves that we can access and that resonates with higher truth and guides us effectively along our path. It is this "I" that represents the authentic inner guru or guide, the true Self, the trustworthy voice of the heart, and the intuition that we strive to live by—yet these are so often obscured by the depth of our unconsciousness.

Thoughts Think Themselves

"Thoughts think themselves!" This shrill pronouncement of my elderly German Vipassana teacher interrupted the lonely silence of the desert and the endless chatter of our minds. I was twenty-two, and it was my first ten-day Vipassana meditation retreat. We participants were sitting on our butts for eighteen hours a day becoming acquainted with our minds: attempting to observe ourselves objectively and without judgment—but more often than not finding ourselves in endless self-created universes full of fantasy, fear, judgment, planning, resentment, hope, and endless repetition.

In spite of my mother's earnest suggestion that I might be more comfortable staying at home and staring at the wall for eighteen hours a day, I suspected that most of us—and certainly I—need to place ourselves in disciplined environments under careful guidance to be willing to face our own interior.

"*You* are not the one thinking," our Vipassana teacher would tell the group again and again. "Thoughts think themselves!" As a concept, this means very little. However, to understand experientially that thoughts think themselves can be a revelatory occurrence for human beings: to become convinced, if only temporarily, that "we"—whoever we imagine ourselves to be—are not the ones thinking our thoughts, but that our minds are endlessly repeating habitual thought forms that result from familial, cultural, and karmic conditioning. Our thoughts largely comprise things we have read, heard, or been told or that others around us think and believe.

Through a dedicated process of learning to observe our minds—a process that often spans decades—we become able to abide in a steady conviction that we are not our thoughts but that thought itself functions automatically. When this happens, we gain the possibility of becoming free from the shackles of our conditioning. When we identify with our thoughts, we become them. Our minds are so powerful that most human beings are slaves to their own conditioned thought patterns, unaware that the arising thoughts are but one minute aspect of who we are.

"We all know how powerful thoughts can be," writes Robert Svoboda in *The Greatness of Saturn*. "Though thought has minimal 'reality' in the physical universe, it is the cause of most of the physical activity that happens there. Our thoughts and emotions are regularly transformed into our physical realities, and our physical conditions generate our emotional and psychological states."[1]

Ego *is* this identification with the mechanical loop of thought-emotion-manifestation. Very few individuals even know that such circuitry exists or that there is the possibility of living outside of its confines.

The I-Thought

"Ego is identifying the mind as yourself," says Patañjali. In Sanskrit, *ahamkāra* is defined as the "making of the utterance 'I.'" We create an identity and then wholly believe ourselves to be that. The moment we are convinced, "This is me. I know who I am," we have confined ourselves to a false and limited identity. The identity is not the problem—identification is how human beings function. Rather, it is the conviction that we *are* what we identify with that confines our existence. "Until you become an unbeliever in your own self, you cannot become a believer in God," said Sheikh Abu-Said Abil-Khair.

Author John Welwood describes ego as the "I-thought," or the thought of "me." He describes the functional ego as a managerial function created by the mind for the purpose of navigating in the world. He says that the tragedy arises when we start to believe that this manager is who we are, not unlike the manager of a business pretending to be the owner. The ego, or "managerial self," is trying to do the right thing without ever really succeeding. He writes:

> Ego, in the Buddhist sense, is the ongoing activity of holding oneself separate, making oneself into something solid and definite, and identifying with this split-off fragment of the experiential field. Continually maintaining this identity project perpetuates a division between self and other that prevents us from recognizing ourselves as seamlessly woven into the larger field of reality. And the more we hold ourselves separate from the world, from our own experience, and from the naked power of life itself, regarding these as other, the more we fall prey to inner struggle, dissatisfaction, anxiety and alienation.[2]

The late U. G. Krishnamurti, one of the great spiritual revolutionaries of our time, used to provocatively blame the identity crisis all human beings suffer on their mothers. "The moment the child comes out from the uterus and the woman says to it, 'You are my child, and I am your mother,' she has ruined the child! From then on the child is brainwashed into believing that it is a separate entity." He suggests that this proclamation of a separate self begins the lifelong sense of separation from the Divine.

This is the same U. G. Krishnamurti who—when I walked into the room where he was staying in Bangalore, India, to interview him—was repeatedly pounding his wrist so forcefully onto a wooden table that I could not imagine how his frail, eighty-two-year-old bones did not shatter. "The only reason this would hurt me," he shouted over the pounding, "is because somebody told me that I was a person, and this was a table, and there is a concept of pain!" He may have said and done unusual things, but his very body demonstrated that he had gained powerful understanding.

Why Ego Can't Die

A fundamental misconception about spiritual life in the Western world is that we are trying to kill the ego. There is much talk about waging war against ego and getting rid of it. "Ego is the enemy. We must conquer it!" proclaim many modern charismatic teachers, and their earnest students attempt to squash and kill these egos that they cannot even see. We somehow imagine that if we meditate enough, or follow our guru with enough devotion, at some point there will be a great explosion and ego will shatter into millions of pieces, and from then on we will live in a state of continual inner peace and grace. Once again, ego has been misunderstood. The underlying sense of psychological badness and self-hatred that so many of us feel is now transferred to spiritual life, with the object "ego" placed upon it, and we set out to destroy the ego, hoping that our sense of badness, or not-okayness, will go away with it.

Ego cannot and does not die. We would not want it to, or we might walk into the middle of the road and be run over, forget how to answer the telephone, lose our jobs, and simply cease to function at the most basic level. Ego's job is to manage our survival, and we need it to function effectively in life. Paradoxically, the ego is very useful in the cultivation of discernment. It can be a valuable tool on the spiritual path.

If our work with ego is effective, our *identification* with the egoic mechanism will become gradually lessened over time and through spiritual practice. If we are fortunate, it may be pierced altogether. Through disciplined meditation and inquiry, we will gain experiential insights into the functioning of our own egoic mechanism and the capacity to function more and more often outside of its dominance. We will learn through experience and self-observation that in every moment there is a tendency for egoic patterns to dominate, and as we gain a capacity to perceive this more clearly, we can choose to act differently in the face of these tendencies, moment after moment. Just as when we learn any new skill, or strengthen any muscle, our ability to work with ego increases. But it requires continual attention, as the tendency of ego is to once again assume control, and the temptation for us to identify with it is relentless.

It is important to understand that the vast majority of us—regardless of what tradition we're involved with and what practices we do—are unlikely to become enlightened and disidentified with ego once and for all and then live happily ever after. Many modern Western traditions sell the promise of "enlightenment," but the product being sold is an imitation or of very low quality. Insight into ego is not hard to come by; many teachers can provide a direct experience of it. And it is stunningly powerful and beautiful to discover that we are not who we imagined we once were and that freedom from this identification is as simple as a shift in perspective. But to maintain such an experience is exceedingly rare. Moreover, such insight is but one stepping stone on an endless path to spiritual integration and maturity.

It is common in spiritual circles to hear the claim that you have to have an ego before you can lose it. I think it is more accurate to say that the ego must be simultaneously strengthened and disidentified with. The ego must be strengthened—for this strength not only fuels our practice but is the mechanism through which many of the fruits of our practice are expressed—but, at the same time, it is being progressively revealed for what it is. The release of ego's control is a nonlinear process in which the ego gradually dominates us less and less. For this to occur, the ego must be at times expanded, at times diminished. To get stuck in perpetually building our egos with the idea that at some time in the distant future we are going to do the work of disidentification is a trap. It is also a trap to try to detach from and transcend the ego before we are prepared to do so, prematurely bypassing necessary human development, a subject that will be discussed in detail in the next chapter.

The Battle between Yes and No

As I said earlier, once a human being consciously chooses to commit his or her life to a journey of uncompromised spiritual transformation, a great unconscious war begins within—Gurdjieff's "battle between yes and no." Consciously, we have perceived a deeper possibility for our lives; we have understood that our lives are essentially meaningless if we do not claim our birthright to become who we truly are and to live in accordance with that truth. But, as we've seen, the commitment to transformation is a death threat to the egoic mechanism that has been programmed to ensure our survival. Our commitment to the path implies an eventual, but definite, annihilation of the egoic mechanism within us that says, "I am separate. I am who I believe myself to be."

"So many people say that they want to become one with everything," says Lee Lozowick, "but what they really mean is that they want to become one with everything pleasant and beautiful, with bliss and love. They do not really consider that the enlightenment they pursue means that they not only become one with all that is light, but also one with all the suffering that exists in the world, with all beings, on all levels."

As we move deeper into the transformational journey on any authentic path, it gradually becomes clear that the journey is not what most of us imagined or fantasized it would be—at least not what ego hoped it would be. Any authentic spiritual process takes the deep unconscious material within us—as well as all of our fundamental confusions and illusions about the human condition and the nature of mind—and brings it to the surface of our awareness, so we can see it for what it is and discover how to relate to it in an effective manner. This is a demanding and lengthy process that often brings us to our knees, at times leaving us wondering if ignorance really is bliss—while knowing that we could not return to that state of ignorance even if we wanted to.

For many years at the beginning of my journey with my teacher, I complained about the same thing: before I engaged the spiritual journey in a profound and committed way, I had been able to passionately feel my desire for truth and God. Once I committed to the path, it was much harder to feel. This is a common experience. It is as if prior to fully committing ourselves to the transformational process we are swimming on the surface of life, alone, calling out for help. Once that help comes, if it comes in the form of an authentic path or teacher, we are suddenly plunged into the turbulent waters of the unconscious; tossed about by waves of emotion; and drawn into the whirlpools of unconscious memories, fears, traumas, and mechanical reactivity. We are sucked into transformational currents we cannot control, often described as "egoic purification," and suddenly the little "me," or egoic mechanism, calls out for safe shores.

French spiritual master Arnaud Desjardins recounts a humorous story that reveals the depth of this unconscious resistance. Many years into his path, when he was already a deeply experienced spiritual practitioner, he slowly sipped a coffee while waiting to board a plane to visit his guru, Swami Prajnanpad, in India. The airport loudspeaker announced, "Monsieur Desjardins, please come to the boarding gate. The doors will be closing." Then, five minutes later, "Monsieur Desjardins, this is the last call for boarding." Meanwhile, he says, he was listening to these announcements and saying to himself, "Who is this Monsieur Desjardins who is about to miss his plane?" Finally, at the last moment, he realized that *he* was the Monsieur Desjardins who, with great unconscious resistance to visiting his guru and the transformation that the visit implied, was about to miss his flight!

Ambivalence, or the coexistence of contradictory emotions, attitudes, ideas, and desires, is an inevitable response of ego in relationship to spiritual evolution. Throughout the years of working with my teacher I have seen countless examples of how ego sabotages transformation: sudden work responsibilities come up before a retreat, people get sick, accidents or flat tires happen on the way. Sometimes students completely forget the appointments they have with the teacher. It is naïve to believe that the ego, whose very survival is threatened by spiritual practice, will joyously and effortlessly agree to its own demise. Instead, we must learn to become aware of, and eventually to work with, the deep resistance we carry even toward that which offers us our heart's greatest desire.

Healthy Ego Development

Because we cannot see or locate ego and we have many misconceptions about it, learning to work with it remains a core challenge throughout our spiritual lives. Since ego cannot and does not die, effective spiritual practice and development must guide us in how to forge a constructive relationship with it.

Michael Washburn, one of the foremost theorists in the field of transpersonal psychology, has formulated a theory of healthy ego development on the spiritual path that he calls a spiral dynamic model. According to this model, growth happens in a spiral with an ongoing relationship between psychology and spirit. It teaches us that we must cultivate keen discernment in relationship to egoic development to optimize our spiritual development.

In the first stage of his triphasic (three-stage) model, known as the pre-egoic stage, the separate, egoic self emerges at birth from its true nature, which he calls the dynamic ground, and begins to discover itself as a separate entity. Yet, it is still closely identified with the dynamic ground, symbolized by its mother or primary caregiver.

In the second phase, known as the egoic stage, the ego must necessarily separate itself from both the dynamic ground and its primary caregiver in order to assert its independence and discover its own identity. This is a natural and healthy phase of human development. But the "great trade-off," as Washburn calls it, is that human beings tend to repress, and often forget, their own deeper nature or identity with the dynamic ground—which he describes as the very "life of the soul," referred to as the Self, Essence, the Divine, or God in other traditions. Most human beings, he says, remain at this level of development throughout their adult lives, having forgotten their true nature. It is this stage of development that is accepted as "normal" in mainstream Western culture: what Abraham Maslow described as "the psychopathology of the average."

However, there remains a greater possibility for human development, which Washburn refers to as the trans-egoic stage. In this phase (which will be discussed in greater detail in Chapter 6) there is a crack in the shell of the egoic dynamic, often catalyzed by crisis, that reveals the underlying dynamic ground. Once in touch with its source again, the ego becomes transformed by the power of the dynamic ground, wedded back to that ground, and even used by the ground as a vehicle of service. This, according to Washburn, constitutes optimal healthy egoic development and human integration. Such human integration is discovered through the capacity to apply clear discernment in relationship to one's inner life.

The nineteenth-century Indian Swami Ramakrishna was approached by one of his students, who said, "Sir, if one gave up the I, nothing whatsoever would remain." "I am not asking you to give up all of the I," Swami Ramakrishna responded. "You should give up only the 'unripe I.' The 'unripe I' makes one feel: 'I am the doer. These are my wife and children. I am a teacher.' Renounce this 'unripe I' and keep the 'ripe I' which will make you feel that you are God's servant, his devotee, and that God is the doer and you are his instrument."

We must remember that even the healthy ego can have its own traps. It is easy to confuse a healthy ego with profound spiritual realization. The achievement of a healthy ego does not mean we have transcended the limitations of ego, and we must be discerning to not mistake one process for another.

As we turn to the subject of ego's relationship to the human psyche and psychology, it is important to remember that ego itself is not a problem. It is part and parcel of the human condition. It is *our relationship* to ego that brings us so much suffering. If we are interested in truth and possess a deep wish to develop spiritually, we are obliged to engage a committed, lifelong relationship with our own egoic mechanism, including its health and strength as well as its unconsciousness, deceit, and traps.

Psychology and Ego

The term *psyche* is derived from the Latin and Greek root *psukhe*, meaning breath, life, and soul. A fully developed psychology should address the very soul of the human being and the core issues we face in achieving our broadest possibility of development. Of course, most of modern Western psychology does not do this.

The awareness of the complexity of the egoic mechanism is not new to humanity, and the need to find intelligent ways to work with it has been understood by esoteric spiritual traditions for thousands of years. Elaborate systems of psychology are found in Buddhist, Sufi, and Hindu traditions. What we in the Western world call psychology is simply one aspect of the study of human consciousness, which ultimately cannot be separated from the spiritual dimension of life. It is only modern Western psychology that has split psyche from spirit, primarily because of the dominant scientific paradigm that splits spirit from matter and acknowledges only what is quantifiable. Although much of Western psychology is empirically and scientifically based, many of the most influential pioneers in the field, from William James to Sigmund Freud to Carl Jung, were well versed in, and in some cases engaged in, the practices of both Eastern and Western esoteric spirituality.

In an ideal circumstance, spirituality and psychology would not be viewed separately; they in fact need each other to provide an integrated model of human development, a subject that will be considered in depth in Chapter 10, "The Union of Psychology and Spirituality." Those who are committed to a path of spiritual development cannot afford to deny their psychological development—as so many in the Western world do—any more than those who are interested in exploring and working with their psychology can dismiss the spiritual dimension of their experience.

Jacques Castermanne, who became a prominent teacher of Zen Buddhism in France, recounts his own discovery of the value of psychology:

> *When I was a young man beginning my studies of Zen with the German master Karlfried Graf Dürckheim, he suggested that I do a course of analysis with a man named Dr. Tolber, who was both a student and friend of Carl Jung. For more than one year I refused, believing that because I did so many spiritual exercises that I didn't need any psychoanalysis. Finally I agreed to meet Dr. Tolber, and he immediately attracted me as a person. He looked so balanced, full of confidence and calm. So I asked him, "What is this unconscious that psychology speaks so much about?" He burst out laughing, "The unconscious is that which is not conscious." I laughed with him, and soon after began my first course of analysis, which shifted my understanding of the spiritual path in a profound way.[3]*

Yogic philosophy suggests that there are five sheaths called *koshas,* or levels of the body, that go from the gross level of the physical body to the subtle spiritual body. *Annamayakosha* refers to the food body or physical body and includes physiological functions; *prānamāyakosha* is the level of energy and life force and breath; *manomayakosha* is the level of the mind, which includes the processing of thoughts and emotions; *vijñānamayakosha* is the wisdom body that lies beneath the thinking and processing mind; and *ānandamayakosha* is the sheath of bliss, or pure being, that surrounds the *atman,* or individuated pure consciousness.[4]

From the perspective of this model, modern Western psychology can be situated at the level of manomayakosha, the sheath of the mind. However, healthy psychology also includes the previous levels of physiology and energy, since obstructions at the level of the physiology, nervous system, and energetic balance of the individual will directly affect and be affected by dis-ease at the level of the mind. Although work at the level of manomayakosha, or psychology, is not the highest level of consciousness we can access, it is the level at which most human beings, whether involved in spiritual life or not, get stuck—and so it is worth our attending to.

Integrated knowledge at each of these levels is dependent upon health at the previous levels; thus, when someone accesses higher levels of spiritual awareness but has not addressed the level of psychology, his or her development will inevitably be lopsided. This is a common occurrence in many spiritual teachers and students. An imbalance in or a disregard for the importance of psychological development is the cause of most of the problems and scandals that serious spiritual practitioners, and teachers, encounter on the path; I will discuss this in the next chapter, "Spiritual Materialism and Spiritual Bypassing."

Mommy, Daddy, and the Labyrinth of Emotion

Many of us who like to imagine ourselves as mature adults have had, the experience of being in a moment of great stress—a car accident, a severe illness, an impending crisis—and instead of responding with intentional breathing, prayer, or rest in a greater presence, we find ourselves longing for our mothers. Stories abound of ordinary men and women, as well as profoundly realized individuals, in the moment of death crying out, "Mommy!"

The imprints we received in relationship to our mothers and fathers, and to a lesser extent our siblings, in the first few years of our lives form the basis of the emotional reality that most of us will carry throughout our adult lives. We would like to believe that ten or twenty years of meditation or spiritual studies would irrevocably alter our emotional patterning, yet the testimony and example of thousands of spiritual practitioners in the Western world demonstrate that it does not. For many of us, one of the valuable fruits of long-term dedicated practice is the appreciation of the depth of emotional wounding to which we remain enslaved, the acknowledgment of which provides a powerful motivation to understand the nature of emotion itself and to learn effective ways of working with it.

One of the primary functions of psychologists is to help us work with emotions, and many tools can be effectively applied to this task, yet very few therapists actually understand the nature of emotion, its relationship to thought, and how the mind functions—precisely because the relationship between these things is only experientially gained through meditation, contemplation, and spiritual exercises. The dynamics of the psyche in relationship to spiritual development is at the cutting edge of Western psychology and is addressed only by newer fields in psychology, including transpersonal and integral psychology.

Swami Prajnanpad was a deeply realized twentieth-century Indian master who lived in the Himalayas in northern India and taught Advaita-Vedanta to his Indian disciples. Eventually, a small group of French students came to study with him, and he faced the challenge of how to help these individuals raised in Western culture address the dense layer of emotional wounding that they had acquired through their cultural and familial conditioning and that blocked them from access to deeper spiritual understanding. Many of the psychological challenges that students from the Western world faced were distinct from those that his Indian students faced, and therefore needed to be approached accordingly. Although the field of Western psychology was still quite new, Swami Prajnanpad devoured the writings of Sigmund Freud, and because of his own deep abidance in an enlightened context, he was able to understand psychotherapy in the context of oneness.

Through an intensive therapeutic process known as "lyings," he helped his students trace the roots of their powerful emotions back to the source of the original traumas and open themselves to what they had turned away from. In this way, they learned to truly "become one" not only with their essential nature but also with the source of their suffering and various aspects of their psychological makeup: to become one with all of themselves. Through this therapy, the unconscious imprints from their past experience would have decreasing influence over their present responses to life.

Swami Prajnanpad made an important distinction between emotion and feeling. As a result of being in a human incarnation, almost all of us, no matter how well we were raised, encountered experiences too intense for our young psyches to digest and integrate. As children, we were not permitted to experience our feelings in a raw, immediate way—allowing them to arise, be sustained for their natural duration of time while we were held, and then subside within a safe context in which we were understood. Unable to digest our experience, we contracted around the feeling by employing a variety of defense mechanisms: repressing the feeling, fleeing into fantasy, blaming ourselves or God, or simply numbing ourselves and erecting invisible barriers in our psyche.

As adults, when these old feelings arise we tend to automatically contract in response to them, as if to say, "What I am experiencing should be otherwise. Reality should be other than it is." We refuse the experience of what *is* in the given moment, yet we cannot make it otherwise. Thus our feeling becomes an emotion, which is in essence the rejected shadow of the raw experience of feeling—replete with accompanying stories, projections, justifications, and dramatization—all as a result of our inability to be intimate with ourselves at the level of feelings. Most of what we call "feeling" in colloquial, as well as psychological, terminology is in actuality emotion.

Gilles Farcet, a French psychologist and writer who is steeped in the teachings of Swami Prajnanpad, explains it in the following way:

> Emotion is a feeling turned savage, gone wild. Whether it is being so madly in love that we cannot pay attention to the rest of the world, or whether we are driven uncontrollably by our hate, greed, anger, or desire, we become completely identified with an event and are driven away from our basic integrity rather than toward it. Feeling, on the other hand, is more subtle. It is the intrinsic quality of an experience, which does not drive us away from ourselves but helps us to be more closely in touch with ourselves. Love, for example, can be experienced as an emotion or a feeling, and the difference is subtle.
>
> Emotion is always associated with thought, mental processes, and an overemphasis and exaggeration, and it is unconsciously linked with past conditioning. The degree of exaggerated response in the present is the result of an unconscious denial of its associations with the past. Practically speaking, very often we switch from feeling to emotion. For example, we look at our child on the beach and feel something real: the innocence of that child. And then quickly it becomes an emotion: "It is my child, and

I am so proud. I hope he or she turns out okay." When
we are stuck in emotion, we are in the loop of our
conditioning, and we can only react, mechanically and
predictably, to circumstances. When we allow ourselves
to feel, we can act and respond to the moment based on
conditions in the present.[5]

The Nature of Projection

"The mark of human maturity is the capacity to withdraw projections," says Jungian psychologist Marion Woodman. Our egoic, cultural, and psychological conditioning is so potent that it causes us to continuously distort reality, reframing it through our projections.

Most of us are so unaware of the encompassing, persistent, omnipresent, insidious nature of projection that it is difficult for us to perceive anything outside of our projections. We project onto our loved ones, often seeing not *them* but our own version and perception of them, and many potentially workable relationships break up because individuals cannot take responsibility for the projections they bring to their partners and circumstances. In spite of our best intentions, we project onto our children—who and how they should be, how they have failed us when they do not conform to our expectations, what they owe us. We project onto the spiritual path and its teachers, insisting on our ideas of where the path should take us and who the teacher is and what his or her function is.

Most modern religions rely on collectively agreed-upon projections of God that are so filtered and distorted they don't really mean anything. We pray to our projection, struggle with our beliefs about our projection, feel guilty, bad, and wrong in relationship to our projection. For most of us the projection is so internalized that we don't even know it is there.

Our emotional reality and the challenges we face with others are largely a function of a profoundly unconscious labyrinth of projections based on often forgotten moments in our past that formed the belief systems that we carry throughout our lives and continue to replay until our deaths. When we cannot take responsibility for our projections, they are expressed in our lives as distorted relationships. "If you can't control yourself, control others," reads a T-shirt printed by E. J. Gold.

Through "lyings," Swami Prajnanpad helped his students appreciate the pervasive degree to which certain pivotal moments and decisions made in childhood continue to distort our relationships throughout adulthood and distort our relationship to the spiritual path. In this therapeutic process that occurs in intensive sessions of two to three weeks and often spans many years, individuals begin with what is called "the exciting cause," any strong emotion that is arising in their lives. They develop a capacity to stay with the emotion with a degree of penetrating presence that, like a rewinding video, gradually takes them back in time to the initial source of the emotion. This original event, experienced by the infant as trauma no matter how well-meaning the parent or circumstance, may be a memory, emotion, bodily sensation, or some combination. The individual attempts to stay present as long as possible with these core events in order to know them, taste them, and truly understand them for what they *were* in the past and experience how they remain alive in his or her psyche in the present.

Once we have enough *experiential* intimacy with the pivotal moments of childhood that become constellated structures in our psyche and are replayed throughout our lives—usually gained through effective psychotherapy or spiritual practices that address the emotional level of our experience—we become conscious of the forces that own us. Each time we withdraw a false projection, we free up energy that is invested in it and allow a clearer perception to be formed. We refine our capacity for discernment and thus are able to live more authentically and function with increasing spiritual maturity. First, however, we need to learn to see the projections.

"Everything that irritates us about others can lead us to an understanding of ourselves," said Carl Jung. As our appreciation of the pervasive nature of projection increases, we begin to be able to use the intensity of our emotional reactions as important clues to help us understand the psychological knots that keep us locked in "my reality" instead of reality. The unconscious manifestations of others may continue to make us uncomfortable when we are in their presence, but the intensity of our reaction is our own. When we find ourselves reacting strongly to another individual, particularly if we are obsessing psychologically, it is an indication that we are operating in the realm of emotion rather than feeling. And the intensity of our reaction suggests it is connected to a projection.

Although we may never be free of all our projections, a powerful emotional reaction to a person or event can help wake us up to distortions in our thinking. I have a friend I used to live with in South Africa who at seventy-five, and after more than forty years of spiritual practice, still actively explores this principle. Sometimes when I would come home and ask her how her day had been, she would say, "Oh, it was a good day. I had some strong reactions to people, and that was the Divine's way of saying to me, 'Gillian, you still have more work to do!'"

Sometimes it is easier to understand certain aspects of our own behavior when we observe them exhibited grossly in others and then slowly allow ourselves to see these traits within ourselves. Author and shaman Carlos Castaneda called people who exhibit such gross and unpleasant behaviors *pinches tiranos*, or "petty tyrants," and said they are of tremendous help to us on the spiritual path: through our reactions to such people we can discover where we remain emotionally conflicted. It is reported that Russian mystic G. I. Gurdjieff consciously chose to invite individuals with provocative and disturbing personalities to live in his spiritual community. They helped his students understand the deeper projections underlying their reactivity, so they might be able to gradually withdraw their projections and take greater responsibility for themselves.

A Karmic Perspective on Psychology

If somebody had to live my life, why did it have to be me?!

—ANONYMOUS

Withdrawing projections is a lifetime labor of love. In each moment when we recognize and withdraw a projection, we are intercepting a pattern of conditioning whose roots extend far into the past and well beyond our personal history. To understand this process and broaden our perspective on the complex forces involved in egoic conditioning, it is helpful to consider the concept of karma. Although karma is a vast and complex principle beyond the scope of this book, appreciating the link between karma and psychology can awaken a broader perspective about the psychological task we face when we enter spiritual life.

Our personal psychology is how our karmic patterns show up in this lifetime. A general Buddhist or Hindu perspective on karma suggests that the individual soul moves through consciousness lifetime after lifetime, incarnating again and again in the school of life in order to complete various tasks and lessons. The conditions and circumstances of each incarnation are based on forces far greater than most of us can conceive of. These forces determine the quality of consciousness we are given, the culture and families we are born into, the bodies we have, and the significant experiences and relationships we encounter. "The accumulated imprints of past lives, rooted in afflictions, will be experienced in present and future lives," writes Patañjali in the *Yoga Sūtras*.[6] If we want to understand the nature of the karma we have earned in past lives, we need look no further than our present life circumstances.

Over great expanses of time, patterns of conditioning repeat themselves endlessly. Psychologist John Welwood describes karma as the transmission of tendencies from one mind-moment to the next. He says that each grasping mind-moment carries forward a previous moment of grasping and passes it on to a successive moment. Our karma arises out of an egoic contraction against the boundless openness of being in order to establish a measure of security and control, establishing "me" as something bounded, definite, substantial, and separate. The karmic viewpoint suggests that we are granted incarnation so that we might find our way through these "knots in consciousness," releasing ourselves from the limitations and suffering that arise from a contracted and misperceived notion of who we are. The situations specific to our lives provide opportunities to learn necessary lessons and unravel the bonds of karma.

Robina Courtin, a Tibetan Buddhist nun from Australia who teaches Buddhism in maximum security prisons, explains that whatever we are experiencing in the present moment is both the fruition of our previous karma and the planting of seeds for future karma. The circumstances we encounter *are* our karma, *are* the expression of our consciousness, and *are* the seeds of our future. We are in a great hologram of karma, and our lives reflect the intersection of our family or genealogical karma, the collective karma of our culture, and, in many cases, a particular set of karmas that is expressed through the teachers and communities we encounter on the spiritual journey.

There are confrontational moments of bare honesty in life during which we perceive clearly that we are reaping the seeds we have sown at an earlier time, whether through accident, illness, or misfortune. An illustration is the case of the father of a friend of mine who ran drugs for many years. When he tried to get out of the business, he was brutally tortured by a group of hit men who had come to his house looking for his hidden stash of cash. He could change his karma, but he could not evade having to experience the karmic seeds he had sown.

More commonly, many of us have found ourselves in a situation in which a seeming white lie, or an act of ignorance or indulgence, comes back to haunt us. At other times, there is a nonlinear ripening of certain past karmas arising from a time or circumstance that is beyond our conscious capacity to perceive. To even consider that the psychological and practical circumstances we face are powerfully influenced by karmic forces requires a willingness to significantly broaden our viewpoint; it also offers the possibility of accepting a degree of self-responsibility that can be simultaneously daunting and liberating.

Bert Hellinger, Alejandro Jodorowsky, and Marianne Costa are among those who have developed intricate psychological processes by which we can literally trace our current psychological challenges not only to our parents but to our grandparents, great-grandparents, great-great-grandparents, and even earlier.

We discover that so many of the deep challenges we face on many levels, and that sometimes feel so devastatingly personal—not only emotional challenges, but relational, physical, and circumstantial ones—are literally passed down through generation after generation and result from a degree of conditioning that is totally impersonal and unconscious.

We may be shocked to realize that many of the powerful experiences we have are influenced in an immediate way by our great-great-grandparents and even far beyond them. These experiences include depression, relationship patterns, illnesses, divorces, and even the age at which we die, as well as many "choices" we experience ourselves making, such as how many children we have, having an abortion, or who we choose to be in relationship with. Only now, they are being lived out in a different circumstance and moment of history. For many people, it is easier to understand and believe the reality of karma when perceived in this tangible and practical way than through the vague notion of a soul moving from lifetime to lifetime.

Many Native American peoples were aware of the karmic implications of their actions. When making important decisions, they would consider the impact on the next seven generations of their families and communities, as well as on their land. The *Guru-Gita,* an important Hindu prayer from the *Skanda Purana,* suggests that when we make significant progress in our spiritual development, our healing affects seven generations into the future and frees the consciousness of seven generations into the past, pointing to the possibility that the bound energy of human consciousness can even be healed outside of linear time.

Robert Svoboda, the author of *Aghora III: The Law of Karma,* says that there are three types of karma: avoidable karma, unavoidable karma, and karma that may or may not be avoided. It can be very difficult, but at times extremely practical, to consider that when seemingly "bad" or difficult things are happening to us, it is in fact our own karmic "payback" that we are experiencing and that it is necessary, even unavoidable, that we endure it.

Several years ago my home in Berkeley was broken into, and the burglars stole much of the jewelry my mother had left me when she died. I felt deeply traumatized and victimized, and I called a powerful healer I know to ask her support in trying to see the event from a larger perspective. She asked me to consider the possibility that perhaps the burglars who had stolen my mother's jewelry were extracting a necessary karmic payment from me for something I could not remember, and that I had been released of karmic weight. She told me the story of the first time she met her healing teacher and arrived at the teacher's home wearing a very expensive antique necklace that had belonged to her great-grandmother. Her teacher took one look at the necklace, ripped it off her neck, and threw it into the fire, declaring, "That necklace is eating up your energy!"

It is not easy to open ourselves to a wider perspective of reality in which challenging questions of justice, victimization, and fairness are seen through such a wide lens. Yet, as with everything, even this perspective can be misused. Here is one example: A friend of mine was kidnapped, badly raped, and almost murdered. Her New Age boyfriend persuaded her to drop the charges, convincing her that she had attracted the situation to herself. Later, she suffered for this premature psychological "bypass" of the trauma she had endured. We cannot presume to understand the full complexity of karma, as it is vast and difficult for anyone to grasp. At the same time, considering a karmic perspective has the capacity to shake loose a narrow and strictly traditional psychological perspective.

A number of therapies concern themselves with past-life traumas, and spiritual students are endlessly fascinated by who they might have been or what they might have done in their past lifetimes, but from a practical perspective we need look no further than our present circumstances in order to address our karma: it is all right in front of us. Whether we were farmers in Mesopotamia, slave traders in the American South, or princesses in Egypt (my college boyfriend used to lament that every woman he ever met who remembered her past life had been a princess of some sort) is ultimately irrelevant. What is important is whether we are able to meet our present circumstance with a clear and discerning perspective and refrain from taking actions that further the endless repetition of unfavorable and limiting aspects of our karmic conditioning. From this perspective, psychology becomes a tool we can use to unlock, work with, and evolve our karma.

Karma or Dharma?

When we become conscious of the powerful karmic forces that dominate us, resulting in a seemingly endless repetition of conditioned patterns, we can begin to make a choice, in any given moment, to act otherwise—a choice that Vedic astrologer Chris Parrot phrases, "Karma or dharma?" *Dharma*, in this sense, refers to the "virtuous path," or lawful duty and service, that is available to every human being who chooses to live a life directed toward her or his highest possibility. To act in accordance with dharma is to take actions that are resonant with the greater structure, or lawfulness, of a divine order or objective truth rather than being moved by the powerful and usually unconscious forces of our karma. It is up to us whether we take an active or passive role in the unraveling of our conditioned circumstances.

."Blessed are you, who opens a gate in every moment, to enter in truth or tarry in hell," writes poet Leonard Cohen in his *Book of Mercy*. The great freedom or truth that so many of us aspire to is only experienced in the moment, and those whom we consider liberated are simply individuals who are routinely able to intercept their conditioning through a choice to practice and act consciously in accordance with their dharma, moment after moment.

"The pains which are yet to come can be and are to be avoided," says Patañjali in the *Yoga Sūtras*.[7] B. K. S. Iyengar elaborates on this point by explaining that we cannot do anything about our past suffering because it is finished. The suffering we are experiencing in the present also cannot be avoided because it is already present, although it can be reduced through conscious attention, spiritual practice, and the application of discerning knowledge. However, he says, the suffering that is still to come can and should be prevented.[8] Future suffering is prevented through intensive self-study and practice that allows us to become aware of our unconscious processes and to intercept them.

This is easier said than done! These patterns that we are attempting to intercept are ancient, and their momentum carries such power that when we try to break them we might feel like a heroin addict going through withdrawal or a poor swimmer trying to swim upstream against a powerful current. Or we may simply feel that something is not "right" because we are so unaccustomed to acting and feeling differently from the way we are used to.

When we pay attention, we discover that at every point there are two choices. When dark thought patterns as familiar as our childhood baby blanket arise, or when we find our buttons pushed and are about to react in the same way we always have to our partner, friend, boss, or child, or when we find ourselves teetering at the precipice of the deep well of self-hatred and self-sabotaging behaviors—if we are able to make the choice of dharma, or practice, rather than karma, we will experience a moment of freedom. If we experience this once, we can experience it again and eventually come to know firsthand how a human being becomes liberated from the cycles of karma. As E. J. Gold said, "At some point you need to decide to live your life so you don't leave a trail of accidents behind you—one of which is yourself."

~~~

If we want to live lives of spiritual integrity rather than leaving a series of accidents in our wake, we must begin to appreciate the nature of our conditioning. We need to understand the basic principles of ego, see how they inform our psychology, and learn to work with ourselves in a way that not only untangles our individual psychological knots but also those rooted in our deeper, karmic conditioning.

If we are serious about the spiritual path, there is no way of getting around ego. We must commit ourselves to becoming intimate with and ruthlessly honest about our own egoic dynamics. We are asked to become skilled mechanics who, little by little, come to understand the intricate wiring of our own psyche: the tricks it plays on us and the stories it creates to avoid the very transformation we have come searching for on the spiritual path.

Many people immerse themselves in spiritual work with the belief or hope that spiritual practice and insight alone will allow them to transcend their psychological labyrinth.

We live in the modern Western world during a time of unprecedented psychological confusion and devastation that leaves almost no one unscathed, including spiritual teachers and communities. In spite of our sincere intention to grow spiritually, our collective psychological blindness often distorts our spiritual perspective. We must learn to perceive how these dynamics function within ourselves, our teachers, and our communities so that we might travel the path with clarity and discernment—and we must support others in doing the same. The next chapter delves into this issue through a discussion of spiritual materialism and spiritual bypassing, two of the most important principles to understand in the development of spiritual discernment.

Chapter 5

~

Spiritual Materialism and Spiritual Bypassing

We have come here to learn about spirituality. I trust the genuine quality of this search, but we must question its nature. The problem is that ego can convert anything to its own use, even spirituality. Ego is constantly attempting to acquire and apply the teachings of spirituality for its own benefit. The teachings are treated as an external thing, external to "me," a philosophy which we try to imitate. We do not actually want to identify with or become the teachings. So if our teacher speaks of renunciation of ego, we attempt to mimic renunciation of ego. We go through the motions, make the appropriate gestures, but we really do not want to sacrifice any part of our way of life. We become skillful actors, and while playing deaf and dumb to the real meaning of the teachings, we find some comfort in pretending to follow the path.

—CHÖGYAM TRUNGPA RINPOCHE,
Cutting Through Spiritual Materialism[1]

M any years ago, after completing *Halfway up the Mountain* and speaking and teaching on the myriad forms of self-deception in spiritual life addressed in that book, I was looking forward to a time in the future when I would be writing books about powerful, esoteric truths, rather than continuing to describe the obstacles to truth.

Eventually, however, my perspective changed as a result of seeing therapy clients over many years who had been profoundly disillusioned by their spiritual teachers, communities, and practices. It changed as I watched spiritual teachers and communities develop and progress over time, and I noticed the commonality of the challenges they faced, regardless of tradition. While teaching at a cutting-edge alternative graduate school, I saw the pervasiveness of confusion about the spiritual path—largely resulting from an egocentric understanding and application of spiritual practices—and also a fundamental lack of available education regarding the spiritual path.

My perspective also changed when, many years after the publication of *Halfway Up the Mountain,* I flipped through the book and discovered I had fallen into most of the traps I had written about, only at a more subtle and less detectable level. I have gradually come to accept that my spiritual practice and the teachings I can share may never go beyond a meticulous and experiential excavation of the countless subterranean layers of false perception and confusion that lie within each of us. Each progressive level of falsity unearths a deeper level of clarity and spiritual maturity that allows us to move ever closer to the truth of our experience with unswerving integrity and groundedness. It is through progressively deeper discernment that clarity is revealed.

In 1973, Chögyam Trungpa Rinpoche, the Tibetan Buddhist master who founded Naropa University, published the groundbreaking book *Cutting Through Spiritual Materialism.* Having come to the West to teach Buddhism in the sixties during the spiritual renaissance in Western culture, he found himself speaking to spiritual seekers who were thirsty for truth and ready to pursue spiritual practice and knowledge with immense vigor, and who were also necessarily confused. Bringing powerful meditative practices and esoteric Buddhist knowledge and technology into a culture that had no cultural matrix to support it, and particularly no foundational understanding about ego dynamics, carried with it a new set of confusions and complexities that Trungpa Rinpoche set out to address. He wrote:

> *Walking the spiritual path properly is a very subtle process; it is not something to jump into naïvely. There are numerous sidetracks which lead to a distorted, ego-centered version of spirituality; we can deceive ourselves into thinking we are developing spiritually when instead we are strengthening our egocentricity through spiritual techniques. This fundamental distortion may be referred to as spiritual materialism.*[2]

John Welwood, a psychotherapist and long-time student of Chögyam Trungpa Rinpoche, coined the term *spiritual bypassing* to refer specifically to the psychological dimension of spiritual materialism. "Spiritual bypassing," he writes, "is using spiritual ideas and practices to sidestep personal, emotional 'unfinished business'; to shore up a shaky sense of self; or to belittle basic needs, feelings, and developmental tasks, all in the name of enlightenment."[3] Spiritual bypassing, therefore, could be understood as an aspect of spiritual materialism that specifically addresses the way in which spiritual concepts and practices are unconsciously used to avoid, rather than pierce, our psychological wounds and challenges.

I am convinced that every serious student of the spiritual path, regardless of his or her religion or tradition, would benefit from understanding the principles of spiritual materialism and spiritual bypassing, not only theoretically but in terms of how these dynamics function in their own lives at increasingly subtle levels. For it is through learning to discern these tendencies within ourselves that we avoid falling into otherwise avoidable spiritual potholes.

One of my graduate students in transpersonal psychology repeatedly complained that she found my emphasis on the subject of spiritual bypassing throughout the semester repetitive and boring. She insisted that she had understood this material long ago—that she was far beyond psychology and frustrated at being asked to study it again. After I had endured a semester of her disgruntled frustration, resistance, anger, projection, and insistence that she was not affected by such psychological dynamics, she told me that she was in fact a spiritual teacher—one who, in my estimation, was clearly unprepared for her function!

We all resist seeing the ways in which we deceive ourselves on the spiritual path. It is an embarrassment to ego, though not to who we really are, to look in the mirror and see ourselves dressed in spiritual drag. Yet we allow ourselves to be exposed for the sake of greater freedom and to become more expansive through recognizing how we are limiting ourselves in the name of spirituality.

Spiritual Materialism

When we were studying the subject of spiritual materialism, Janice, another student in my transpersonal psychology class, raised her hand and said, "I know I am really drawn to spiritual life, and somehow what stops me is this really cool black-leather jacket I bought in Italy. I think that if I really give myself to spiritual life, I will have to give up my jacket, and I know it sounds ridiculous, but it really holds me back."

Janice's leather jacket was a material possession, but we all have something—a reason, possession, or something we tell ourselves that prevents us from looking at ourselves more deeply—that can keep us away from the path for our whole lives. For many of us, in spite of our best intentions, our spirituality itself becomes one more layer of subtle armor behind which we shield ourselves from deeper truth.

Judith Lief, a close student of Chögyam Trungpa Rinpoche who has been teaching for many years, describes spiritual materialism this way:

> *Spiritual materialism is an attachment to the spiritual path as a solid accomplishment or possession. It is said that spiritual materialism is the hardest to overcome. The imagery that is used is that of golden chains: you're not just in chains, you're in golden chains. And you love your chains because they're so beautiful and shiny. But you're not free. You're just trapped in a bigger and better trap. The point of spiritual practice is to become free, not to build a trap that may have the appearance of a mansion but is still a prison.[4]*

There are infinite ways in which our spiritual materialism can be expressed. On the most obvious level, spirituality can be, and is, used to make money, as we talked about in Chapter 1. Given that global culture has been turned toward materialistic values in a way unprecedented in human history, it is inevitable that this same ethic would infiltrate our approach to spirituality. We live in a culture that values accumulation and consumption, and it is naïve of us to assume that simply because we are interested in spiritual growth that we have relinquished our materialism—or even that we necessarily should. There is nothing wrong with having an "Om" symbol on your T-shirt or being an avid practitioner of meditation while also enjoying moneymaking and big business, but it is useful to explore, understand, and check your integrity in relationship to your choices. Spiritual materialism is not a matter of the things that we have, but of our relationship to them.

We also use spirituality to gain power, prestige, recognition, and respect and even to avoid our own troubles. And we misuse the very teachings, practices, and all the spiritual things we do and think to increase our awareness to avoid a deeper intimacy with the truth we seek. We use our practices, paraphernalia, and concepts to support ego rather than truth. Even a monk on a mountaintop can be attached to his robes or begging bowl as a way of creating a false sense of spiritual security.

The ego wants to think of spirituality as something it can "have" once and for all, and then we do not have to do the continual work of showing up and practicing moment after moment for the rest of our lives. The ego creates a whole identity around one's spiritual self. This is part of what we all do on the spiritual path, but it is helpful to learn to see it in ourselves.

There are many forms in which spiritual materialism may manifest:

- The spiritual resumé refers to the list of important spiritual people we have met, studied with, done a workshop with. At times we might find ourselves reciting our spiritual resume to impress ourselves or somebody else.

- Spiritual storytelling takes the form of reciting narratives about our spiritual experiences. While they may be interesting, we often hide behind our stories to shield ourselves from the vulnerability of deeper human connection.

- The spiritual high often manifests by going from workshop to teacher to beautiful place in order to stay on a perpetual high and avoid our own shadow, which is a different form of spiritual bypassing.

- "Dharmacizing" refers to using spiritual jargon to account for our confusion and blind spots and to avoid relationship. If we're a dharmacizer and someone tells us they feel tension around us, we might counter with a truism such as, "It's just a passing phenomenon. Who is there to experience tension anyway?"

- Spiritual shopping sprees are characterized by accumulating initiations, empowerments, and blessings from saints the way others collect cars, yachts, and second homes. We need to feel that we are always getting somewhere—that we're becoming richer and better. Some people unconsciously believe that if they collect enough spiritual gold stars to become enlightened, they don't have to die.

- The spiritualized ego imitates, often very well, what it imagines a spiritual person looks and sounds like. It can create a glow around itself, learn eloquent spiritual speech, and act mindful and detached—yet there is something very unreal about it. I remember going to hear a particularly well-known spiritual teacher talk. He was trying too hard to act and talk spiritually—saying profound things and wearing a certain "knowing" smile—yet his message was empty of feeling and dimension. His ego had integrated the spiritual teachings, but he had not.

- The bulletproof ego has assimilated constructive feedback and integrated it into its defense structure. If someone shares an opinion about us, we may say, "I know it appears that I'm being lazy and selfish, but I'm actually practicing just 'being' and taking care of myself." A spiritual teacher with a bulletproof ego may justify verbal abuse or economic extortions from his or her disciples by saying he or she is trying to cut through the egoic mechanism or trying to teach them they must learn to surrender all they have to the Divine. The problem with people who have spiritualized and bulletproof egos is that they are extremely slippery and difficult to catch—and it is particularly difficult to see how this spiritual defense mechanism operates within ourselves.

It is important to understand that spiritual materialism is less about the "what" and more about the "how" of relating to something—whether it's a teacher, a new yoga outfit, or a concept. It is not a question of wealth or money but rather of attitude. I have encountered numerous *sadhus,* or holy men, in India who live as renunciative beggars, yet waved their fists at me when they felt the donation I gave them was insufficient. Others' attachment to the pilgrim's staff they carried was as prideful as many bikers are about their prized Harley-Davidsons. As we penetrate deeper into the layers of our own perception, we discover that the origin of all forms of spiritual materialism rests in the mind. We find that we can relate to information, facts, and even profound understanding in such a way that it precludes the emergence of deeper wisdom. At this most subtle level, in which even knowledge itself becomes a barrier to wisdom, our sword of discernment—the deep desire to see ourselves clearly and the willingness to take feedback from others—can cut through our confusion.

Spiritual Bypassing

Psychologist John Welwood brought the concept of spiritual bypassing to the attention of the Western public as a way to help people understand how the ego can, and does, co-opt spiritual ideas and practices by attempting to bypass, rather than work through, the wounded, confused, and even damaged aspects of our psyches. Spiritual bypassing operates at all levels of spiritual development, from beginning seekers to advanced yogis and spiritual masters. Access to spiritual truth, when not integrated, is a very dangerous weapon whose primary hazard is that we can effectively fool ourselves into believing we are more realized than we are and miss the deeper possibility that is available to us. And if we are in a position of power, we are likely to bring this confusion to other people.

The egoic mind is a highly intelligent mechanism, and we should not underestimate its extreme cleverness and the absolute efficiency with which it carries out its task of obscuring the recognition of our deeper nature, thus protecting its identity. In its managerial function, the ego keeps us safe and organizes our lives, work, and families—and it is capable of creating and destroying civilizations. One of the goals of all esoteric spiritual traditions is to become free from the stronghold of egoic identification and domination, and yet we must realize that, for the most part, it is this same egoic mechanism that manages and guides us along the spiritual path.

What this means is that those of us who are deeply serious about spiritual practice find ourselves in an authentic predicament; for the very ego that motivates and sustains much of our spiritual direction and practice must also be carefully scrutinized and worked with. As the soul experiences the glory of awareness of its deeper nature, the ego simultaneously experiences the possibility of authentic transformation as a literal death threat. In its great intelligence, the ego co-opts the language and concepts of truth and transformation to ensure that this transformation does not happen, but it does so *in the name of truth.* Its very defense structure, described earlier as the spiritualized ego, is made of concepts, ideas, and even unconsciously concocted imitations of spiritual auras, energies, and insights. This is the domain that the principle of spiritual bypassing addresses; due to the subtlety of its expression, it is a concept best understood through examples, several of which I offer in the remainder of this chapter.

If It's All an Illusion, Why Do I Have to Work on My Mommy-Daddy Issues?

We cannot assume that simply because we have had profound experiences of spiritual illumination or enduring insights, all aspects of our psychology have been touched by our awareness. It is a great temptation to imagine this, but it is rarely the case. Our increased awareness can certainly impact our psychological dynamics, offering us a wider perspective on our conditioning or giving us the courage to go deeper into that which is still unilluminated within us. But rarely does heightened awareness take the place of the necessary and humbling task of learning to feel and digest our own psychological pain, or of the gritty challenges of dealing with human relationship, self-hatred, shame, sexuality, and intimacy with others. Spiritual insight can, but often does not, penetrate psychological conditioning. When we have not learned to manage our psychology, our psychology will continue to manage us.

Many of us have unconsciously come to spiritual life as a way to transcend the painful suffering that remains from our childhood conditioning. And, indeed, authentic transformational work can, should, and in many cases does help alleviate this suffering. By learning how the conditioning of the mind functions, we gain an increasing capacity to observe and dis-identify with its incessant repetition of thought patterns and to see that we are something other than our perceived identity and familiar story. But there is a very fine line between practicing the necessary process of nonattachment and falling prey to a neurotic detachment from life that is more a protective mechanism based on fear than an expression of spiritual clarity.

I once went to hear an American Zen Roshi speak. He was a revered and respected teacher in his community, and we expected to hear a classic "dharma" talk about Zen teachings, but he had another story to tell us. He had been practicing intensive Zen meditation for thirty years, often doing *sesshins* of several weeks or months at a time, and gradually he became very skilled at quieting the mind, detaching from his thoughts, and observing the multitude of precise rituals that are a part of Zen practice. Then his wife left him, and he found himself in a state of such profound grief and enduring depression that even his practices could not help him, and he began to explore his own personal past.

As a child, both of his parents worked, and he spent long periods of time alone. He had difficulty making friends and recalled that he would spend hours sitting in his mother's rocking chair, staring at the wall, lost in his own inner world. He had learned in childhood to use his breath to calm the tremendous anxiety and loneliness he felt at night. He shared with the three hundred people gathered for his talk that his success as a Zen teacher was largely a function of an unconscious redirection of defense structures he had learned in childhood. Fortunately for him, his wounds had found a constructive outlet by leading him to the path of Zen, but his practice had also supported him in avoiding huge areas of his psyche that needed attention and that had eventually resulted in the destruction of his marriage. He found the help he needed with this aspect of his transformational process from psychotherapy, not from meditation.

Egosyntonic refers to those behaviors and attitudes that are compatible with our preexisting egoic structure and tendencies. It is useful to explore how the practices we choose are egosyntonic with our personalities and how our approach to spirituality can support us in avoiding important areas of being that need attention. For example, do we use our meditation practice to escape life or become more intimate with it? Do we use spiritual concepts to avoid feeling or to help us feel more deeply?

In 2002, I published an article called "Zen Boyfriends"[5]—a term that refers to a man who "skillfully uses spiritual practices and ideals to avoid the challenges and demands of authentic human connection with an intimate partner." A typical dialogue with a Zen boyfriend might include something like the following, which occurred when my boyfriend, whom we will call Jivan, returned from India believing that he was enlightened.

"I truly believe in nonduality," Jivan told me. "We're all one. I can feel it now."

"What exactly does that mean?" I asked.

"It means that you or I don't exist separately from any animate or inanimate object. There's no separation."

"And yet, you don't really listen to me," I told him. "I need you to be really here and not so detached."

"But who is the 'you' that wants to hang out with this 'me'?"

"Damn it, Jivan, *I* am the *me*, and *you* are the *you*."

"There's no difference, so we can never really be alone, or apart. It's all the same," he retorted.

"You're full of shit."

"Who is the 'me' that is full of shit?"

"You!"

"And who's getting angry?" he insisted.

"I'm getting angry!"

"Look into my eyes. What do you see?" he continued.

"You."

"Look deeper. Now what do you see? Can't you see yourself? Can't you see everything?"

"I see a lonely man who thinks he is enlightened," I told him finally. "I want to have an *intimate* relationship, and frankly, I'd rather hang out with myself than hang out with somebody who thinks he's nobody."

Jivan eventually got into therapy to work on his mother issues, and I continued to work on the father issues that kept attracting me to men who were not emotionally available, but the interaction that prompted our breakup was characterized by the classic psychological defense mechanisms originally set out by Sigmund Freud—including repression, denial, rationalization, isolation, and splitting. We had simply borrowed the clothing of spiritual truths to buffer ourselves from the vulnerability inherent in human relationships.

In the worst-case scenario, our spiritual bypassing can potentially undo or destroy the effects of the effort we have given to our spiritual practice. Such was the case with Mercedes, a Spanish woman I know who was raised in a small farming village in the south of Spain. Mercedes's father was physically, sexually, and verbally abusive to her and her sister when they were young, and her mother was insecure and passive, never defending her children. When Mercedes was nineteen, she read about meditation in a book. Soon after she started experimenting with the practices, she began to have powerful experiences of altered states of consciousness. Nobody in her home environment could understand her, so she went to live at an ashram in northern India.

Once in India, Mercedes undertook an intensive course of spiritual practice that spanned more than two decades under the supervision of a small number of powerful teachers. Among the thousands of spiritual aspirants I have met and interviewed, perhaps no one practiced with as much discipline, ardor, and vigor as Mercedes, who performed spiritual austerities, service, chanting, and contemplation regimens that only great realizers usually undertake. She experienced great states of enlightenment and was revered by all who knew her.

Perhaps the only challenge Mercedes did not undertake was a confrontation with the ghosts of the past she had left behind, never looking back, focusing all of her energies into her spiritual practices. Many years into her practice and over a short period of time, Mercedes experienced several difficult events, including the deaths of all of her main teachers and her mother. When yet another teacher, who had taken Mercedes under her wing during this vulnerable period, suddenly died, Mercedes experienced a schizophrenic break. She became completely withdrawn, stopped speaking and bathing, and remained in states of unconsciousness and despondency for weeks at a time, dangerously depleted and ill. When people tried to help her, she became aggressive and reported that she was in deep states of spiritual union and did not want to be disturbed. Eventually, Mercedes had to be hospitalized and treated for psychosis and depression, yet she remained uninterested in pursuing therapeutic work.

It is interesting to note that childhood abuse often results in extraordinary spiritual sensitivity and awareness. The imperative to escape from one's immediate surroundings often propels young children to explore their inner world and discover domains of consciousness that are more peaceful and safe. In fact, for many spiritual seekers, it is the dysfunctionality of their broken homes and wounded psyches that wakes them from the spiritual slumber of contemporary culture. Motivated by their inability to effectively deny the pain that permeated their psyches and families—the pain that pulses through all of contemporary culture—they are propelled to ask the deeper questions in life.

Paradoxically, childhood trauma and even the increasing anxiety and peril of modern culture can be a great gift that wakes us up individually and collectively to a deeper possibility. But if once committed to the path we do not eventually address these issues, either our spiritual realization will be incomplete and perhaps distorted, or the unworked issues will come back and demand our attention, often at highly inconvenient times.

Spiritual Bypassing in New Religious Movements

Spiritual bypassing is not a phenomenon limited to individuals; it impacts entire spiritual communities and traditions. The past decade has seen an epidemic rise in the prevalence of spiritual bypassing in Western spiritual movements. A palpable growth in tension, depression, fear, superficiality, and materialism can be felt around the world, as well as a low-grade collective panic and a desire to find fast-acting, accessible solutions that offer a panacea for our confusion and pain. This urgent need to find relief is reflected not only in the popularity of certain spiritual movements but also in how we think and talk about spirituality. There is a sense that life is moving so fast that we must find techniques that do not require the investment of time, practice, discipline, and long-term commitment. As one of my young psychology students who was resistant to the meditation practice we did at the beginning of every class said to me, "I'm looking for a quick fix, and it's very clear to me that meditation is not going to provide that."

The New Age movement is fraught with such tendencies, with much of its focus on transcendence, ascension, and what my writer friend Jorge Ferrer calls "heart-chakra-and-above" spirituality. While most New Age traditions and practices are based upon objective truths, the realities they represent have often been selectively chosen to include only the pleasant truths. There is a full range of workshops, approaches, and teachers that trains people to touch the heavens at the cost of losing their grounding in the earth and in the most practical aspects of human experience. People move toward the light while being unwilling to descend into the dark, murky dredge of their own emotions and relational challenges. The result is an ungrounded, partial, and lopsided version of spiritual awareness.

On one hand, it is certainly healthier for people to trip out on rainbows and crystals than take crystal meth, and from a purely practical standpoint, the truth is that most people are not willing to engage the discipline, commitment, and authenticity that genuine transformation requires. On the other hand, the popularity of such movements generates great confusion in contemporary culture as to what spirituality really can offer, both to sincere seekers and curious onlookers.

Another example of how spiritual bypassing can impact an entire spiritual community is found in what is commonly referred to as the neo-Advaita, or satsang, movement that has become increasingly popular around the world. With notable exceptions, many of the teachers of this approach—who often claim that they are not teachers because there is no "one" to teach or to teach to—offer a temporary experience of pure consciousness and nonseparation that is experienced as very powerful by their followers. Many teachers in this movement do not advocate spiritual practice and discipline, and in many cases they shun it, telling their adherents that the striving nature of the belief that we need to *do* anything, rather than to just *be*, takes us out of the present moment.

Once again, such a philosophical stance is irrefutable, and yet observing both students and teachers in these movements for over more than two decades, I have not been impressed with the widespread results of these approaches in terms of spiritual maturity and discernment. One result of this new spiritual movement is that it has left thousands, if not tens of thousands, of individuals believing they are enlightened—in many cases they go off to teach others these same techniques long before they are prepared for such a responsibility. Since most of them do not call themselves teachers, and certainly not gurus, they do not take adequate responsibility for the dynamics and projections that arise in their communities, always returning instead to the point that it is all simply the play of mind.

I have heard hundreds of stories similar to the one I told about my Zen boyfriend Jivan—stories of intimate relationships that have gone haywire because one of the partners continually uses the concepts and jargon of enlightenment to avoid intimacy and the very real challenges that human relationship implies. Approaches such as neo-Advaita and many New Age spiritualities are fraught with a tendency toward spiritual bypassing and have become so popular that they are actually distorting our Western collective understanding of enlightenment and undermining the possibilities for authentic spiritual maturity.

In the late 1990s I went to hear a talk given by Ram Dass, the former Harvard professor and author of *Be Here Now,* one of the most influential spiritual books ever published in the West. His book describes the revelations that were catalyzed by his encounter with his guru, Neem Karoli Baba, and his powerful teachings about the importance of being in the present moment. In the more than thirty years since the publication of that book, Ram Dass had been on a remarkable and humbling journey, including having had a recent stroke, and had become intimately acquainted with his own tendencies toward spiritual bypassing, which he referred to as "vertical schizophrenia."

That evening, a very sincere young spiritual seeker raised his hand and asked Ram Dass if he still felt that the practice of "being here now" was the highest ideal to aspire to. With great warmth, Ram Dass told the young man that he still agreed with that philosophy of "be here now" at the essential level, but that his understanding of what "now" referred to had expanded to include the need to be present with all levels of his experience, including painful emotions, interpersonal human challenges, and the suffering of the earth itself and its citizens and leaders. He said that he now believed we must learn to be present with everything that exists in the here and now, not excluding anything. For true spiritual growth to occur, we must understand that even a commitment to being in the present moment can be used as a means of avoidance.

When Spiritual Teachers Haven't Dealt with Their Stuff

Perhaps in no area of spiritual culture do we experience the impact of spiritual bypassing as strongly as the arena of spiritual teachers. For most of us, the subtle ways in which we bypass our psychological dynamics impact only our own process of integration and perhaps those who are close to us. When we have any type of teaching function, however, the obscured pockets in our psychological awareness become deeply intertwined with our sharing of the teachings and can result in confusion—even great harm—to those whose lives we influence.

The vast majority of spiritual scandals are a result of spiritual teachers who have had a certain degree of realization in some areas but remain imbalanced in their psychological or sexual development. In my own research over the course of many years, I have had the opportunity to speak with, counsel, and receive detailed accounts from spiritual seekers all over the world who have been affected by spiritual bypassing in their teachers. I have also known a few instances of individuals who once believed themselves to be enlightened and were in teaching functions, but who later denounced themselves when they recognized that they were not prepared to be spiritual teachers.

Generally, the most detrimental behaviors teachers enact in relationship to their students can be traced directly to psychological wounds and blind spots resulting from childhood trauma, abuse, or less than optimal parenting. These unaddressed wounds are expressed primarily through distorted relationships with sexuality, power, or money, and an inflated sense of their own realization. In some cases the effects of a teacher who bypassed his or her own psychological work manifest in massive scandals in which communities fall apart, lawsuits ensue, and—in the most extreme cases—individual or group suicide is committed. Often the manifestations are more subtle and gradual, invading the psyche like an undetected cancer that is only discovered after great, and sometimes irreparable, damage has occurred.

Philosopher Ken Wilber's discussion of developmental lines can help us understand how someone can have a high degree of realization in one or more areas but remain highly undeveloped in others. Wilber explains that development occurs in distinct lines, or streams, including but not limited to morals, needs, affect, interpersonal capacity, cognition, sexuality, motivation, and self-identity. In any given individual, some of these lines may be more developed and others less so; thus human development is an uneven process. Wilber writes, "These lines are 'relatively independent,' which means that, for the most part, they can develop independently of each other, at different rates, with a different dynamic, and on a different time schedule. A person can be very advanced in some lines, medium in others, low in still others—all at the same time."6

Many spiritual scandals arise when teachers demonstrate uneven development with respect to sexual issues, which may be further complicated by the cross-cultural factors involved when Eastern teachers attempt to transplant their traditions into Western soil. There are countless tales, past and present, of spiritual scandals involving Tibetan Buddhist monks or Indian male yogis who were raised in monastic environments or in cultures whose cultural imprint for male-female relationships did not prepare them for the sexually seductive, beautiful female disciples they encountered in the West. They found themselves deceiving their disciples and pretending they weren't in fact having numerous affairs. These Eastern teachers might justify their sexual promiscuity as "initiations" or claim they are practicing "tantra," rather than being honest with themselves and their disciples and admitting that they are exploring their own sexuality or cannot control their sexual impulse.

The problem is not that individuals serving in teaching functions are not integrated on every level; expecting this to be true of others or oneself is unrealistic. The harm comes when teachers lack the ability or willingness to examine themselves with ruthless self-honesty at each level of their experience and adequately assess whether their weaknesses could harm others and in what ways. Pretending that they are more developed than they actually are is a great disservice to themselves and their students.

Another phenomenon that arises when spiritual teachers haven't dealt with their psychological knots is the tendency to attract students with a similar set of issues. Just as in intimate relationships in general, like qualities tend to attract each other. So it is fairly common that those areas of the teacher's psychology that he or she has not come to terms with connect with similar tendencies in the student. A type of spiritual codependency, called mutual complicity, develops. (This subject was introduced in Chapter 1.) The weakness in the psychology of the student plays off the weakness in the psychology of the teacher, and vice versa.

I can offer an illustration of how this works from my own life. When I began my spiritual search in my late teens, I found myself repeatedly drawn to older male teachers who were powerful individuals but who had not handled their own psychological issues in relationship to power, authority, and manipulation. Over and over again, I found myself replaying aspects of my relationship with my father that I had not resolved, which landed me in very uncomfortable, sometimes scandalous situations that I myself had helped to create. I became endlessly disillusioned with my teachers and repeatedly suffered past traumas that I kept replaying in my spiritual life. Eventually, the dynamic repeated itself enough times that I finally said to myself, "This could not be happening over and over again if it were not reflecting something within myself." At that point I became very serious about my own psychological work and began my formal studies in psychology.

This very same phenomenon of spiritual bypassing finds its way into the dynamics of entire spiritual communities. Of course, all communities will, to some degree, reflect the collective psychological disposition of their members, but some communities suffer a thicker, more complex set of dysfunctional dynamics than others. There may be unspoken agreements that it is okay to physically hurt others in the name of the teachings, or that nothing the teacher (in the projected role of Mommy or Daddy) says or does can be questioned, or that the authority of the hierarchy in the community cannot be challenged. Any number of unhealthy family dynamics can show up in the community around the teacher, and it is inevitable that some degree of dysfunction will arise. The question is whether we can bring awareness to this tendency toward dysfunction, which exists in all spiritual communities, and develop discernment with respect to those we encounter and are attracted to so that we might make wise decisions regarding our degree of participation in them.

When a spiritual group professes not to believe in psychology—particularly if it cursorily dismisses psychology in the name of truth, suggesting it is *maya,* ignorance, or ego—the group is more apt to fall into collective aspects of spiritual bypassing, including mutual complicity and spiritual codependency. When the role of psychology is denied or undervalued, individuals within a community will not work to understand their own contribution to the psychological dysfunction of the community. This does not mean it is not happening, only that it is not being examined.

Finally, a consideration of spiritual bypassing among teachers must recognize that, at a very practical level, it is unrealistic to expect everyone who functions as a spiritual teacher to be fully integrated at a psychological level. There is a great need for spiritual help in the world, and there are not enough perfected, integrated human beings to address the task at hand. I have heard many stories about great upheavals that arise in spiritual communities when the teacher is having marital problems, experiencing depression or illness, or is going through a particularly challenging aspect of his or her own human development. Such situations often activate fears within us at a very primal level, not so different from a child's shock upon hearing that his or her parents are divorcing or upon realizing that a parent has weaknesses and doesn't know everything. These psychological upheavals give rise to questions such as "Can my teacher help me through my most difficult life challenges if he or she hasn't been able to handle his or her own life?" or "Does my teacher really embody what he or she teaches?"

These are not questions that are easily answered, but such issues do come up, and we must deal with them. Given the times we are living in, when almost no one, including genuine and powerful teachers, has been raised in a healthy and balanced environment either at home or within his or her cultural, political, and educational climate, even sincere teachers will have blind spots. Our concern must be whether a given teacher is qualified to work with us at the level on which we have agreed to work together. We must assess, as honestly and clearly as we can, whether our teachers' personal psychological challenges get in the way of their capacity to teach us effectively. Part of this assessment, which is admittedly very difficult given the deeply intimate and vulnerable nature of the student-teacher relationship, involves recognizing whether our own psychological weaknesses tend to collude with those of the teacher. This subject will be addressed further in Chapter 11, "The Question of the Teacher."

Those of us who have committed to the spiritual path find ourselves on a never-ending journey in which each level of expansion and awareness we achieve is accompanied by new levels of complexity. And increasingly subtle levels of self-deception arise as we gradually move toward stabilizing ourselves in an increasingly integrated perspective. Understanding this, the importance of cultivating discernment becomes a necessity rather than a luxury.

It is important to remember that spiritual materialism and spiritual bypassing *will* arise as part and parcel of the spiritual path. Understanding their dynamics and learning to identify them as they arise is how we protect ourselves from falling into their traps. Avoiding these traps allows us to move forward on our respective paths with consistency and integrity. Spiritual life is, among other things, a continual revelation about what spiritual life is not.

The next chapter, "The Healing Crisis," takes us more deeply into an aspect of the spiritual path that touches many of us, sometimes repeatedly at various times in our lives. A lifelong path of spiritual practice includes many trials and tribulations—times of deep crisis and shocking circumstances that crack open our comfortable shell, allowing us to become more deeply authentic and of greater service to life.

Chapter 6

~◌~

The Healing Crisis

*Cosmic love is absolutely ruthless and highly indifferent:
it teaches its lessons whether you like/dislike them or not.*
—JOHN LILLY, *The Dyadic Cyclone*

I t almost always catches us off guard, and it comes in ten thousand forms. The body suddenly breaks down at a too-young age, and we receive a diagnosis of an illness we unconsciously believed only happened to other people. A car accident leaves us with physical trauma and reminds us of our own death in a very real way. We are betrayed in an intimate relationship, or our spouse announces a desire for an unexpected divorce. Somebody close to us dies, and our pain is beyond consolation and does not lift. An addiction sneaks up on us, and we are suddenly consumed by it. It could be anything. Often, such events come in succession; no sooner have we landed back on our feet when we find ourselves thrown to the floor once again. Whatever it is, it *always* feels as though it has come at a bad time. Our capacity to see and act clearly is tested to the limit, and we find ourselves feeling as though we are failing miserably. It is precisely during the major crises of our lives that our capacity for spiritual discernment is most useful—and will be most severely tested.

For many of us, the initial opening to our own spiritual potential paradoxically arises in the midst of grief, loss, trauma, illness, or a near-death experience—trials that prompt us to turn inward in search of deeper wisdom and understanding. It is not that we should covet such crises, or that they provide the only means to grow and cultivate discernment, but it is sometimes only through such shocks that we are jarred out of the narrow confines of our conditioned and routine lives. Shocks have the capacity to crack us open to a new world that is unfamiliar and frightening but also compellingly real and immediate—a world we recognize as being truer than the one we have previously known. Our previous beliefs and ideas—"spiritual" and otherwise—are tested and often disassembled. If we do not give up and allow this dismantling to occur, our capacity for discernment and clear vision is paradoxically deepened and refined.

For others of us there is no one dramatic event we can point to, but the crisis is equally powerful. We fall into a depression we cannot crawl out of. Our fear of death cannot be contained and becomes an obsession. We discover that we do not really know how to love or how to feel, or we become aware that we have constructed a personality that is not a reflection of who we truly are. Or we suddenly realize that we have invested our life energy in vanity and excess, and we cannot find meaning in our lives. Or aging comes with new fears, sorrows, and the recognition that we are entering the latter stages of life and have not acquired the spiritual wisdom, insight, and understanding we had hoped for. Such crises are often correlated with developmental rhythms, ages, and stages, including the increasingly documented quarter-life crisis, the Saturn Return (in astrology), the midlife crisis, menopause (no longer exclusive to women, some suggest even men pass through a parallel stage), and the profound challenges of old age.

On the surface, our lives may be sane, and we may feel we have nothing to complain about, but internally we find ourselves moving through deep, and often very dark, periods of an inner process for which we have no road map and no way to make sense of what we are experiencing. It is often during these periods that even self-proclaimed agnostics or those who have had no prior interest in spirituality find themselves exploring spiritual subjects and practices. For Siddhartha Gautama, who later became the Buddha, leaving his castle for the first time and encountering old age, sickness, and death had such a powerful impact that he renounced his family, wealth, and life as a prince in order to search for what was true beyond the confines of space and time.

"We will die how we live," a friend of mine who worked in hospice once commented. It is wise to cultivate spiritual discernment sooner rather than later. This chapter explores the universal theme of the healing crisis and its function in cultivating discernment.

The Crack

There is a crack, a crack in everything
That's how the light gets in.

— LEONARD COHEN, *"Anthem"*

In the winter of 2004, I experienced such a crack. I was wrestling with an undiagnosed illness that had persisted for more than a year, and I was also recovering from a recent heartbreak. One afternoon, after teaching a full-day seminar at John F. Kennedy University, I was driving a cheap rental car in the pouring rain during evening rush hour on Interstate 580 in Oakland, California, on my way to pick up my car from an auto-body shop called Karmakanix, owned by a Buddhist mechanic. Suddenly, a man in the next lane moved toward me; I was in his blind spot as he was changing lanes. I veered to the right into the next lane to avoid being hit and found myself hydroplaning across the highway. I turned sharply again, this time to the left, desperately trying to avoid a crash. At that point, however, my car spun 180 degrees, and I was suddenly flying backward, out of control and at great velocity, toward the median.

In that state of suspended time that is common in near-death experiences, I took a full inventory of the situation, trying to recall what the person at the rental car agency had told me about the extra insurance I had not purchased and the potential implications. I realized I was about to crash into the median and would either be killed on the spot or have lifelong injuries and accompanying financial issues. With no recourse or hope of salvation, I called out, from the most earnest place within me, the mantra my teacher gave me. I did not want to be alone at the moment of impact.

No sooner had I uttered the mantra a single time than my car came to a sudden halt, the engine off, pointing into oncoming traffic. I sat in stunned silence, looking straight into the headlights of four lanes of stopped cars as they shone through the rain. Not a person or car was touched by the drama. I was in a cosmic "freeze-frame." I wanted to get out of my car and fall to my knees on the highway in gratitude, but quickly realized that was not a practical gesture. So after about thirty seconds, I restarted the engine, turned the car around on the highway, drove to the mechanic, picked up my car, drove home . . . and cracked. I did not fall apart—I was cracked wide open. Not only the shock but the profound grace of having my life spared left me disassembled from my ordinary state, and wide open to life. For the following weeks,

I felt profoundly connected to grace and the suffering of others, and I experienced a deep sense of protection and gratitude. Then, slowly and predictably, my psyche reconstituted its familiar shell of security until the next opportune time arose for it to be cracked open once again. But that experience taught me a very powerful lesson about the possibilities of crises becoming an opportunity to cultivate deeper discernment.

We do not "plan" to get cracked open. We do not wake up one morning and say to ourselves, "Today is a good day for a nervous breakdown. Bring it on!" or "I've got myself together enough that I can bear a cancer diagnosis now." Life just isn't like that. The deep psyche's need to be revealed by having its armor cracked open has its own timing, and it's seldom convenient. In reality, there is never a good time for a breakdown.

Like the driver who nearly hit me, we all have blind spots, hidden corners of our psyche that we cannot ordinarily see. Zen masters, physicians, presidents, great yogis—we all have places inside where we cannot see ourselves clearly, and it is usually from those places that we end up hurting ourselves and others. Many of us spend our entire lives—many traditions would argue multiple lifetimes—avoiding dealing with these deep patterns of conditioning, known in Sanskrit as *samskaras* and expressed in this lifetime as psychological wounds and weaknesses.

"They make the red flags red, so you can see them!" a friend once told me while lamenting that she had fallen once again for an unavailable man. But how often do we actually see the red flags? We get so caught up in our routines and our busyness—keeping our lives, finances, and relationships together, as well as unconsciously protecting ourselves from the dismantling of our illusions—that we are not available to allow a deeper transformational process to arise in us. Sometimes we need a serious kick in the butt to wake us from our slumber, and life offers no shortage of such opportunities.

When I was a child, my older brother had a pet tarantula. About every six months, when it had been properly fattened up through its diet of mice and crickets, it would go into a very still space for several days, at the end of which its skin would fall away and it would emerge in its new form. Human beings are very much like that. We must shed our previous identity in order for something greater, deeper, and more authentic to emerge. "Breakdown precedes breakthrough," says spiritual teacher Lee Lozowick. Although we may wish it were otherwise, the reality is that human beings often learn more from pain than from pleasure, and the most potent and life-changing lessons we learn, as well as the most significant breakthroughs we experience, often arise on the other side of breakdown. In *The World of Shamanism,* psychiatrist Roger Walsh writes:

> *Developmental crises are periods of psychological stress that accompany turning points in our lives. They may be marked by considerable psychological turmoil, sometimes even of life-threatening proportions. These transitions can occur spontaneously, as in adolescent and midlife crises, or can be induced by growth-accelerating techniques such as psychotherapy and meditation. These crises occur because psychological growth rarely proceeds smoothly. Rather, growth is usually marked by periods of confusion and questioning or, in extreme cases, disorganization and despair.*[1]

Disillusionment, though deeply painful, offers an opportunity for cultivating discernment and healing unhealthy patterns and tendencies in a way that few other things do. What is brighter, more essential, and more true can shine forth when we break down the illusions we have overlaid onto reality. At such times in our lives, a deep interior need compels us to try to discern what we have previously been unable, or unwilling, to see. In seeing, there exists the possibility to take far greater responsibility for our lives, to open ourselves to more understanding, more heartbreak, more challenge, more expansion, and also to serve humanity in progressively deeper ways. Although we may have felt we were looking inward in years past—and we always have been doing so to the degree that we were capable of at the time—we now find ourselves turning more deeply toward our true selves than we ever have before.

Each layer of spiritual development brings with it its own set of challenges. This is how the unfolding process works. It is why, as we get into psychotherapy or any kind of serious healing, things often get worse—or seem to—before they get better. We must allow the buried dis-ease to rise to the surface and invite that which is unconscious to be brought to consciousness, so it can be understood and related to in a more significant way. The wound is uncovered, so it can be worked with. Sometimes we do this consciously, but more often, life simply breaks us open.

Understanding Crisis as Opportunity

Not long after passing through the strongest series of crises I have ever known, I visited Llewellyn Vaughan-Lee, a Sufi sheikh and mentor I have known for many years. "It was quite a liberating experience you went through?" he inquired as he greeted me.

"It was very painful!" I told him.

"When is an extremely liberating experience not painful?" he asked.

Intellectually understanding the spiritual possibilities inherent in breakdown and disillusionment does not always make the reality any easier to deal with, but knowing that it is a well-traveled path and a necessary passage can sometimes bring with it a measure of comfort and courage. Like the mythical Humpty Dumpty after his fall, we find ourselves cracked into small pieces and strewn about the ground, with no idea how we will possibly come back together again. It can feel as if our life is over, that the pain and damage have gone so deep there is no hope of repair. I remember that at one such point in my own life I called a psychologist friend. "Tom, do you think I'll ever be able to crawl out of this hole?" I asked him. I was certain that this was it. At the ripe age of thirty-six, I was finished, no hope for brighter days. He calmly assured me that in his work with thousands of individuals during three decades, he had seen many who found their way out of comparable or even more difficult crises than the one I was passing through. And sure enough, within a few months my life was back on track.

Crises, depression, and breakdown are part and parcel of the spiritual path and of every journey through life. Buddhist nun Pema Chödrön's book *When Things Fall Apart* became a national bestseller because she was speaking to the reality, rather than the dream and fantasy, of our passage through life and the need to learn to transform difficulties into opportunities for growth. The current statistics on depression are astonishing. According to figures published by the National Institute of Mental Health, in a given year depressive disorders affect approximately 14.8 million American adults, or about 6.7 percent of the U.S. population age eighteen and older,[2] and women are twice as likely to be depressed as men.[3] The fact that we practice meditation or have devoted our lives to spiritual work does not exempt us from contributing to these statistics. In fact, immersing ourselves in the purifying power of spiritual practice often surfaces our wounds more readily, and with greater intensity, than maintaining a life filled with psychological buffers and staying within the confines of conventional paradigms of mainstream culture.

Among spiritual practitioners and meditators there is often a tremendous amount of shame and denial that arises when we find ourselves in a state of anxiety, depression, or other kinds of psychological breakdown. It's as if the fact that we have studied spiritual teachings or have meditated for five, ten, or twenty years means that we should have transcended our psychological wounds. In such cases, we may try to deal with arising unconscious psychological material with more meditation and spiritual practices, rationalizing our troubles away by reciting spiritual teachings or engaging other classic forms of spiritual bypassing. In the article, "Optimal Healing: What Do We Know about Integrating Meditation, Medication, and Psychotherapy?" transpersonal psychiatrist Roger Walsh and his colleagues write:

> Somewhere along the path we ran into a problem: reality. It gradually became apparent that many classic accounts of spiritual life are idealistic and unrealistic, not unlike the Hollywood sagas of boy meets girl, boy and girl fall in love, ride off into the sunset, and live happily ever after. Anyone who has ever been in an intimate relationship knows that something has been left out of the story.
>
> In short, spiritual practice turned out to be far more complex and demanding than it first seemed. True, there were many gifts and graces along the way, and the glimpses of our spiritual potentials were awe inspiring.

But covering these potentials were layer upon layer of difficult emotions, demanding motives, compulsive conditioning, and countless old wounds, fears, and phobias. And ironically, spiritual practice often made these challenges more apparent and difficult to deny.[4]

Paradoxically, sometimes it is the fruition of our spiritual practice that allows us to see where deeper discernment needs to be cultivated. Theravadan Buddhist teacher and author Jack Kornfield often recounts having lived as a monk in Southeast Asia as a young adult, returning to the United States feeling very holy, and getting into a romantic relationship—only to discover that his years of meditation had not addressed large areas of his unconscious and had produced far less equanimity than he would have dared imagine. In fact, most of the spiritual teachers, psychiatrists, and psychologists I have met and interviewed say that the single most frequent cause of psychological breakdown among spiritual practitioners, as well as among renowned teachers and even monks and nuns, results from issues involving intimate relationship, sexuality, heartbreak, and betrayal. It is these circumstances that most powerfully open up the unhealed wounds from childhood around love, survival, and basic needs.

We would not ordinarily consider that unhealed wounds surfacing could be the result of the fruition of our practice and the successful removal of psychological buffers that block us from feeling life at progressively deeper levels, rather than from something within us going awry. Breakdown offers the possibility of allowing false structures to be disassembled so deeper discernment and clarity can emerge, particularly if we have a context of spiritual teachings, practice, and community to support us in mining the spiritual possibilities of breakdown. During such times in our lives, a doorway opens that may not stay open for long, and whether the crisis is respected and worked with from a context of spiritual transformation or it is seen as a pathology that must be suppressed, hidden, and rejected will often determine whether it is an ordinary crisis or a healing one that presents a doorway to greater discernment.

Spiritual emergence is a term coined by Stanislav and Christina Grof to describe "the movement of an individual to a more expanded way of being that involves enhanced emotional and psychosomatic health, greater freedom of personal choices, and a sense of deeper connection with other people, nature, and the cosmos."[5] Sometimes, however, the insights, experiences, energies, and phenomena associated with the powerful emergence of unconscious material overwhelm an individual to the point of experiencing unmanageable stress and turmoil. The resulting crisis is referred to as *spiritual emergency.* The Spiritual Emergence Network (SEN) and the Institute of Spirituality and Psychology (ISP) are organizations that offer referrals to licensed mental health professionals for individuals experiencing difficulties with psychospiritual growth.

One of the primary factors that determines whether a given crisis will be experienced as a nervous breakdown, or what yoga teacher Bhavani Maki calls a "nervous breakthrough," is the environment in which we place ourselves during such times. What sources of formal and informal help do we turn to? What contextual framework of spiritual and psychological understanding do we have access to that helps us understand what is arising within us? What company do we keep? Crisis becomes opportunity when we learn to place our predicament in a larger context of growth and extract knowledge and meaning from the process. "It is important to realize," write Stanislav and Christina Grof, "that even the most dramatic and difficult episodes of spiritual emergency are natural stages in the process of spiritual opening and can be beneficial if circumstances are favorable."[6] Sometimes the greatest gifts we receive from going through a period of crisis are the recognition of our own vulnerability to life and a deeper capacity to empathize and support others who are suffering, as we now understand this aspect of our shared humanity.

In our naïveté, we might believe that devoting our lives wholeheartedly to a path of uncompromised spiritual growth means that we will experience progressively deeper peace, tranquility, harmony, and good fortune, and that if we practice diligently and sincerely enough we will somehow be exempt from the suffering that befalls the rest of the human race. In some cases this may be true, but once again, we are dealing with vast forces of karmic conditioning that often extend farther back in time than the intellect can conceive. And if our aim is to discover truth, the path will bring to the surface all that is untrue within us. We are tempered and refined through spiritual practice and through our own lives, and in this way, spiritual discernment dawns.

Once when I was attending a concert on a beach in Kauai, I noticed a striking young woman dancing wildly in the warm evening air, a large black tattoo that read "INVINCIBLE" in Gothic-style capital letters printed across her lower back. I ached when I thought of the shock and sorrow this young woman would inevitably encounter when she learned that neither she nor anyone else is invincible. Werner Erhard, a leader in the field of self-development, used to tell his students that the reward they would receive for learning to solve their problems would be even bigger problems to solve, and that the reward for learning to digest their own suffering would be to learn to digest the suffering of the world. Often, those who have the strongest intentions and who have made the most profound vows of transformation—usually consciously but sometimes even unconsciously—pass through the most severe tests, initiations, and "trials by fire" on their path.

The Dark Night of the Soul

"For a tree's branches to reach to heaven, its roots must reach to hell," says a medieval alchemical dictum. We cannot know what awaits us when we make a commitment to the spiritual path or an internal vow to discover the truth within ourselves. The beginning of the path is often marked by a flood of new insights and revelations about the magnitude of one's own spiritual potential and the magic of life—insights that may be accompanied by powerful mystical experiences, physical phenomena, and changes in the body. Beginning meditators regularly encounter experiences of great bliss, quietude, and equanimity, when they suddenly gain access to universes they previously believed to exist only in myths or thought were reserved for great mystics. At this point on the path, it is common to feel that we have a special, even unique, relationship to the spiritual domain—that we have been hand-plucked by the great Divine Intelligence itself to grow in its garden and be bestowed with gifts of wisdom and grace. In his classic book *Dark Night of the Soul,* the Spanish mystic Saint John of the Cross writes of this phase of the path:

> *I remained, lost in oblivion; My face I reclined on the Beloved.*
> *All ceased and I abandoned myself, Leaving my cares forgotten among the lilies.*[7]

For others of us, the initial awakening to our spiritual potential is not so extreme or ecstatic; nonetheless, it is accompanied by the dawning of great possibility. It is as if we have waited our whole lives to hear the teachings, to learn about the path, and to begin practice. We are profoundly touched by the possibilities of our mundane lives being converted into something extraordinary, of finding relief from our suffering and responses to our soul's questions that we dared not ask for fear there were no answers. We are told that much of spiritual life involves a continual shedding of ideas and ideals about the path as well as limiting self-concepts, illusions, and identities. It all sounds adventurous, liberating, and meaningful, and we are anxious to get to the heart of things. We begin to practice, often with great passion and zeal.

The initial remembrance of our divine nature is not unlike the great passion of falling in love. At such times, the reflection of the divinity in the other is so apparent that we often spontaneously say, do, feel, and commit to things that will have lifelong repercussions. Our initial "re-union" with the Divine carries this same intensity of consuming emotion and the promise of infinite possibility, only its nature is even more subtle and sublime; thus its pull may be even more powerful. Yet these divine moods are not designed to last forever.

"Run as fast as you can, if you can!" my spiritual teacher told me when I first encountered his spiritual school and was swooning in the ecstasy of my reunion with a forgotten aspect of my deeper self. I remember feeling that I was being teased and that my commitment was being tested. I didn't even glance backward.

The path seems to be designed such that we cannot know in advance the trials that await us—it would frighten us away from what our innermost being most deeply desires. The Divine, or Truth, seduces us with its unparalleled beauty, so we may glimpse the true nature we have been estranged from by our karma and conditioning. Once we have sensed our deeper origins and have committed to the path, we begin a profound and enduring process in which everything that keeps us from perceiving and abiding in our deepest nature is brought to the light of conscious awareness, so it can be understood, addressed, and assimilated.

For many people, this process, often referred to as "purification," is gradual and relatively undramatic. For others there are stages of purification that are so challenging that even the greatest of spiritual warriors feel that their sanity, and sometimes even their lives, are being put to the test. "The dark night of the soul" is how Saint John of the Cross described a period of time in the life of the mystic in which the Divine puts him or her through intensive trials and challenges that may include aridity of soul, disenchantment, or even a total loss of connection with God or the Divine—all designed to burn away any obstacles that stand in the way of union with divine intelligence. Discernment often emerges from the ashes of the purifying fire that burns away what is untrue within us.

Although most people will not experience the degree of the dark night that Saint John and many of the world's great mystics describe, many people do pass through varying degrees of profound spiritual crisis. "Regression in the service of transcendence" is the phrase transpersonal psychology theorist Michael Washburn uses to describe an evolutionary stage in the development of the soul in which the individual undergoes a great descent into the dark night, which Washburn proposes is a necessary process for further development to occur. In his developmental model, outlined in *The Ego and the Dynamic Ground,* he suggests that most people never grow beyond the stage of being fully identified with the egoic self. For the stronghold of egoic identification to be weakened so it can be progressively reclaimed by the dynamic ground—which is likened to divine intelligence—the ego must undergo an intensive and often "dark" process of purification.[8]

During this period of "regression in the service of transcendence," which Washburn says is often correlated with a midlife crisis, worldly goals lose their meaning, and the individual undergoes an intensive and often difficult process of purification in which the protective shell of ego is cracked open, and he or she is flooded with enormous amounts of previously unconscious material. In the first stage, profound disillusionment, despair, emptiness, and meaninglessness pervade the individuals' experience, often leaving them feeling as though they are losing ground in their development and perhaps even devolving. In the second stage, there is a breakthrough during which profound mystical states often arise—experiences that Washburn says people often mistake for enlightenment, or think mean more than they actually do. Rather than being an end in itself, this stage of development is preliminary to the eventual integration of the ego with essential nature, or dynamic ground.

Some of the most inspirational spiritual teachers and role models are those who have suffered the most challenging personal and spiritual crises. Mother Teresa of Calcutta is one such example. Although she was known to the world as a beacon of light and compassion, internally she endured devastating degrees of darkness, loneliness, and estrangement from any type of divine connection. Throughout her life, she kept this fact hidden from the world, sharing it only in writing with a few close spiritual mentors. Only after her death did these confidants choose to share her letters with the world, to demonstrate by example what is possible to offer and achieve in life in spite of a painful internal reality. *Come Be My Light,* a biography of Mother Teresa's life, includes letters written to her mentors during a period of darkness that extended for several decades. In one of these letters she wrote:

> *Now Father—since 49 or 50 this terrible sense of loss—*
> *this untold darkness—this loneliness—this continual*
> *longing for God—which gives me that pain deep down*
> *in my heart.—Darkness is such that I really do not*
> *see—neither with my mind nor with my reason.—the*
> *place of God in my soul is blank.—there is no God in*
> *me.—When the pain of longing is so great—I just long*
> *& long for God—and then it is that I feel—He does not*
> *want me—He is not there..God does not want me.—*
> *Sometimes —I just hear my own heart cry out—"My*
> *God" and nothing else comes.—The torture and pain I*
> *can't explain.*[9]

Irina Tweedie, a Russian-born Sufi master who experienced great heights of union and a profound capacity to influence the lives of others, said of the trials and tribulations on the spiritual path, "The ego does not die with laughter and caresses; it must be chased with sorrow and drowned with tears." In *Daughter of Fire,* she shared the story of some of the intense internal states she endured while with her guru, B'hai Sahib.

> *The body was shaking . . . I was biting my pillow not to*
> *howl like a wild animal . . . I was beside myself—the*
> *craziest, the maddest thing one could imagine, so out*
> *of the blue, so sudden, so violent! . . . The mind was*
> *absolutely void, emptied of its content; there was no*
> *imagery, only an uncontrollable fear—primitive, animal*
> *fear. And it went for hours. I was shaking like a leaf . . .*
> *a mute, helpless trembling jelly, carried away by forces*
> *completely beyond any human control. A fire was burning*

inside my bowels . . . I don't know how long it lasted or
whether I slept out of sheer exhaustion, or if I had fainted.
The whole body was shaky and trembling in the morning.[10]

In *Dark Night of the Soul,* editor Mirabai Starr comments:

The divine lays siege upon the soul in order to make her
new and to make her divine, stripping her of habitual
affections and attachments to the old self to which she had
been reconciled. The divine disentangles and dissolves her
spiritual substance, absorbing it in deep darkness. In the
face of her own misery, the soul feels herself coming undone
and melting away in a cruel spiritual death. It is as if the
soul were being swallowed by a beast and disintegrating in
the darkness of its belly, like Jonah when he was trapped
inside the whale. She must abide in this tomb of dark
death until the spiritual resurrection she is hoping for.[11]

From this example, we see that during the dark night of
the soul the human being undergoes a powerful training in
discernment at the deepest levels of his or her experience. I
suspect that we came into this world with certain "contracts"
with the Divine. Each of our contracts is unique, depending upon our individual karma and our soul's destiny, but it
seems as if in some dimension, at some time long before this
time, decisions were made, and a kind of fate was sealed. The
intensity of the purification process often, though not always,
correlates with the degree of our conscious and even unconscious commitment to the spiritual path. Some who aspire to
great spiritual heights will need to endure a profound degree
of suffering. When we have awakened the light within us, that
very light becomes focused inward in order to illumine that
which remains "dark" or unconscious. Each spiral of growth
involves moving through and addressing another level of

obscuration so that more of our inner light can be known. It seems that the deeper our exposure to the light, the more intensely we experience our estrangement from it.

I have been surprised to discover how many of the spiritual teachers and mentors in my life whom I consider to be very advanced practitioners have passed through truly harrowing crises in their lives on the path—including months or years of depression, existential despair, and periods of profound psychosis in which they lost all sense of sanity and purpose. It is often through these experiences that they have discovered the deeper truths of our shared humanity and have learned how to work with the psychological and spiritual aspects of the human experience.

Lama Palden Drolma, an American teacher of Tibetan Buddhism, explains that according to karmic law it is possible that practitioners of very intense spiritual aspiration who wish to serve others in a powerful way might find themselves passing through severe personal spiritual crises and "dark-night" trials in preparation for such service.

> *Very highly developed people sometimes enter into different situations to liberate that karma for themselves, to liberate that kind of karma for all beings in general, and also to learn how to work that kind of karma so they can help others who experience a similar type of karma. According to Tibetan Buddhism, a lot of times if you awaken really easily in a given lifetime, you don't have the same capacity to help other people to awaken. You don't really understand what other people go through unless you've been through it.*[12]

Whatever term we use to describe it, when the great intelligence of the universe responds to our soul's deepest yearning by taking away from us rather than giving to us, what keeps us going forward? Can we still believe in the Divine, ourselves, and life? Can we go deep within and travel on a hairsbreadth of faith that what is occurring is somehow part of the path rather than a betrayal by the path? If not, can we simply endure, staying in place long enough to allow the process to do its work on us?

Groundlessness

The bad news is that you are falling through the air, there is nothing to hang onto, and you have no parachute. The good news is that there is no ground.

—CHÖGYAM TRUNGPA RINPOCHE

Powerful breakdowns, healing crises, and dark nights—times when we feel bereft and disillusioned, stripped of all we thought was solid in our lives and with nothing to replace what was lost—give us a direct experience of what the Buddhist tradition refers to as "groundlessness." We find the apparent solidity of the ground beneath us to be made of shifting sand. The beliefs and identities we have hung our lives upon are revealed to be empty constructs that have no objective meaning.

While experiences of groundlessness may be very uncomfortable, particularly among people who are accustomed to using intellectual knowledge to maintain a semblance of control in their lives, according to Buddhist tradition they are valuable because they offer an immediate experience of undeniable reality. Paradoxically, it is from an intimacy with groundlessness that we are able to make discerning choices in relationship to the decisions we make and actions we take in the world of duality, or "ground." When we are unafraid of groundlessness, we can make bold, radiant, and clear choices about our lives.

"Reality is groundlessness," says Lee Lozowick, "and the only place to stand is in groundlessness." Human beings need organizing principles around which to develop their lives. We build houses, families, and retirement accounts. We work; make lists and schedules; create routines, goals, and projects. We construct identities, meanings, experiences of continuity, obsessions, addictions, and even problems in order to create a sense of safety, protection, and ground beneath our feet, to feel that we exist and that life has meaning. Yet, the greater truth is that there is no final security, nothing that is fully known, no ultimately solid ground, nothing that will not fade.

Buddhism speaks to this phenomenon of groundlessness through the principle of *impermanence,* the recognition that there is no essential substance or concept that is fixed and endures permanently. Everything is continually in flux and destined to fade. Dzongsar Jamyang Khyentse, a Bhutanese Buddhist master, writer, and filmmaker, suggests that although impermanence is a difficult aspect of reality to entertain, much less accept, within it lies a portal to human freedom. He writes, "Fearlessness is generated when you can appreciate uncertainty, when you have faith in the impossibility of these interconnected components remaining static and permanent. You will find yourself, in a very true sense, preparing for the worst while allowing for the best. You become dignified and majestic."[13]

In 2002, I spent several days in the company of U. G. Krishnamurti, a spiritual revolutionary whose very being was an expression of groundlessness. In his presence there was no ground to stand on: not a theoretical one, not an emotional one, not a spiritual one. During my efforts to interview him, he undermined every question and concept I had, revealing the essential emptiness and groundlessness behind my motivations, efforts, concepts, and beliefs. Here is an example of our interchange.

Me: "U. G., how . . ."

U. G. (instantly interrupting): "The moment you say *how* you are in a concept, just looking for another one to replace it."

Me: "But how can I not do that?"

U. G.: "Don't try to not do anything!"

Me: "But . . ."

U. G.: "The very idea that you need to be something different than you are, the idea that there is something you can get, all that was placed into you!"

Me: "Can I get rid of it?"

U. G.: "No! You can't get rid of anything."

Me: "But how can I proceed along the spiritual path?"

U. G.: "There is no spiritual path! There is nothing outside of you!"

Many of us are drawn to the spiritual path because we want to be happy, and we believe that discovering deeper truths about ourselves, and even objective truth itself, will bring about that happiness. It can therefore be both shocking and sobering to find ourselves experiencing moments of groundlessness, emptiness, and impermanence. A friend of mine heard the Dalai Lama speak about the first time he glimpsed the state of emptiness, described by Buddhists as the recognition that nothing possesses an essential, enduring identity. My friend said that when the Dalai Lama spoke about it his whole posture contracted and his voice hushed. Emptiness was a difficult aspect of reality to bear even for His Holiness.

"Incense and candles are exotic and attractive," writes Dzongsar Jamyang Khyentse, "impermanence and selflessness are not."[14] It is at these junctures on the path that many people choose the comfort of illusion, even spiritual illusions, rather than allowing deeper realities that can only be discovered through letting go into groundlessness to be revealed.

"Security is not the cure for insecurity," announced E. J. Gold to a group of us seated around his dining room table early one morning. The nature of being human *is* insecure. Depending on the environment in which we were raised and how we were parented, existential insecurity may be coupled with and magnified by psychological insecurity, leaving us with a gnawing feeling of lack that continually prompts us to grab at straws of security, whether material, conceptual, or psychological.

Yet no amount of security will fill the hole of psychological or existential insecurity within us. We see too well from the example of many of the world's materially wealthy but spiritually impoverished individuals that no amount of wealth or security will bring happiness or spare us from death. In too many cases the walls we build up around ourselves to protect us from insecurity become the prison that prevents us from exploring deeper possibilities for inner freedom. Tantric scholar Robert Svoboda suggests that one of the primary motivations for the accumulation of wealth is a deeply unconscious belief that we can somehow purchase immortality.

"If security is not the cure for insecurity," one of our group inquired of Gold during that winter morning meeting, "what is?"

"Drop the issue of security altogether," he told us. The great spiritual challenge is to drop our identification with the experience of the separate self that believes it exists and must protect itself at all costs. The only cure for insecurity is to recognize its insubstantiality, to turn our backs on that within us which insists on seeking security despite the futility of the search, and to step forward into the unknown without looking back.

Facing the reality of groundlessness is like the spiritual student standing on the high-dive board over an empty swimming pool as the master says, "Jump!"

"I can't jump!" the student says. "There is no water there!"

"Jump first, and the water will appear," says the master.

Of course, most of us will not willingly jump into the unknown because we have read in some spiritual text that the universe will somehow cast a safety net beneath us before we crash, or that we cannot crash at all because the ground will recede into the infinite. Yet many circumstances of life—accidents, psychological crises, severe illness, the very real dangers of terrorism and global warming—confront us with the reality of groundlessness and impermanence, and one of the functions of spiritual practice is to help us learn to stay present and open in the face of the reality of profound uncertainty. Certainly, the moment of death will be the great test of our ability to release ourselves to groundlessness. And it is unrealistic and impractical to believe that we can spend our whole lives clinging to the security of comforting concepts, limiting identities, and a universe that we manipulate and control only to suddenly find ourselves at death's door able and willing to release ourselves into the unknown.

Groundlessness is, paradoxically, very fertile ground from which new creativity can arise. The Hindu trinity, or *trimurti,* of Brahma, Vishnu, and Shiva symbolizes the principles of creation, sustenance, and destruction that continually operate in relationship with each other throughout the cycles of our lives, in nature, and in the cosmos itself. As we become able to experience the reality of groundlessness, making space within ourselves to allow for continual creation and dissolution, we become more fluid and spacious. We recognize that we live in a universe without walls, and from this spaciousness arises a wellspring of creative potential that knows no bounds. The domain of our discernment widens, as we must not only discern between variables and choices that are known to us, but also include in our awareness the continual presence of the unknown.

The Grief of Ego

"Nobody talks about the ego's grief, as it is called, to let go of all it has held to for dear life," my friend Gillian said, reflecting on her fifty years on the spiritual path as we sat on her porch outside her home in South Africa.

Insight into spiritual truth is not difficult to come by, but the purification and the shattering of illusions that must be undergone by those who commit their lives to the integration of that truth is a momentous undertaking. Most of the great tasks of spiritual life, the heroic inner leaps that every spiritual warrior is asked to make, are far more easily reflected upon than accomplished. "Simple but not easy," say the masters of all traditions. Whether we are talking about the need to drop the sense of insecurity, disidentify with ego, let go of the hope of salvation, or allow our concepts and constructs about what spirituality is to fade, these are processes that span many years, even if we have first had very clear insight into their principles.

There are times when the process of disidentifying with ego is so powerful that we become convinced we are literally dying, and we may even manifest certain symptoms of death. We unconsciously believe that if we are not who we have always believed ourselves to be, we do not exist, and death is imminent. Something is dying inside us, but *we* are not dying. This is the critical point of discernment we must understand at these times.

I am intimate with this process from my own experience. Following a great emotional shock catalyzed by profound betrayal by a loved one, I found my sense of identity fragmented into what felt like thousands of splintered pieces spread throughout the universe. The emotional shock precipitated a series of powerful physical responses in my body, and I was certain that I was dying. Fortunately, I was in my teacher's ashram during this period, where my crisis could be understood in a spiritual context. I recall sitting on the floor with a dear friend, sharing with her that I thought I was dying. "*You* are not dying," she told me, "something within you is dying." She repeated this to me many times, over days and weeks, and gradually I was able to perceive the difference between the death of my dreams, beliefs, and various identities and the death of my body.

Many of us come to the path and say that we want to be free of our illusions, yet these illusions make up most of our reality. Again, it is not life that is an illusion, or maya, but our relationship to life that is clouded with projected images, false perceptions, and endless levels of subjectivity and beliefs—all of which we assume to be real. This illusory relationship to ourselves, to life, is what we truly believe we are, no matter how brilliantly we talk about the false self, how deep into the silence of meditation we go, or how many *satoris* we have. As we considered in Chapter 4, although this process is sometimes referred to as "ego death," the ego itself cannot and does not die. It is the identification with whom we believe ourselves to be that will be revealed as deceptive and false, while the ego itself remains, bearing witness to the dismantling of the false self. There is tremendous grief and fear involved in this loss.

"Your dharma usually involves you killing yourself at some point," says yogic scholar and author Robert Svoboda. It is no joke when it is said that the "I" that enters this path does not come out the other side. The path is an actual death sentence for the "I," the only question being how prolonged the trial will be. What we must contend with is whether we will be able to endure the dismantling of whom we believe ourselves to be with some degree of dignity.

The ego's grief as it witnesses the demise of our identification with it is rarely written or spoken about in dharmic circles. The spiritual books we read are usually written by spiritual masters who write from the perspective of having already shifted their identification to a nonegoic context, by teachers who have had enlightenment experiences but have not undergone the dismantling of ego and subsequent psychospiritual integration, or by sophisticated spiritual dilettantes who paint a picture of the spiritual path as a glamorous adventure—but who have no idea what they are talking about.

There are too few accounts of long-term spiritual practitioners that detail the despair, depression, patience, fortitude, and endurance involved in maintaining a lifelong commitment to the spiritual path once the blush of the great reunion with the forgotten truth of our deeper experience has passed. There are often long periods on the path—months or even years—when our naïve hopes and assumptions about our spiritual greatness have been revealed for what they are, and we feel ourselves becoming stagnant, even backsliding. There are times when our illusions of who we are and what the path is have been dismantled and have not yet been replaced with anything else. T. K. V. Desikachar describes the Sanskrit term *alabdhūmikatva* as the experience of "just as we've been thinking we have made some progress, we suddenly notice how much there still is for us to do. We can grow very disappointed at this point and become fickle in mood. We suddenly have no interest in trying again, in finding another way to begin, in taking the next step."[15]

"Ninety percent of spiritual life is just hanging in there," says E. J. Gold. And while we are hanging in there, enduring the often too-slow process of transformation, we must also endure inevitable and sometimes lengthy periods of grief and sorrow. We would like to believe that the spiritual path brings about increasing joy, bliss, and clarity, and I believe that it does increase our capacity to perceive these aspects of life more vividly and directly. However, the path to truth must necessarily reveal what is untrue, and with these insights grief comes to ego as the false self becomes dethroned in the service of an eventual abidance in the real.

The healing crises we pass through in life can serve as powerful lessons that teach us true spiritual discernment. These passages, when integrated, become the resource from which we are genuinely able to help others because we really do understand what they have passed through. We have opened the doors and entered the rooms of our own sorrow, heartbreak, hopelessness. We have learned to live with them, and thus we are emotionally, energetically, and empathically able to support others as they navigate the labyrinth of their own hidden worlds. Our crisis is an initiation into discernment and wisdom, and as we embrace the archetype of the wounded healer, our challenges are converted into deeper clarity. This transmutation of energies within us, of learning to turn crises and confusion into greater discernment and clarity, is the essence of the tantric principle, which we will explore in the next chapter.

Chapter 7

∼

The Tantric Principle

If you bring forth what is within you, what you bring forth
will save you. If you do not bring forth what is within you,
what you do not bring forth will destroy you.

—JESUS CHRIST, *The Gospel of Thomas*

"O ne reaches heaven by the very things which may
lead to hell," says the *Kularnava Tantra*. Translated
as "continuity," "fabric," "to weave," "technique,"
and "method," *tantra* teaches us to weave the totality of our
experience—what we consider to be both good and bad—
into one continuous fabric of awakened awareness. To relate
to and make use of the tantric principle, we must have keen
discernment, so we can make clear distinctions and transform ordinary reality into extraordinary reality. Treading on
a razor's edge of transformation, it is our clarity of perception
that will guide us.

The tantric principle is an approach found in many religions and spiritual paths even if it is not named as "tantra."
Therefore, this chapter is not about Buddhist or Hindu tantra,

but rather a principle of spiritual transformation that is particularly valuable to consider in our understanding of spiritual discernment, as it opens our eyes to important distinctions that are not highlighted in other paths. At its core, the tantric approach offers a philosophy and a method by which one might become an integrated, unified human being. It does this by teaching us how to relate to all experience as fertile ground for uncompromised spiritual transformation. Through this approach, we learn to perceive and consciously engage the potent energies that weave through all aspects of life—from the most mundane, challenging, and dense levels of our lives to the powerful force of emotion at the core of our psychology and relationships with other people, to the subtle, often imperceptible energies of mystical perception and experience.

Providing concrete information on Hindu and Buddhist tantric traditions is a task beyond the scope of this book, and one that I do not presume to be qualified to address. This chapter instead explores various perspectives on the underlying principle of tantric transformation—a principle that is found within specific esoteric aspects of many religions and spiritual traditions. Although the term *tantra* is most commonly associated with Hinduism and Buddhism, the core principles of transformation are found in Judaism, Christianity, Sufism, alchemy, hatha yoga, martial arts, and a variety of other spiritual traditions and psychological methods. As it is approached in this chapter, the essence of the tantric principle is an approach to transformation that is nondenominational and that transcends conventional religion while still drawing from, and aligning itself with, many religious rituals and practices.

Before we further explore the principle of tantric transformation, it is important to be clear about what tantra is not. Tantra is not spiritual sex as popularized in New Age publications and workshops and increasingly marketed in spiritual circles around the world. "I don't mind people having good or even great sex," says Robert Svoboda, a scholar and practitioner of Ayurvedic medicine and tantric yoga. "People should have wonderful sex, but *please* just don't call it tantra!" Buddhist scholar Steven Goodman comments, "There is less sex in tantra than in most good marriages." The past few decades have given rise to a brand of "neo-tantra" in the Western world that draws upon and isolates specific terms and sexual practices found in Hindu and Buddhist tantra while omitting of the vast context of tantric practice and tradition. There are prerequisites that include commitment to a lineage, the guidance of a guru, codes of moral and ethical conduct, and a firm foundation in meditation and other practices before one is qualified to be initiated into esoteric sexual practice.

Unfortunately, the popularity of neo-tantra confuses people, leading them to believe that exotic sexual practice is the whole of tantra. This confusion means that many sincere spiritual practitioners miss out on an opportunity to be exposed to an encompassing body of highly refined knowledge and practices that may be very useful to them, regardless of what religion or spiritual practice they adhere to.

When one is steeped in an experiential understanding of the tantric principle, the capacity to apply this to sexual experience comes naturally and organically, as a by-product of integrating tantric wisdom. Conversely, learning tantric sexual techniques without understanding the broader principles of tantric transformation and practice holds little possibility of integrating tantric knowledge into all aspects of one's life. When the focus is on sexual technique—without those techniques being embedded in a larger context of study, daily discipline, and consistent guidance—any mystical experiences that may arise remain isolated within the narrow body of sexual experience. As extraordinary as that is, the sexual aspect is only a fraction of what tantric wisdom can teach us. To make any real use of tantric philosophy and practices requires keen discernment on the part of the practitioner.

The Inseparability of Nonduality and Duality

To begin our exploration of the tantric principle, it is useful to consider the relationship between nonduality and duality. Most esoteric traditions recognize a nondual, formless source at the core of all experience, whether they refer to it as emptiness, *purusha,* soul, essence, advaita, divine intelligence, or a God that is beyond name and form. Many traditions and religions then go on to distinguish between this formless essence and the manifest world of duality. These traditions consider human beings and the world we inhabit as separate from this greater intelligence, often referred to as God. Some traditions tell us we have fallen and are residing in a state of sin; others suggest that our lives are an illusion; still others insist that God, or the Divine, is unknowable. There is usually a primary text and an accompanying set of moral and ethical guidelines to follow for those who adhere to the particular religion and philosophy that they represent. The world is full of frustrated card-carrying members of religious traditions who sense that the version of truth they are being sold somehow undermines their own internal sensing of a divine presence and connection.

The tantric approach offers a radically different perspective, suggesting not only that ultimate reality is knowable and accessible through our own direct experience, but that the very facets of our experience that many religious traditions label as mundane, illusory, "dark," or otherwise separate from the Divine—aspects we so often dismiss and reject—are in fact the doorway through which we can experience union with ourselves, the Divine, and therefore others and all of life.

Ngakpa Chögyam, a Tibetan Buddhist teacher from Wales, offers a perspective on nonduality that includes all of life as a direct expression of the nondual core of truth. He explains that nonduality, or emptiness, has two facets: one is the empty, or nondual, and the other is form, or duality. Therefore, duality is not illusory but is instead one *aspect* of nonduality. Like the two sides of a coin, the formless reality has two dimensions—one is form, the other is formless.[1] When we perceive duality as separate from nonduality (or nonduality as separate from duality), we do not engage the world of manifestation from a perspective of oneness, and thereby we fall into an erroneous relationship with it. From this perspective it is not "life" or duality that is maya, or illusion; rather, it is our relationship to the world that is illusory.

The teachings of the inseparability between nonduality and duality are found in many traditions, both in their philosophical treatises and in their art and symbology. The *Heart Sūtra,* the best-known sūtra of Mahayana Buddhism, states that "matter is not different from emptiness, and emptiness is not different from matter." Hinduism is full of representations of the relationship between multiplicity and oneness, vibrantly portrayed through the Hindu pantheon that maps the human psyche and its relationship to the Godhead. The *Pratyabhijnahridayam Upanishads,* one of the doctrines of Kashmir Shaivism, states, "The Lord has the universe for a body." The *lingam*, a phallic symbol that represents Lord Shiva, or the masculine principle of formless truth, always sits at the base of a *yoni,* which is roughly shaped like a vagina and represents Shakti, or the feminine principle of manifestation. Together they represent the point of enlightenment.

We can see that throughout the esoteric teachings of many traditions the great nondual insight of oneness, in its optimal expression, pervades all of duality. In *Wearing the Body of Visions,* Ngakpa Chögyam writes, "The limitless multiplicity of the world of form is seen as providing limitless opportunities for the realization of nonduality: emptiness is presented *through* form."[2] In *The Sacred Mirror,* John Welwood affirms:

> *Letting the relative be as it is, then, reveals the absolute. Thus there is no need to give absolute being a special status apart from the relative process of form evolving in time, for these are inseparable. Realizing this frees us up to move fluidly between engaging with our experience and discovering its spacious indefinable nature, without regarding either side as more real than the other. There is no need to set up any divide between duality and nonduality.[3]*

For many people, an intellectual understanding of the relationship between nonduality and duality as represented from a tantric perspective seems natural and organic once it is understood. Yet learning to access experience at this degree of subtlety and integrating it into our daily lives remains the single most challenging aspect of spiritual life, even for those who agree at a conceptual level about the importance of valuing both relative and absolute, or nondual and dual, reality.

Many contemporary spiritual traditions tend to favor either the dual or the nondual aspect of reality. The first few decades of Theravada and Zen Buddhism in the West, for example, have favored a nondual stance of dwelling in emptiness, silence, and detached observation of the mind rather than engaging the messy, unpredictable, and relative domain of human psychology.[4] On the other end of the spectrum, many contemporary shamanic and spiritually based psychological traditions tend to favor duality and the world of form as the inroad to spiritual understanding, at times undervaluing the reality of emptiness, impermanence, and groundlessness.

Similarly, in our own individualized approaches to spiritual practice we are likely to favor one aspect of reality over the other. On one extreme is the tendency to spiritually bypass, spiritualizing away our responsibility to ourselves and others, which results in an incomplete process of development. "If you betray the earth in yourself, you will never attain the heaven in yourself," writes Arnaud Desjardins in *The Jump into Life*.[5] On the other end of the continuum is a narcissistic obsession with ourselves and our own history and personal process, accompanied by a life of endless searching and attempts at self-improvement, none of which address the essential nondual essence of life.

"Everything has two sides to fall off of," said my friend Jeff after we had been debating for months on this subject. Truer words have never been spoken in relation to the perception and practice of spiritual truth. Exploring the relationship between duality and nonduality, in our own consciousness and in our own experience, is a continuous dialectic, an endless dance along the razor's edge. Constant attention is required to be aware of the moments of awakening that arise in our lives and the perspective they provide while simultaneously attending to the needs of the deep psyche and the life that surrounds us.

Turning Poison into Medicine

One man's food is another man's poison.

—SWAMI PRAJNANPAD [6]

Tantric practice teaches us to turn poison into medicine. According to the tantric perspective, everything, including those things we most dislike and fear, can be used or misused. If we use it, we gain energy from it and grow; if we misuse it, it depletes us and deepens our confusion. The key to discernment lies in how we relate to any given circumstance. Learning to extract medicine from poison requires a training of attention to subtlety that takes many years of practice. Through this training, we learn to work with the energies within ourselves; then, by a natural extension of our practice, we are able to make use of the potent and intense energies we encounter in our external lives, including the stresses of daily life and the negativity of others as well as the subtle energies of sexuality, imagination, and profound states of spiritual awareness.

The first place we learn to work tantrically is with our emotional body. Many of us involved in spiritual work have tasted vast possibilities for spiritual awareness and may long to merge our individual consciousness with universal awareness. Where we get stuck, again and again, is in our emotional bodies, which are informed by the basic structures of ego and our personal psychological conditioning. Great spiritual thinkers and writers who have inspired us both past and present have repeatedly suffered and caused suffering to those around them because they did not learn to use their spiritual insight to address the more basic structures of their psychology and emotional body.

Many spiritual traditions tell us that our neurosis is, in essence, unreal. There are powerful and effective meditation techniques that teach us how to observe these energies when they arise and to cultivate an attitude of detachment from them so they do not dominate our experience. My personal opinion is that these techniques work only for some people and at certain times in their lives. They rarely stand the test of relationship and sexuality, and they often result in a very detached relationship to life rather than an integrated psycho-spiritual transformation. Tantra differs from these approaches in the belief that the cure for the wound lies within the wound itself. Through learning to turn toward what we ordinarily hide from, we form a relationship with it, touching the very core of its energetic makeup with conscious awareness, releasing blocked energy, and allowing this direct experience with previously unknown aspects of our experience to inform us at progressively deeper levels. In *Tantra: The Path of Ecstasy,* Georg Feuerstein writes, "In their endeavor to reach the One, the Tantric practitioners inevitably must traverse those intermediate realms, which are invisible to ordinary sight but nonetheless as real (or unreal) as the material world."[7]

"Your neurosis is your enlightenment," said Buddhist master Chögyam Trungpa Rinpoche. How can this be? Because at the core of our neurosis lies a storehouse of buried energy that has limitless capacity to transform us at a very deep level. Tantra teaches us to turn toward this gold mine of confused experience and extract the pure energy of the life force contained within it. From a tantric perspective, our neurosis is not a limitation. What limits us is contracting and turning away from pockets of our internal experience that are so potent we are afraid to feel them—wounds so tender that we have repressed them from conscious awareness, fears so unconscious and convincing that we would rather live limited lives than open ourselves to them, repressed feelings of terror or anger so virulent that we fear we might actually kill someone if we allowed them expression.

"If every defensive pattern contains hidden intelligence and resources," writes John Welwood, "this means that we do not have to reject the defensive personality. We need to crack it open so that we can discover and gain access to the intelligence and resources that lie hidden within it."[8] Through studying and practicing with the tantric perspective, we gradually learn how to turn toward all that is dark and frightening within us and within life. We learn to use those things to expand ourselves, a subject explored further in the following chapter, which specifically addresses working with our shadow material. From a tantric perspective, our personality itself is not a limitation—it's our refusal to keep growing beyond our personality that is the problem.

To work tantrically involves using our awareness and attention in a new way. The neurosis may not change, at least right away, but through our attention and intention it becomes refocused in the service of transformation. Part of us continues to enact the same mechanical, conditioned behavior in daily life— eating, thinking, freaking out, working, being confused, trying to love those near to us—while the very base of our experience, orientation, and attention is being slowly redirected toward a transformational experience. Along the way, our weaknesses are co-opted into the service of a greater reality, and we are released from the stronghold of their neurotic grip as they gradually purify and channel into expressions of creativity and growth.

Robina Courtin, a Tibetan Buddhist teacher I referred to earlier, once lectured a group of graduate students on tantra at the university where I teach in San Francisco. Describing her life before becoming a nun, she told the group she had been an "angry, Marxist, radical-lesbian biker chick" before meeting her teacher and beginning a life of practice. She was still full of anger, she told us, but now it was turned toward fighting ignorance within herself and teaching Buddhism to convicts in maximum security prisons. Her lifelong sense of not belonging led to a life of public teaching in which she traveled throughout the world addressing thousands of people who were thirsty for spiritual teachings. Her anxiety and restlessness resulted in the creation of spiritual centers and large-scale service projects, and she edited multiple books for her teacher. Through a lifelong commitment to tantric practice, Courtin's weaknesses became assets, not only to herself but to others, benefiting thousands of people who are touched by her presence.

Tantric practice reveals the hidden gifts within what we perceive to be our weaknesses. If we are greedy, we do not stop wanting things, but we become greedy for knowledge, wisdom, or opportunities to serve. Our anger becomes an intense motivation to address our own ignorance and see clearly the ways we hurt others unconsciously; our sorrow becomes empathy and compassion for those who suffer as much or more than we do. Our fear becomes awe of the majesty of the divine process; our loneliness is converted to longing; our joy and gratitude give rise to the need to share our good fortune with others. Our attention is always absorbed in something. The question is, "What do we choose to be engaged in?" The tantric principle instructs us in how to shift our self-absorption in such a way that we become absorbed in increasingly more encompassing levels of reality, transformation, and service. It is our capacity for discernment that determines whether something is poison or medicine.

The Practice of Non-Rejection

If you want to know silence, take great interest in the noise!

—ARNAUD DESJARDINS

Non-rejection, according to Lee Lozowick, is one of the primary principles of all tantric practice. Tantra has often been regarded as the "dangerous" path, or a slippery slope, precisely because it allows for, and makes use of, substances, energies, and activities that many other spiritual paths renounce and reject as being unspiritual, impure, or dangerous. The tantric perspective challenges the dichotomies of spiritual/unspiritual, sacred/mundane, pious/profane. It calls upon us to learn to respond appropriately, effectively, and with a deeply informed integrity in all circumstances.

It is important not to mistake non-rejection for undiscerning awareness. This is a trap common to those who engage tantric principles and practice at a superficial level and regard tantra as a philosophical justification for indulgence. To "not reject" does not mean that we accept everything we are given with open hands and eat it whole. One of the greatest purposes of tantra is to teach us to develop the discernment necessary to engage all the elements of life—from the ordinary, to the challenging, to the extraordinary—in a productive and useful way. Our capacity to digest our experience becomes refined such that we do not have to close ourselves off from any aspect of life. We trust ourselves to be able to handle the circumstances life brings in a way that always results in growth, even if such growth at times feels very uncomfortable.

In *The Book of Secrets,* Bhagwan Shree Rajneesh, also known as Osho, elaborates the principle of non-rejection:

> Don't try to go against anything because you will move
> to something which belongs to it. It looks opposite, but
> it is not. Don't move from sex to brahmacharya. If
> you are trying to move from sex to brahmacharya, your
> brahmacharya will be nothing but sexuality. Don't move
> from greed to no-greed because that no-greed will again
> be a subtle greed. That is why if a tradition teaches to be
> nongreedy, it gives you some profit motive in it.[9]

To say "yes" to life is the primary practice that students of Advaita-Vedanta teacher Arnaud Desjardins are asked to do. As we learn to open slowly and skillfully toward that which we have an aversion to, adversarial emotions and conditions lose their power over us. In *Jump into Life* Desjardins explains, "Once the ego no longer finds an adversary, then the ego is no more. From birth, what characterizes the ego is *being against* . . . that is why the word yes is the absolute weapon against the ego. This is not only true for disciples of a Hindu or Tibetan master, any psychologist who has studied the genesis of the ego in childhood will agree."[10] Where there are two, there is duality, and therefore opposing aspects of our consciousness. When we say "yes" to all of our experience, the duality inherent in our resistance to ourselves and to life dissipates into a union that arises out of complete acceptance of our life and our experience as it is.

Kenny Johnson, a former prisoner who founded This Sacred Space,[11] an organization that supports prisoners in learning to access their spiritual wisdom, speaks in a similar fashion about being in prison after he'd had a profound spiritual awakening catalyzed by meeting his spiritual teacher. Although still incarcerated for the two years following the meeting with his teacher, he experienced a period of profound contentment, and his consciousness stabilized in nondual awareness, enjoying the security of having a place to sleep and food to eat. At one point he spent two days in the back of a maximum-security bus being transported to another federal prison. The other prisoners in the bus were agitated, angry, and afraid, and they challenged Johnson's apparent sense of well-being, trying to provoke him. Yet no matter what the others said, or what the circumstances were, his experience of union with all of life was unwavering.

The tantric practice of non-rejection teaches us to cease resisting our experience and trying to force it to be something else. This allows our awareness to rest in a state of nonseparation and brings us into profound communion and a sense of oneness with our experience. When we learn through attention, practice, study, courage, and tremendous perseverance to say "yes" to what is real, however undesirable it might be, all of life becomes a vibrant field of transformational possibility.

Restraint and Sublimation: The Tantric Brahmacharya

By passion the world is bound; by passion, too, it is released.

—*Hevajra Tantra*

The tantric principle teaches us how to consciously utilize energy for transformational purposes. Through tantric practice, we learn to engage potent energies within ourselves and harness them in order to access deeper layers of experience. The Sanskrit term *tapas,* referred to earlier, literally means "heat" and refers to the fire of transformation that is catalyzed through intentional spiritual practices. The inner heat that is generated within us can burn through dense and otherwise impenetrable layers of unconsciousness.

In yogic psychology, the term *brahmacharya* suggests someone whose life is devoted to the realization of Brahma or God. In a traditional yogic sense, a brahmacharya is someone who practices sexual celibacy for the purpose of sublimating and redirecting sexual energy to support spiritual realization. Spiritual celibacy has been practiced in a variety of mystical and monastic traditions throughout time, to greater and lesser degrees of effectiveness in terms of its stated purpose: to redirect one's full energies toward

God, to evoke spiritual insight, or to engage in the esoteric transformation of sexual energy.

I have met and interviewed hundreds of spiritual practitioners of celibacy from a wide variety of spiritual traditions—whether they practice brahmacharya in the context of a Hindu ashram or a Catholic monastery. For the majority of them, the sexual energy they attempt to restrain becomes repressed, blocked, or misdirected rather than sublimated and transmuted. The Western psyche relates to sexual energy with an immense amount of confusion and distortion due to a variety of factors, and it is this confusion that is responsible for many spiritual scandals, which often occur in the guise of "tantra" or "special initiations."

When sexual celibacy is combined with potent spiritual practices—particularly when practitioners have not explored their own sexuality or unpacked their psychological baggage relating to it—it often results in physical, psychological, and psychic blockages that are expressed through a wide range of manifestations ranging from depression to illness to aggression. In the case of the spiritual teacher, these blockages are often responsible for scandalous and problematic behavior. (This circumstance is distinct from temporary celibacy, which may be appropriate for studying one's own relationship to sexual energy, for healing purposes, or because life circumstances necessitate a period of situational celibacy.)

For the majority of contemporary practitioners of Western spirituality, the principle of "restraint" may be more effectively considered as the practice of learning to take responsibility for the power and creativity of our own sexuality. We learn to make conscious and discerning choices in relationship to it rather than succumbing to the unconscious forces of repression, seduction, and manipulation that are so common in contemporary Western culture. When we learn to access, understand, and direct our sexual energy, it can be used for any number of purposes, including accessing higher knowledge, supporting creative endeavors, simply enjoying the precious gift of human pleasure—and manipulating and controlling others. Teachers and students of sexual "tantra" need to be particularly discerning about how they use their sexual energy and charisma. In Western culture, whether we are interested in spirituality or not, a conscious relationship to sexual energy is usually something that is learned and cultivated, often through an extensive process of inquiry, exploration, healing, and discernment.

An interesting and simple way to begin exploring our relationship to energy is to inquire, within the context of our daily lives, how life-force energy, often referred to as *prana* or *chi,* works within our bodies. We start to explore which circumstances, individuals, relationships, and interactions take energy from us and which give us energy. Repeatedly throughout a given day, we ask ourselves, "Does this situation/person/activity give me energy or take it away?" As we begin to take inventory of how we use our physical, emotional, and sexual energy—learning which types of interactions and circumstances nourish us and which deplete us—it gradually dawns on us that we are largely unconscious with respect to how we relate to the energy of our own life force, beginning with the fundamental energy of breath and extending into the arena of mental, physical, and sexual energies. We learn to be more discerning about the functioning of our own energy body, the energetic mechanisms of others, and our tendencies in relationship with others, particularly in regard to our power, sexuality, desire, and needs. It is not that we should not engage in activities that take away energy, but that we gradually take responsibility for our energy and thus use it more effectively and efficiently.

Until we have learned to perceive our own life force and understand our energetic relationship to the most fundamental aspects of life, it is unrealistic and impractical to believe we are ready to engage the spiritual practices prescribed by sexual tantric techniques as they were intended to be used. A premature engagement with sexual tantric techniques without the proper initiation and guidance of a teacher may result in more potent sexual relationships—which can be a wonderful thing, as long as individuals don't think they are masters of tantra. But tantric sexual techniques can produce an inflated sense of power, and some teachers of such practices, as well as their organizations, are fraught with emotional breakdown, divorce among "tantric couples," and confused spiritual knowledge.

When a practitioner has embodied a deeper sense of the tantric principle and practices within his or her own personal experience, the most minimal guidance or practice with simple sexual techniques can yield powerful results. As with any other type of yoga or body discipline, when we engage very simple practices with intention and discipline over many years, the practice begins to inform us, and it unfolds and instructs us from the inside out. The quality of insight and experience gained from approaching sexuality from a deeper context of spiritual practice far exceeds, in both depth and value, the dazzling but short-lived experiences learned through technique-focused workshops.

When we sense the depth of possibility available through tantric work, we see that leaping into tantric sexual practice without an adequate spiritual foundation creates a high probability of falling into the trap of spiritual bypassing. Through tantric sexual techniques, we may gain access to extraordinary spiritual states and mistake them for spiritual achievement, not realizing that tantric practice is about learning to work in a transformational capacity with all states of consciousness.

As we will continue to consider throughout the book, discernment is the cornerstone of all effective and integrated spiritual transformation. Disciplined practice strengthens the body so that it becomes a container for transformational energy and prepares the mind to make clear observations and distinctions. Having a teacher—both to initiate the student in the appropriate practices for his or her level of development at the right time and to guide the student through the practice—is often an invaluable support to our practice. The "checks and balances" provided by a community of practitioners keeps the individual practitioner from getting confused and carried away by the mystical and often seductive states of consciousness and experiences that arise as a result of evoking potent energies.

The tantric brahmacharya walks the middle way, *madhyamā-pratipa* in Sanskrit. It is not a boring, monotonous middle way, where everything is measured and whispered and detached, but a passionate approach to a life of practice in which everything is made use of and relished and nothing is rejected, yet all is done consciously and within appropriate limits. Whether we are practicing in relationship to sexuality, work, child raising, or our own emotions, our use of energy is intentional, disciplined, and always referenced in a greater context of transformation and service. In *Dakini's Warm Breath: The Feminine Principle in Tibetan Buddhism*, Buddhist teacher Judith Simmer-Brown writes:

Realizing the true nature of passion . . . transforms ordi-
nary passion into the basis for the experience of great bliss,
which greatly accelerates the removal of emotional and
conceptual obscurations in one's practice. The purpose of
exploring the nature of passion is to bring about realiza-
tion where it has not already occurred; from this point
of view, the experience of bliss is a great expedient in the
practice of tantra. . . . Bliss melts the conceptual mind,
heightens sensory awareness, and opens the practitioner to
the naked experience of the nature of mind. [12]

The tantric approach to transformation can be found in countless traditions, and it is helpful to see it from a variety of perspectives in order to understand the principle more clearly. Whether we are practicing saying "yes" to all conscious and unconscious circumstances of our lives from an Advaita-Vedanta perspective, as Desjardins suggests; using our breath and awareness to meet energetic blocks and resistances within us, as hatha yoga teaches; transmuting aggression into power and peace, as experienced through Aikido practice; discovering how to turn toward and befriend the shadow aspects of our psyche, as deep psychology offers; learning to evoke and sublimate sexual energy, as taught by sexual approaches to tantra; or simply practicing doing mundane chores or facing boredom with absolute awareness, acceptance, and freedom from resistance, we are engaging a tantric approach to life that will teach us to become increasingly more effective with our energy and consciousness and to become more potent agents of transformation and service in the world.

It would require volumes of writing to begin to do true justice to the sublime and complex subject of tantra. Nonetheless, in our process of learning and refining our capacity for spiritual discernment, it is worthwhile to consider the valuable principles tantra offers for deepening spiritual discernment in our lives. The next chapter, "Pandora's Secret," draws on tantra to help understand the importance of learning to practice discernment in relationship to the darker, shadow aspects of our experience.

Chapter 8

Pandora's Secret: Demystifying the Shadow

Perhaps all the dragons in our lives are princesses, who are only waiting to see us act, just once, with beauty and courage. Perhaps everything terrible is, in its deepest sense, something helpless that needs our love.

—RAINER MARIA RILKE, *Letters to a Young Poet*

The Myth of Pandora Revisited

It is through discernment that we learn to traverse the domain of our psychological shadow and make use of its gifts for our spiritual process. The myth of Pandora is an instructive metaphor for the importance of learning to work with our own shadows to cultivate spiritual discernment and integrated transformation. In the traditional story, the mythical woman Pandora had a special "box" that she was warned not to open, but because of her dark, dangerous, and insatiable disposition as a woman, she could not control her curiosity. She opened the box and released evil into the world.

What many people do not know, however, is that the contemporary myth of Pandora most of us are familiar with is, in fact, a distorted version of the original myth that was changed through the influence of the fathers of the Church and an eighth-century Greek poet named Hesiod, probably in accordance with the collective subjugation of women and feminine power during that time. What follows is a revisioning of the Pandora myth that provides a useful illustration of how the tantric principle is applied to work with our own shadow—the unconscious, rejected, and often repressed aspect of our psyche. When we are able to apply discernment in relationship to our shadow, we have a great asset on the spiritual path, for we can navigate not only the light, but also the dark.

According to ancient Greek myth, Pandora was the first woman, fashioned by the gods themselves. Her name means both "the all gifted" and "the all giving." Hephaestus, the blacksmith of Olympus, created for Pandora a dazzlingly beautiful body, the vessel of her consciousness. Athena gave her a soul and breathed the life force into her. Aphrodite, the goddess of love, gave her uninhibited sensual desire and a seductive beauty that would captivate every heart. Hermes, the messenger of the gods, gave her the art of eloquent speech and subtle persuasion.

Hera, Zeus's wife, gave Pandora a most interesting gift. She placed an insatiable curiosity into the core of Pandora's being. Once the blacksmith Hephaestus had completed her body—a vessel which only much later, in the rewriting of the myth, would be replaced by an external "box"—Pandora was cautioned not to look within herself. Opening the "lid" to her inner being would have irreversible consequences difficult to bear.

But Pandora's curiosity was greater than her caution. How could it not be, as Hera had placed into her restless inquisitiveness and longing? In an act predestined by the gods themselves, she carefully lifted the heavy lid. What a surprise awaited her! From within the vessel of her body surged the cosmic laws of incarnation, duality, and the karmic mandate of cause and effect. The realities of old age, sickness, and death rushed into her conscious awareness. She was flooded with lust, jealousy, rage, heartbreak, hatred, grief, terror, and flashes of insanity. Attachment, aversion, confusion, pride, and existential angst gushed forth. This was what she had been warned about should she dare to open the lid to her own dark interior.

She reached desperately for the lid, certain she had made a terrible mistake, but just as she was about to seal the vessel forever, she heard a voice. Hauntingly beautiful, it arose from beneath the dark pit of her sorrow and rage, prior to the notions of good and evil, right and wrong. Its name was Hope, and in a voice so faint and subtle that it could be discerned only by using every faculty of perception to hear it, it whispered a message. It told her that the cure to all the imagined "evils" she had released by opening the vessel that held her inner darkness could be found by meeting each and every one of them with the light of awareness, acceptance, and love.

Why We Fear the Darkness within Us

Most of us are not prepared to deal with the reality that the forces of darkness and evil we find in the exterior world—the causes of war, oppression, corruption and abuse—also exist within each of us. Organized religion projects the forces of "darkness" within us onto the outside world rather than teaching us to navigate the inner worlds. To understand and take responsibility for our own unconsciousness is something few of us are interested in hearing about. Yet to develop the discernment required to integrate our experience, we must be willing to turn toward the darkness within us.

Regardless of how we interpret Pandora's myth, something about her and her mysterious box has an archetypal appeal. We find it both alluring and repelling. We all know there are inner universes we keep hidden from ourselves. If we do not acknowledge them during our lives, we will most likely have to face them as we die in the form of intensified emotional suffering, confusion, and regret. Yet for most of us, Pandora's box—which represents the great mystery of our inner shadow—remains unopened. Why are we so afraid of facing ourselves?

To begin with, we have never been taught to deal with the contents of our personal emotional interior, much less the immense social, cultural, archetypal, planetary, and universal forces we are subject to. In contemporary culture, we lack traditional sources of wisdom: guides and role models who show us we are capable of navigating such depths. Our shadow—both personal and collective—remains repressed and denied. We project it onto others, lacking the trust and confidence to believe that we have the capacity to navigate and integrate the darkness within us.

Another primal fear that most human beings share, consciously or unconsciously, is that if we open up to the "dark" forces within us, we will literally go mad. We are afraid that if we acknowledge the shadow aspects of our existence, our lives will fall to pieces; we will experience intolerable degrees of terror, pain, and anger; or we will simply disintegrate under the weight of our own suffering. We fear that opening Pandora's box will release a metaphorical zoo of dangerous and uncontrollable beasts that live within us, and we fear that if we allow these dark forces to be known and felt, they will take control and ruin our lives and relationships. We resist our darkness because we fear that looking at it will shatter us, but the opposite is true: when we look at it, it shatters only our false identification with it, leaving us more authentic and whole.

"We are more afraid of change than we are of death," claims author Caroline Myss. As we discussed in Chapter 4, the ego is programmed for survival, and it constellates itself during childhood into a series of defense mechanisms to protect us from circumstances, feelings, and aspects of reality that are too overwhelming to bear during that stage of our development. The ego's job is to maintain the stasis of the false self; from its perspective, authentic transformation equals death. What dies is not the physical body but limited belief structures about who we are. The ego, however, does not understand this, and it interprets the transformation that comes from facing the shadow as actual death. Failing to realize that we cannot access our light without accessing our darkness, most of us make the fundamental mistake of keeping the lid on the box closed, thereby succumbing to lives of mediocrity in which our greatest potentials remain unrealized.

We long to live truly passionate lives and to know our own totality, and we intuit that much of our life force remains hidden from ourselves. It is only the true warrior of the spirit who chooses to undertake the "hero's journey" and plunges into his or her own depths because the thirst to know is greater than the fear of what may be found. Like Pandora, we are endowed with the gift of curiosity to know ourselves. It is our divine birthright. Sometimes it is only the pain of our own limitations, or seeing how our shadow unconsciously produces endless suffering for ourselves and others, that motivates us to change. Anaïs Nin wrote, "And the day came when the risk to remain tight in a bud was more painful than the risk it took to blossom."

The Psychology of the Shadow

What is the *shadow,* and why is it so important to address the unconscious content of our psyches? Psychologists have been asking this question since the inception of psychology Carl Jung brought the term to popular awareness as one of the primary and necessary archetypes every human being must encounter on the path to self-knowledge. World religions have addressed the shadow through myth, art, and story. Mystical cultures have practiced esoteric rituals and meditative techniques to teach people how to work with these challenging aspects of their psyches.

The majority of humans live and die largely unconscious of their totality. To see ourselves clearly, with eyes wide open, we must learn to face ourselves objectively and unsentimentally, denying nothing and being willing to meet each new layer of the psyche as it progressively reveals itself to us. "Everyone carries a shadow, and the less it is embodied in the individual's conscious life, the blacker and denser it is," wrote Jung.[1] To enter into the shadow of one's interior is a conscious decision available to each human being—a choice made not once but again and again by one who longs to become fully conscious.

All mystical journeys involve a descent. Without it, integration is impossible. We travel into the darkness to demystify it and free ourselves from our fear that if we face it, it will consume us. To face one's shadow is a process of conscious descent for the greater purpose of higher integration, or what

Michael Washburn describes as "regression in the service of transcendence." The trek into the shadow world is a voyage of retrieval. We undertake this voyage to reclaim aspects of ourselves that we perceive as too painful to allow ourselves to feel, yet these repressed parts are repositories of our transformational potential. In his poem "Turning Point," Rainer Maria Rilke wrote that even when we have learned to see clearly, we must still do the work of the heart on the undigested images within us, "for you conquered them: but now you don't know them."[2]

Where do these shadow images come from? Our personal psychological shadow contains all the memories and feelings from childhood that were too intolerable to feel, too threatening to consciously remember, or simply beyond the developing psyche's capacity to digest. Although repressed, these images, emotions, and bodily sensations remain recorded in our psyche, sometimes reemerging with such vivid clarity that they seem to be occurring in the present. In dreams we see people who may no longer be alive and places from our past where we have not been for decades, as if frozen in time. Powerful moments of love, fear, and trauma remain etched in the timelessness of the psyche, waiting to be resurrected and owned.

As an extreme example, I once had a student whom I took on one of my study-abroad trips to India. He had been severely abused on many levels as a child, and he walked around in a world of abusive and scary ghosts that he recreated everywhere we went on the trip. He would see flashbacks of his father and grandmother abusing him as if it were occurring just then, and he would interpret comments that were intended to guide his safety as verbal attacks. Left undigested, his shadow transformed into psychosis. Although most of us do not suffer to this extreme, our unseen shadows from childhood continue to affect us and block our capacity to see clearly.

In similar fashion, the collective shadow consists of beliefs, ideas, emotions, and paradigms that our culture, socioeconomic group, and religion teach us are not okay to think and feel. A culturally programmed collective ignorance about the functioning of mind, emotions, and ego teaches us it is dirty, bad, or wrong to have a full spectrum of emotions that includes rage, violence, and terror; to feel a wide range of sexual desires; and to think as global citizens rather than as members of one particular country or religion. While we operate under the illusion of being separate and independent human beings, the rest of the world suffers the impact of our individual and cultural choices; the more sensitive we become, the more we feel the suffering of human beings everywhere—and of the earth itself.

There is also a shadow born from the existential nature of what it means to be human. Aging, illness, death, the "big questions" about meaning, faith, and the existence of God or a divine intelligence are examples of existential issues we repress, with the collective fear and denial of death being the most prominent. Ernest Becker's Pulitzer Prize–winning book, *The Denial of Death,* suggests that much of modern civilization is constructed as an elaborate defense mechanism against the recognition of our own mortality. My own experience as a therapist confirms this and has demonstrated to me that the fear of death is more pervasive and less conscious than most of us imagine. All this and much more constitutes our shadow. It is important to recognize that there are shadow elements at each level of spiritual development. It is something we cannot avoid and must include in our process of spiritual development if we hope to become integrated human beings.

"To penetrate the darkness we must summon all the powers of enlightenment that consciousness can offer," wrote Jung.[3] We build our light, and then dedicate some of it to working on the shadow. Through this work, we find that the dark and frightening inner material we have been so afraid to feel is "dark" not because it is objectively evil or destructive, but because it has not been met with the light of our conscious awareness and acceptance.

The necessity to engage our own darkness with acceptance and love is one of the most powerful laws, or secrets, of psychological and spiritual transformation, and it is the essence of tantric and alchemical practice. It is what poet Rainer Maria Rilke meant when he talked about the dragons of our lives really being princesses once we have seen them and loved them. It is the esoteric message of fairy tales such as "The Frog Prince" and "Beauty and the Beast." The "kiss" of our own acceptance and love transforms what is ugly into that which is beautiful.

It may seem paradoxical that we voyage into the shadow to discover and recover the bright light and radiant energy that is stored there, but this is how the shadow is retrieved and integrated. The light that will heal the world will shine brighter to the degree that we are willing to know and accept our own darkness. The more fully we are able to face what is true of us and take responsibility for it, the brighter and lighter we become. The challenge we face is acknowledging that a whole human being comprises both his or her higher *and* lower natures. To access our totality as human beings, we must come to know both. As we free the vital and emotional energy that is locked up in our shadow, we gain access to a wellspring of creativity, release the shame and self-denial we have kept locked away, and connect with our personal and sexual power.

No matter who we are, we must learn to work consciously with our own shadow. Politicians, gurus, monks, scientists, and ordinary people of every race and profession face the same task, and the greater our position of power and authority relative to others, the more deeply our shadow impacts both our immediate world and the world at large.

Working with the Shadow

There are many ways to work with the shadow and many levels at which it can be explored. Alejandro Jodorowsky, the Chilean filmmaker, created an approach to healing called "psychomagic," in which the individual performs specific ritualized actions in the outer world in order to reorganize the symbolic language and orientation of his or her psyche. For one of his clients, he prescribed that she sit by the Seine River in Paris with a bucket of soapy water and wash people's shadows for the price of one euro. As an activity for one of my psychology classes, I hosted a "Dark Side" party in which I asked students to come dressed as, and act out, their shadow selves. A crew of strippers, black magicians, flaming narcissists, pimps, love vampires, murderers, egomaniacs, and adulterous priests shared an evening allowing the most hidden, ashamed aspects of themselves to be brought forth, so they could be explored and witnessed in a context of safety and shared investigation. As Claudio Naranjo explained:

> Sometimes we purify ourselves of some of our sick attributes by living them to the hilt. Letting them ooze out, being as crazy as we can be. Wisdom comes sooner in this way. You see your craziness for what it is only to the extent that you're willing to act on it.[4]

Certainly the most common and safest arena to begin exploring one's shadow is in the psychotherapeutic environment.

Often, the first level of the work is simply to admit to another human being all the thoughts, feelings, desires, and fantasies we believe we should not think or feel. We need to "confess" to the therapist all the bad things we have done. We unconsciously believe that the presence of such forces within us means that we are inherently bad, and we repress them and hide them even from ourselves. This causes a burden on the psyche, which expresses itself as depression, psychological disorders, and psychosomatic symptoms.

Whereas psychotherapy seems to be the most effective venue for unburdening the mind and body in this day and age, it arises from the same need that is at the root of the Catholic tradition of confession or the Jewish ritual of Yom Kippur. These religious rituals tend to be ineffective for most people, as most modern priests and rabbis don't have the knowledge to guide people psychologically and spiritually through them. Regardless, whether we begin our foray into shadow work with a therapist, priest, or shaman, the act of confession—to disclose or admit—is often very healing.

Once we have unburdened ourselves of the secrets we have shamefully kept hidden, a therapeutic investigation deepens into a process of uncovering the unconscious shadow material within us. In an ideal therapeutic circumstance (which unfortunately is rare), we skillfully learn to access and experience deeply buried emotions, memories, traumas, images, belief systems, and even physical knots and illnesses that are buried deep within the physical and subtle levels of our bodies and energy systems (the koshas discussed in Chapter 4). Unfortunately, many psychotherapists have not worked deeply enough on their own shadow material to be able to effectively help others, but there is also a growing number of innovative and effective approaches to working psychospiritually with trauma and shadow material. Some fine schools that do such work include: The Diamond Approach, The Hoffman Quadrinity Process, and The Landmark Forum. Body-centered approaches include Somatic Experiencing, Lomi Somatic work, and Hakomi trainings.

Shadow work can occur at increasingly deeper and more esoteric levels. There are tantric techniques and practices ranging from simple visualization processes to intricate and intense ceremonies that have been performed for centuries to work with the shadow, not only on a personal but on a universal level. (See Robert Svoboda's *Aghora: At the Left Hand of God*.) To work with shadow material on this level requires the guidance of a skilled teacher who has demonstrated a consistent degree of integrity in overseeing these processes in his or her students.

Regardless of where we begin our shadow work, it is clear that it requires effort. If there were not a tremendous benefit to be gained from the work required, most of us wouldn't do it. It is a labor of love to become intimate with one's shadow, involving ruthless self-honesty as well as a considerable investment of time and often money. In spite of our most sincere intentions, we need help to take the risks involved in traversing our own interior landscape. Yet once we begin to taste the freedom that comes when we release the shadow and bring formerly hidden material into consciousness, we become willing to explore it more deeply because we have experienced its value in our lives.

When we refuse to deal with our shadow elements, there are consequences, particularly if our aim is self-knowledge, and even more so if we are in a position to teach or direct others in any way. To refuse to live with our shadow means that it will insist upon living with us, unconsciously controlling and manipulating our psyche to its desired ends.

Some people can coast a long time in life without being made to face their shadow. For others, there is an awareness of the shadow but a lack of willingness to do anything about it, either because life is working well enough or the task seems too overwhelming. Often it is others who suffer our failure to work with our shadow material, as our neurotic manifestations may be more evident to others than they are to ourselves. Sometimes this failure shows up in an inability to be deeply intimate with others, since repressing one's shadow elements often means repressing other emotional and relational aspects of oneself as well.

In many cases, repressed shadow elements can lead to physical illness. The fact that many physical diseases are the result of psychological imbalance is becoming increasingly well documented. The health of the body is intimately connected with the health of the mind, emotions, posture, and breath. Not only can unaddressed shadow elements lead to chronic pain, immune deficiency, ulcers, and cancer, they are the primary cause of most mental disorders, ranging from depression and anxiety to schizophrenia and severe psychosis.

On a spiritual level, failing to deal with one's shadow often results in scandal, as well as coercion, manipulation, and abuses on many levels. This is rampant in spiritual circles, as even those who work with very high and refined levels of consciousness still have shadow elements that must be dealt with. There is a common misconception in those who have achieved insight into the nature of mind and its essential insubstantiality that they are no longer under the influence of their unconscious shadow. This is a grave oversight that has resulted in countless acts of corruption related to power, money, manipulation, and sex.

Extreme examples of refusing to confront the shadow both on a leadership and community level include the Jonestown massacre in 1978 and the group suicide of Heaven's Gate followers in 1997. In both cases, a leader's unconscious shadow connected with his followers' unconscious shadows, resulting in disastrous consequences. Although rarely so extreme, there is often an element of mutual complicity in spiritual communities in which shadow elements interact under the guise of spiritual teachings. The more we work with our own shadow, as individuals and within groups, the healthier the overall psychology of the group will be. Unfortunately, many spiritual leaders, practitioners, and communities are not aware of, or willing to work on, their individual and group shadows to the degree necessary to protect the group.

The tendency toward psychological denial in many spiritual circles cannot be underestimated. Even if they remain obscured from our awareness, our shadow aspects are always affecting us. The shadow is there. The question is whether or not we will choose to see with eyes wide open and assume the task of becoming conscious of it.

Revisioning Sin and Abolishing Shame

"There is no sin, there is only childishness. All sins are manifestations of our childishness," said Arnaud Desjardins. Yet most of us in the Western world live filled with feelings of sin, shame, wrongness, badness, unworthiness, not-enough-ness, and what writer Joseph Chilton Pearce calls "the feeling that something was supposed to have happened that didn't." Learning to see our shadow material clearly, and make important distinctions within our psyches in relationship to it, has the capacity to transform deeply internalized beliefs of our own "original sin" and to release shame that has been embedded in our minds and bodies.

The notion of "sin" that has penetrated Judeo-Christian religion in all its forms has also infiltrated contemporary spiritual alternatives and contaminated the Western mind. Until we allow the repressed parts of ourselves we have labeled "sinful" to surface and be faced consciously, we remain enslaved by the fear of our own impulses and desires. Only when we dare to open ourselves to them can we discover what they are made of, what deeper longing they are expressing, and what transformational possibilities they hold.

Transpersonal theorist Michael Washburn explains that a stage of ego development he calls "primal repression" is an almost inevitable process of human development in which the emerging ego-self must repress the awareness of its own true nature—which Washburn calls the "Dynamic Ground"—so the next step of human development can occur. It is this forgetting of our true nature and the subsequent identification with the false self that is the root of "sin." Although this repression is an inevitable stage of development, Washburn suggests that most people get stuck in primal repression far longer than necessary, often an entire lifetime. In *The Ego and the Dynamic Ground,* he writes:

> *Hence, even though primal repression is at first a necessity to be regretted rather than a wrong to be condemned, it becomes, in time, an unnecessary and unwarranted obstacle to the ego's higher developmental destiny. In time, it becomes a way in which the ego is held back— or rather,* holds itself back—*from meeting its ultimate spiritual Ground. In short, primal repression becomes a way in which the ego refuses God. It becomes sin.*[5]

Primal repression itself becomes the sin, and from that psychological fragmentation the child's ego begins to absorb all kinds of conditioned neurotic responses from its family and environment; it is for this reason that "the sins of the parents will be visited upon their children."[6] It is therefore important to ask ourselves whether the greater sin lies within our darkness and shadow or in the act of repressing it. From this perspective, our sins can essentially be seen as crimes of unconsciousness, against ourselves and against the Divine. Sufi sheikh Muhammed Abu Hashim Madani writes: "There is only one virtue and only one sin for a soul on the path: virtue when he is conscious of God and sin when he is not."

The tantric principle reveals to us that by acknowledging and accepting the repressed elements of self and learning to express them in healthy ways, a potent process of transformation occurs. Learning to fully accept and become one with all aspects of our experience—to become fully conscious of *everything*—is an alchemical process in which each of the imagined evils within us gradually becomes transformed into beneficial attributes: heartbreak becomes longing, fear becomes awe, greed becomes a tool used to acquire knowledge and pursue transformation, anger becomes organic empowerment, lust becomes a passionate relationship to all of life, sorrow becomes empathic compassion. Through this tantric principle, conventional morality leads to the expression of universal ethics, and neurosis transforms itself into a creative vehicle by which we express our unique gifts.

When somebody asked the late Tibetan Buddhist master Chögyam Trungpa Rinpoche what he did when he found himself in the hell realms, he said he tried to stay there as long as he could. To learn to manage the hell realms within ourselves is to gain the power to live in truth, honesty, authenticity, and integrity in any and all circumstances, including the transition into death.

I once asked Robert Beer, the Western world's foremost expert on the sacred art form of Tibetan *thangka* painting, about the different effects of having paintings of wrathful versus peaceful deities in one's home. He looked at me as though he did not understand the question. "Wrathful and peaceful, dark and light," he sighed. "They just don't mean anything to me anymore." When we fully acknowledge the shadow within us, there is a place where dark and light come together and where the constructs of good/bad, right/wrong, sacred/profane, worldly/spiritual collapse into a more unified field of continually changing experience. When we are able to viscerally connect with a level of our own awareness that lies beneath or beyond these constructs, we discover that our nature is what Chögyam Trungpa calls "basic goodness," radical Episcopalian theologian Matthew Fox calls "original blessing," and Advaita-Vedanta teacher Arnaud Desjardins calls "intrinsic dignity."

I have met a few individuals who have freed themselves from shame to a great degree. It is powerful to see how free and unapologetic someone can be in relationship to their own actions while at the same time being accountable and responsible for the effect of those actions on others. These are the fruits of the self-knowledge that comes from seeing and owning the dark, unconscious shadow elements within ourselves.

The notion of sin and the essential insubstantiality of shame has been addressed not only through philosophy and mysticism but also through art. I believe that most forays into the domain of the taboo are attempts—conscious or unconscious—to challenge the notions of internalized sin and free ourselves from shame, and artists of every medium have perennially addressed the shadow world through painting, sculpture, theater, writing, and music. Yet whether through philosophy, art, myth, or psychology, the message is the same: we must face our own darkness in order to be free, and redemption comes from within and not from without. To feel the totality of our experience we must deconstruct the internalized constructs of conventional morality, good and bad, right and wrong, spiritual and mundane.

Many of us fear that if we release our internalized notions of sin and shame we will act in wildly immoral ways and say and do horrendous things. Yet the truth is that such actions are more likely to express themselves when we are laboring under the repression of shame and sin rather than when we have learned to accept and have compassion for ourselves.

Although we are not essentially bad or wrong, we are responsible for all of our actions: past, present, and future. If we have hurt others, we are responsible for finding a way to apologize. And we must make sincere and intelligent efforts to transform those parts of ourselves that bring pain to ourselves, others, and even the environment. Tantric practice destroys notions of conventional morality, giving rise to deeper clarity and an organic desire to bring warmth, joy, benefit, and healing through all of our attitudes, thoughts, and actions. Decisions are not based on right and wrong but on seeing oneself clearly, so we can determine what action, or restraint of action, is most effective and beneficial in each given moment. This radiant response to life arises when we are able to embrace paradox on every level.

A revisioning of the notion of sin suggests that we are already pure—the precise opposite of original sin, Matthew Fox's aforementioned "original blessing." Essential purity is our natural state, and the reality that there is an inevitable process of polishing the mirror of our already pure consciousness does not taint our purity. And still, while we remain unpolished we will bring suffering to ourselves and others. It is never a question of good and bad but of more loving and less loving, more effective and less effective actions, more and less communion with life.

I once imagined that the spiritual path was about transcending one's own darkness. Now I believe it is about learning to know and accept all parts of ourselves, to know and feel everything within ourselves so that we can live radiantly and powerfully. We become one not by leaving any aspect of ourselves or of life behind, but by accepting ourselves, and all of life, as it is.

Learning to navigate and discern our way through our own darkness brings us tremendous empowerment as human beings, for we have become intimate with our own single greatest threat: the shadow of our own unconscious. A sense of organic and unshakable confidence arises within us, for we have met all the demons of the world through our own experience, have looked them in the face, and have named them. By turning toward our own shadow and gradually overcoming its power over us through our acceptance, we begin to become truly integrated human beings.

As we bring to a close our consideration of the shadow, we return to the myth of Pandora and see that she was truly the all-gifted one. Her intense curiosity and longing not only allowed her to express those human traits that are conventionally recognized as "good," but helped her embrace and transform the emotions and qualities we consider shadowy, sinful, and immoral. Pandora lives within each of us. Her gift is the curiosity to know ourselves completely, and when we are willing to face the shadow within us, it no longer owns us. There is only the unconsciousness of the fragmented psyche waiting to be illuminated by the light of our own discernment, awareness, acceptance, and love.

With a divine body to contain the contents of consciousness, the insatiable curiosity to know all that lies within, and the skillful means with which to steer a course through the journey of embodied life, the myth of Pandora demonstrates how human ignorance and unconsciousness can be transmuted into divine expression by applying discernment to our shadow material. She reminds us that it is our birthright and destiny to go within, that the way through darkness is discernment, and that divine consciousness can be expressed through our own bodies. The next chapter, "The Body as Bodhi Tree," further explores the imperative of learning to integrate spiritual wisdom into the body, both to serve our own process of psychospiritual discernment and integration and to become effective agents of healing in the world.

Chapter 9

~⌒

The Body as Bodhi Tree: The Imperative of Embodiment

Welcome is every organ and attribute of me,
and of any man hearty and clean
Not an inch nor a particle of an inch is vile,
and none shall be less familiar than the rest.

—WALT WHITMAN, *"Song of Myself"*

Just prior to his enlightenment, Gautama Buddha approached the famous Bodhi Tree, circumambulated it seven times, and sat down to meditate, resolving that "even if my blood should run dry I will not leave this seat until truth has been realized!" Renouncing the needs of his body and resisting the lures of the demon Mara, who attempted to distract him with all that is beautiful, alluring, and pleasant, as well as that which is terrifying and monstrous.

Despite these temptations, the Buddha stayed in place until the clarity of enlightenment emerged from within.

In contemporary times, extended tree sitting is not what most people need in order to realize the truth of their own nature. Our task is different. We have already renounced our body's needs and repressed its wisdom, but, unlike the Buddha, we've done so in the wrong ways and for confused reasons—to attain the perfectly slim body or to try to transcend the emotional pain stored within our bodies—and the results are not healthy. We have disconnected from our bodies, from the organic rhythms and cycles of the earth, and from the seasons of our soul's unfolding. We have numbed ourselves in order to repress the rage, pain, and fear stored within our bodies, and in so doing we have also repressed our deeper nature. The more alienated we become from nature and the natural cycles of life and the more stress that emerges from intense economic, political, and environmental issues and our lack of collective emotional intelligence, the further we alienate from our bodies.

In contemporary culture, where alienation and dissociation form the backdrop of our collective psychological landscape, our own body *is* the sacred Bodhi Tree that calls to us, inviting us to dwell deeply within its sanctuary and to stand unwavering in the face of the modern demons of self-hatred, self-denial, self-abandonment, shame, unworthiness, helplessness, and neediness until the essence of our own embodiment reveals itself, and we reclaim our bodies as our rightful home. When this happens, our blood, rather than running dry, will run hot to boiling, our bones will be infused with strength, our skin will emanate a natural radiance, and a wellspring of unshakeable solidity and contentment will arise from within. In our journey toward discernment and learning to see clearly on the spiritual path, our bodies serve as an invaluable reference to guide us toward making wise choices. The more deeply we are able to embody our experience, the more effectively our bodies will support us in discerning wisely and expressing the wisdom of our discernment.

What Is Embodiment?

Within me even the most metaphysical problem takes on a warm physical body which smells of sea, soil, and human sweat. The Word, in order to touch me, must become warm flesh. Only then do I understand—when I can smell, see, touch.

—NIKOS KAZANTZAKIS, *Report to Greco*

The first time I was told that I needed to "get in my body," I was twenty-three, studying to be a psychologist, and undergoing therapy for the first time. "If I'm not in my body, where am I?" I asked my therapist in response to her seemingly absurd suggestion. Little did I know that this apparently simple question would ignite a fire that would burn stronger with each passing year, resulting in a lifelong investigation into the nature of healing and embodied spirituality. It is quite remarkable that we can spend years clothing, feeding, resting, exercising, and moving our bodies while having so little intimacy with and knowledge of our own interior.

One afternoon while I was lying with my mother on her deathbed as she endured the agonies of her body being ravaged by cancer, she turned to me and said, "I've been alive for almost sixty-five years. I gave birth to three children and traveled the world. Yet I never knew what the inside of my body felt like until now."

To choose a path of conscious embodiment is to choose not to wait until we are dying to discover the mysteries contained within our bodies. The Bauls of Bengal, an obscure sect of spiritual practitioners from India, describe their practice of embodied spirituality as *kāyā sadhana,* which means "the practice of ultimate realization *in the body* in this lifetime." They believe that the Divine dwells within the body of human beings and that the most effective way to know the Divine is through one's own embodied experience.

Embodiment refers to the integration within the body of all levels of emotional, mental, and spiritual development. Jorge Ferrer, author and professor of comparative religions, writes:

> *Embodied spirituality regards the body . . . as the home of the complete human being, as a source of spiritual insight, as a microcosm of the universe and the Mystery, and as pivotal for enduring spiritual transformation.*[1]

"Your body is the vehicle of your consciousness. Are you going to take up the reins?" shouted my yoga teacher during our teacher training program. In my experience, both as a therapist and as a teacher of transpersonal psychology and yoga, there are not many disciplines that have effectively integrated the body, psyche, and consciousness in a profound way. For all the lip service we give to mind-body-spirit integration, most of the body disciplines do not know how to integrate the content of the Western psyche or access spiritual domains. Mainstream Western psychological disciplines do not understand the role of spirit or the necessity of incorporating body awareness into psychotherapy. Many spiritual traditions and practices prematurely transcend psychological development and discount the psyche as unreal, and not all body-based traditions adequately take into account nondual awareness.

When I was researching my last book, I attended a conference that featured a panel of some of the world's great holistic physicians and medical researchers. One of the panelists, the author of several best-selling books on holistic health, sat on stage hunched over his laptop, his skin gray, his clothing unkempt, as though it had been slept in, while he proceeded to give a very eloquent discourse on holistic approaches to health and integrative medicine. The lack of integration demonstrated by his body posture, appearance, and demeanor is not uncommon. It is very difficult to practice what we preach. Taking up the reins of consciousness in relation to our body is an intentional, experimental, and ongoing process for each of us, and it involves work at the physical, psychological, and spiritual levels of our experience over a sustained period of time. We must work through our imbalances at each of these levels as we take the necessary steps to restore aliveness, consciousness, and balance within the body.

As we progressively embody our experience, our bodies become physical and energetic matrices that contain and absorb the energies involved in transformation. As we engage a process of physio-psycho-spiritual integration, we become increasingly sensitive to more subtle levels of energy, both within ourselves and in the world that surrounds us. A strong energetic matrix in the body itself is needed to contain these energies and to digest and integrate the potent fires of spiritual transformation.

You've Got to Feel to Heal

"I am astonished, disappointed, pleased with myself. I am distressed, depressed, rapturous. I am all these things at once and cannot add up the sum," wrote Carl Jung, expressing the powerful experience of being open to the full range of one's inner life. If we want to live fully, we must also feel fully, and although many of us experience a continual fluctuation of intense emotions, we still have not learned to feel at a deep level. In order to feel, we must learn to touch and taste the great pulse of life that moves through our bodies, deep psyches, and hearts. In order to experience our own love, we must learn to face the other principle emotions: pain, anger, and fear—fear being the most difficult to feel and face. It is through feeling the totality of our experience that our bodies become alive and radiant, and we learn to perceive deeper truths with greater clarity.

We are afraid that if we open ourselves to feeling, our lives will fall apart, and we will not get over the suffering. Yet, paradoxically, it is the fear of feeling—the resistance and contraction away from feeling rather than the feeling itself—that causes so much of our suffering. To inhabit our body and integrate spiritual wisdom we must turn toward everything, embrace everything, learn to like—and eventually to love—everything. We must learn to open to that which hurts us, especially when we want to close.

One of the primary aims of spiritual life—far from our fantasies of an eternal Disneyland—is simply to open to all that is unconscious within us. This includes our denied suffering, as well as the great sources of hidden love. As we deepen our capacity to dwell within the totality of our own embodied experience, we will feel *everything* more deeply—the "dark" as well as the "light"—and learn to be at peace with both. We long to experience the wide-open heart; yet, in truth, our heart is already open. We need only dismantle the walls of protection that enclose it. We do this through our willingness to feel.

The *Yoga Sūtras of Patañjali* describe a five-fold progression by which the emotions surface and are eventually integrated.

In the first stage, known as *prasupta,* the emotions are repressed. This is the "quiet desperation" that philosopher Henry David Thoreau wrote about—often felt as a quality of inertia, depression, numbness, or flatness that characterizes much of modern American culture. As repression is lifted and the dark, unconscious material breaks through into consciousness, there is often an explosion of emotion, called *udāra,* and we may find ourselves impulsive, moody, and erratically tempered. In the stage of *viccina,* our emotional life fluctuates up and down or remains somewhat flattened but punctuated by profound insight as we learn to navigate the process of opening to our emotional world. Most people do not move past this phase in their emotional development. In the fourth stage, called *tanu,* our capacity to navigate our emotions becomes refined as we learn to digest the potent energies of the external environment as well as those arising from our own unconscious. *Nirodha,* the fifth stage, is the experience of quiescence, or fluid peacefulness, in relationship to one's inner and outer life.

Cultivating discernment with respect to our emotional interior gradually allows us to experience increasing refinement and well-being. Learning to manage emotions and open to feeling are great tasks, yet we can begin quite simply with a wish to open accompanied by the intention to follow through. The process is not complex, but our conditioning is powerful; for most people it requires dedicated and consistent practice.

"Pain is inevitable; suffering is optional," teaches Buddhism. Much of our experience of pain is in how we relate to it; whereas we cannot escape pain, learning to feel it more and more deeply will decrease unnecessary suffering. We arrive at a point on our path where we have a certain appreciation for pain, for we have experienced its transformative power. It is not that we like pain as much as we learn to fear it less and open to it more, because we know this to be the most efficient way to move through it.

One thing is clear: nobody will do the work of feeling for us. It is deep soulwork, one of the most challenging and important aspects of our human experience. Difficult feelings are often the doorway to our healing.

Embodying and Balancing the Three-Centered Being

There are many philosophies, systems, and methods to describe the various levels of awareness, but all seem to recognize that a human being comprises at least three primary centers: the physical (body), emotional (feeling), and mental (mind). Some traditions consider the "spiritual" center, or the center of consciousness, as the fourth center, whereas others suggest that "spiritual" refers to the more developed level of each of the three main centers. A variety of other yogic, Ayurvedic, spiritual, and psychological maps further divide these centers according to slightly different and more complex schemas, but all converge in agreement upon the need to integrate body, heart, mind, and spirit.

People tend to have a bias toward and a strength in one or more centers, yet they neglect the others, which can result in lopsided development and difficulty with integration. For example, imbalance in the physical center may manifest as tension, contracted body posture, aches and pains, immune-system collapse, or disease. An imbalanced emotional center results in intense emotional fluctuation, depression, and overall psychological instability. Mental center imbalance is marked by a lack of clarity and discernment and an inability to perceive truth and reality. As these centers are intimately related, an imbalance in one center strongly influences the balance of the other centers.

The physical center, or moving center, is the body. "We access our consciousness through our tissues," said T. Krishnamacharya, the forefather of all modern hatha yoga. Or as my friend Laura tells her yoga students, "The issue is in the tissue."

There are very dense pockets of wounding, trauma, and sorrow stored within our bodies. For many of us, these repressed wounds and traumas eventually reveal themselves in the form of emotional and physical illness, lopsided posture, decreased and uneven energy, and a lack of radiance. Every traumatic moment we have ever experienced is stored within the cells of the body, and it is this same body that contains the possibility for unbounded bliss and pleasure, as well as the potential to reveal and express profound spiritual realization. It is often through processing the pockets of stored traumatic material that the body begins to reveal deeper levels of pleasure, bliss, and understanding from within. As this embodied awareness deepens, our breath becomes more full, our posture changes, and we begin to express increasingly expanded states such as pleasure, vibrancy, love, compassion, and generosity of spirit. We gradually learn to identify with the larger bodies of humanity, with the earth and its creatures, and perhaps even with the cosmos itself.

The energetic core, the heart, is the center of feeling that ranges from conditioned emotional reactivity to the capacity for empathy to sublime experiences of universal love, dignity, unity, empathy, and compassion. Intimately connected with the mental and physical centers, the heart is the center through which we can experience and digest the full range of human feeling.

The heart is not only a potent emotional center, but a biological axis of intelligence. Studies produced by the Heartmath Institute suggest that the heart is so intimately linked with the brain's intelligence that it has an actual "heart brain." A summary of the Institute's findings suggest that:

The heart and brain maintain a continuous two-way dialogue, each influencing the other's functioning. Although it is not well known, the heart sends far more information to the brain than the brain sends to the heart, and the signals the heart sends to the brain can influence perception, emotional processing and higher cognitive functions. This system and circuitry is viewed by neurocardiology researchers as a "heart brain." [2]

The intelligence of the heart is known by mystics of all traditions. The heart is powerful on every level. It is the center of our very being. It keeps us alive and is a direct access point to ourselves, each other, and mystical insight and experience. Many people are "collapsed at the heart" because they have not processed their feelings, and there is a backlog of undigested pain that needs to be felt in order to "unblock" their heart. When the heart is diseased or imbalanced, we are prone to imbalance in mind and thought, as well as to physical illness and pain.

The mental center is the domain of the mind and intellect and the seat of higher knowledge. When our mental center is not developed, our capacity for basic cognitive functions is compromised and the potent capacities of the mind to perceive higher knowledge are inaccessible. We are unable to discern truth from falsity. The mental center, which includes our intellect but also higher functions of mind, allows for the intellect to become integrated at increasingly refined levels, leading to the development of conscience and wisdom.

Vikalpa is the Sanskrit term that refers to verbal or intellectual knowledge that is devoid of substance and not integrated or embodied. B. K. S. Iyengar, in the *Yoga Sūtras of Patañjali*, writes:

> *Playing with fanciful thoughts or words and living in one's own world of thoughts and impressions which have no substantial basis is vikalpa, a vague and uncertain knowledge which does not correspond to reality. . . . If vikalpa is brought to the level of factual knowledge by analysis, trial, error, and discrimination, it can awaken a thirst for correct or true knowledge, and delusion can be transformed into vision and discovery. Unless and until such a transformation takes place, knowledge based on imagination remains without substance.*[3]

To embody our mental center is to study our minds, learn to observe ourselves, and to develop and act with discernment and conscience. For many people, it can initially be very disturbing to become more honest with oneself and deal with the intensity and content of one's mind. Over time, and with conscious effort, the mind becomes more relaxed, porous, and balanced. Deeper levels of integration at the mental level result in the capacity to access higher knowledge—the ability to perceive deeper truths about the nature of reality itself that we may have previously believed were inaccessible to us. Mystical and esoteric knowledge can be perceived with clarity through our own awakened mental center, yielding profound understanding at increasingly deeper levels. "The possession of knowledge does not kill the sense of wonder and mystery," wrote Anaïs Nin. "There is always more mystery."

Balancing the Three Centers

As we become aware of the importance of balancing each of our three centers, we need to consider what the most effective practices are to help us work with our imbalances and express the more awakened aspects of each of these centers.

To work with the physical center, we must engage the body. Spiritually oriented body disciplines, including but not limited to yoga, aikido, tai chi, qigong, and certain types of dance and martial arts have been intelligently developed to awaken awareness through the body. Through breath, movement, intention, discipline, and attention, such practices open the blocked places within us and liberate stored energy, also referred to as life force, prana, or chi. Prana is highly intelligent and naturally flows where it is needed to heal, strengthen, and balance the body.

Spiritually oriented body disciplines are distinct from other forms of physical activity in that they have been precisely designed to penetrate not only the physical body but the more subtle levels as well. As deeply held patterns of trauma and psychological conditioning are released, the practitioner becomes open to increasingly subtle layers of spiritual awareness. When we penetrate the body's contractions with our own awareness, the effects of stored illness and trauma are lessened, and we become more energetic and enlivened.

Another way to approach working with the moving center is through body-centered healing therapies, ranging from acupuncture and Rolfing to many of the newer somatic approaches to psychotherapy. Whereas such methods do not replace the value of spiritually oriented body disciplines, they can be very helpful in processing trauma stored in the body and awakening awareness through the body.

Deep psychotherapy can help the practitioner work with and rebalance the feeling center and support the mental center. Clearly, some forms of psychotherapy and some psychotherapists are more effective than others. It is ideal, but not always necessary, for those committed to spiritual life to find a psychotherapist who has a solid foundation in his or her own spiritual practice, a subject discussed further in the following chapter.

When psychotherapy is effective, we begin to understand the deep unconscious structures that form our individual psyches. A result of our personal history, ancestral conditioning, and the cultural context in which we were raised, these structures continue to repeat themselves as painful and sabotaging patterns throughout our adult life. Effective psychotherapy helps us turn toward and digest emotions and experiences that might otherwise be difficult to access. The creation of a safe and trusting relationship with a therapist serves as an externalized template for clarity, compassion, and loving regard in relation to our inner life—a template that we can gradually internalize. As we discover that what we most fear within ourselves will not overwhelm or kill us if we face it, we become more flexible psychologically, and the heart opens and rebalances.

It was not so long ago when psychotherapy was associated with a certain stigma. A person with "mental problems" would go see a "shrink." Many people still hesitate to enter psychotherapy for this reason. Yet more and more people engage in psychotherapy as a means to more deeply understand themselves. The majority of the pioneers in spirituality and psychotherapy whom I most respect have intermittently engaged in psychotherapy throughout their lives. As we will explore further in the next chapter, spiritual understanding does not replace psychological work, and for many people this means engaging an effective course of psychotherapy for an extended period of time.

For developing the mental center, there is no substitute for meditation practice accompanied by contemplation and study. "To go up alone into the mountains and come back as an ambassador to the world, has been the method of humanity's best friends," wrote Evelyn Underhill, the twentieth-century Christian mystic and writer in mysticism. All esoteric branches of the world's religions prescribe some type of meditation or contemplation practice for their adherents.

A new therapy client came into my practice telling me that his psychiatrist had diagnosed him with attention deficit disorder—a diagnosis that is becoming devastatingly common in the modern day—and was treating him with strong medication to help him concentrate. Like so many other millions of Americans, this man was overworked, underslept, overcaffeinated, excessively stimulated through technology, television, and the consumption of unhealthy food, and suffering from depression.

Today, when most of us are overstimulated, undernourished, and imbalanced on a variety of levels, our attention is highly fragmented. Focused and clear attention is a capacity that is cultivated and trained; meditation, contemplation, and the body-centered spiritual disciplines discussed above offer an ideal way to begin to train our attention.

There are many types of meditation, each offering particular benefits. Some practices cultivate awareness—helping the practitioner connect with and anchor him- or herself in a degree of spaciousness and consciousness that is wider than, and encompasses, the egoic-thinking mind. Other meditative practices train the mind in concentration, in an effort to learn to steady attention and awareness. Meditative practices that train the individual to focus on transcendental consciousness and/or leaving the body are less effective in the quest for integration and embodiment.

It is seemingly paradoxical that the vehicle of the mind is used to teach us to go beyond the mind. When the mind is focused and aware, it can be consciously directed to release the body. Like so many spiritual practices, the value of meditation is only experienced through sustained, disciplined practice over a period of time. The practice itself possesses a deep intelligence that cannot be understood by the ordinary mind. Rudolph Steiner, a German mystic and the founder of anthroposophy, wrote:

> *When we raise ourselves through meditation to what unites us with the spirit, we quicken something within us that is eternal and unlimited by birth and death. Once we have experienced this eternal part in us, we can no longer doubt its existence. Meditation is thus the way to knowing and beholding the eternal, indestructible, essential center of our being.*[4]

There are few systems that offer fully effective models of psychospiritual integration and practices to support them; therefore we must learn to understand ourselves deeply enough to discern and pursue integrated courses of development that address our indiv̶i̶d̶ and spiritual goals. Transpersonal ps̶ nd his colleagues conducted impor research on the integration of psyc d medication in order to reevaluate ma and diverse therapeutic disciplin

*Being willing to face the unavoidable pains of life may be
a sign of courage and wisdom. But being unwilling to use
effective therapies to relieve unnecessary pains may be a sign
of misunderstanding and of a spiritual superego run amuck.
After all, Buddhist psychology regards happiness and joy as
healthy, beneficial, spiritual qualities.*

*What we and our troubled world need is to carefully
assess and optimally use the unprecedented array of therapies now available to us. Only such an open-minded,
multi-pronged approach can hope to address the diverse
sources of suffering that afflict us, and thereby optimize
healing and awakening for us and our world.*[5]

We need to learn to understand and seek out an optimal
and integrated combination of lifestyle choices, psychological and spiritual practices, and medical treatment in order
to balance ourselves and move toward increasing wisdom
and embodiment.

Jangalykayamane: The Jungle Physician

There exists within each of us the capacity to heal ourselves. This
"inner healer" can be cultivated and worked with. In yogic philosophy, the inner healer is referred to as *Jangalykayamane*, or
the jungle physician. He represents the human being's capacity
to heal him- or herself of ailments of body, mind, and spirit. He is
the inner physician that exists within each of us whose task it is to
create healing, wholeness, and ultimately spiritual awareness.

When the yogis went to the forest to do their practices
in an attempt to achieve spiritual realization, there were no
doctors to heal them of all their physical ailments or of the
wounds that afflicted their souls. They had to learn to discover their inner healer, and they did this by means of yogic
practices, including posture, breath, movement, purifications,

awareness, meditation, diet, and cleanses. They did not avoid all illness or the physical challenges that came with age, but they did learn to heal themselves of many ailments, including the deeper ailments of psyche and spirit.

Jangalykayamane is the Lord of Embodiment. He is the physician of the three-centered being. From a yogic perspective, he is the healer of all the koshas, or sheaths of our physical and psychic bodies, from the grossest to the most subtle levels of our experience.

I learned about my own inner healer during a three-year illness that no doctor could accurately diagnose or help me with and that was slowly killing me. During this time, my friend Roger, a successful human rights lawyer in South Africa, told me how he had cured himself from chronic fatigue syndrome only when he was willing to see that there was some part of his soul he was not tending to and that was out of balance. He was only able to heal himself by making changes within himself. I remember being very disturbed because I knew what he was saying was true for me, and I had great resistance to restructuring a lifetime of habits and ways of living in relationship to my own body and energy. My health was going to depend on me.

I realized I had to try to locate my inner physician or quite possibly die. I learned to access my body more deeply through yoga and breath and then to listen to my body's prescription for my own healing process. Through yoga, diet, and simply listening to and following the clues my body gave me, I learned how to heal myself from within, and I fully recovered my strength. Through listening and acting on what is heard, the jungle doctor within me came alive and taught me how to heal myself.

While meeting with various healers throughout my illness, I encountered an osteopath who worked in a small clinic in the West and who, I eventually learned, was also a high healer in the Mormon church. Dr. J's capacity to heal people had made him a local legend. Although he subtly adjusted people's bones, and offered some kind of energetic healing, what he actually taught them to do was to contact their inner healer. He taught people four essential laws of self-healing:

1. **I will heal if I live by my heart. There is no other way to heal.** In teaching people this law, Dr. J pointed to the human being's need to discover his or her own heart and to follow its calling. If we fail to do this, our hearts become sick, which gradually leads to physical symptoms.

2. **I can trust what I feel in my heart. There is nothing else I can trust.** We must relearn to trust our own feelings and listen to the inner healer, which is no other than our own heart.

3. **I will like the results if I follow my heart; I will not like the results if I violate my heart.** Dr. J suggested that when we are listening to our inner healer, it will generally produce positive results.

4. **All of my actions are perfect for my learning and growth.** This law addresses the healing power of self-acceptance. He explained that spiritually oriented people are particularly susceptible to illness because the "spiritual superego" often places a demand on them to live according to certain spiritual ideals they cannot possibly achieve, and their lack of self-acceptance and disappointment can make them prone to illness.

In one way or another, we are all ill. We all have our weak spots. We are wounded at the karmic, or soul, level, and such wounds can take a long time to heal. There are things only the inner healer can tell us. The true physicians—whether spiritual teachers, psychologists, or doctors—are guides who teach us how to contact our inner physician through practices, words, or medicine.

One of the remarkable qualities of accessing the inner healer is that we learn to protect ourselves and heal from body ailments while also learning to heal deeper wounds of the soul. "Why fear illnesses? They are our allies. Bodily ills reveal problems that we dare not face and heal the illnesses of the spirit," writes Alejandro Jodorowsky, quoting his Zen master, Ejo Takata.[6] We all know that some of the most powerful life lessons are learned from the deepest moments of illness and tragedy. Such experiences often crack us open; in the opening is feeling, and in the feeling is healing.

As we begin to understand and sense our capacity to heal ourselves, it is important to remember that not every illness can be healed. It is tragic when people who have discovered powerful New Age truths begin to fault themselves for not being able to heal themselves, adding unnecessary suffering to their experience. We are working with very deep patterning and karmic processes as well as the reality that all bodies must eventually die of something.

At the highest levels of healing, the body is literally transformed into prayer, and this transformation can occur even in the midst of disease, when one is ravaged by pain and illness. It's also the goal toward which many sexual and yogic practices aim. On a more subtle level, the body can express prayer through the way one holds one's child or cooks a meal. The fully embodied human being, resonant and aligned within him- or herself and the great life force, expresses prayer and divinity through all the actions of daily life.

I was told a story about the yoga master B. K. S. Iyengar's first visit to America. He asked his host to take him to the Grand Canyon. Upon first viewing at the wonder of nature, he exclaimed, "I must pray!" He then hopped over the guardrail to a precipice above the canyon, and with the precision and confidence that could come only from someone who had deeply unified his body, he did a headstand.

~

The first time I heard someone talk about the human body as a temple, I thought it was a bit of New Age exaggeration. And yet, when we are faced with grave illness, impending death, mystical sexual experience, or simply moments of profound embodied experience, we know the truth of this experience. Our bodies are the temples that host our consciousness. We can learn to respect and treat them as literal sanctuaries that the Divine can come to occupy and where the ego can come to rest.

We must nourish our bodies with good food, exercise, and breath; our minds with rich learning; our hearts with kindness and warmth toward ourselves; and our spirits with disciplined practice and inquiry. We must do whatever work is needed to clear out negative patterns and the unconscious ways in which we hurt ourselves and others. We can then fill our bodies with kindness, elegance, and radiance—and experience what Arnaud Desjardins calls our "intrinsic dignity."

It becomes clear that as our discernment penetrates our bodies, a deeper integration emerges, and spiritual maturity gradually ripens from within us. The next chapter, "The Union of Psychology and Spirituality," further explores the importance of integrating spiritual awareness into all aspects of our experience.

Chapter 10

~

The Union of Psychology and Spirituality

Do not seek only the supra-conscious state found in meditation,
a state in which you feel detached from everything—even if
this is a real state which will one day underlie your entire
existence, no matter what trials life may bring. Although you
have every right to long for it, you will never attain this state if
you refuse the way in which it is expressed. And it is through
the shakti, the almost terrifying life force which sustains you,
that this supra-conscious state expresses itself.
—ARNAUD DESJARDINS, *The Jump into Life* [1]

I magine a comprehensive psychology that embraced our widest spiritual potential as human beings while simultaneously addressing the most intricate and subtle blocks in the psyche. A psychology that could penetrate the mind and its wounds, weaknesses, and blind spots and also help us understand the nature of the mind and the mysteries of our

THE UNION OF PSYCHOLOGY AND SPIRITUALITY   219

incarnation. Then imagine a spirituality that did not deny or prematurely transcend any corner of our existence: a spirituality that offered a window into a vast mystical vision and provided a context in which to address the dark, hidden, and challenging cobwebs of the psyche with penetrating clarity and compassionate perspective. Whereas some people will approach this possibility through formal psychotherapy, and others through a variety of forms of internal and interpersonal inquiry, such an integration requires keen discernment into the psychological aspect of our experience.

Pioneers in the fields of both psychology and spirituality have begun to address these issues in the past few decades, but I believe that the psychology of the future—a comprehensive, spiritual psychology that takes into account the unique complexity of the Western psyche and the role of the body in integrated transformation—is still being created. It will increasingly emerge as the work of a growing body of dedicated and highly discerning spiritual practitioners who understand, value, and undertake their own embodied psychospiritual transformation, and who further articulate theories and methods by which this can be taught and applied to others.

In 1992, James Hillman and Michael Ventura published an important book titled *We've Had a Hundred Years of Psychotherapy—And the World's Getting Worse*. In it, they effectively argue that psychotherapy in its current conception lacks the adequate means to deal with many of the afflictions that face the Western psyche and also ignores the challenging realities and needs of the external social and political worlds. I believe that Hillman and Ventura's critique is accurate, but they fail to consider that we have had *only* just over a century of Western psychotherapy. This is a very short time for the evolution of any new discipline, much less one like psychology, whose task is to address and unwind the Western psyche in accordance with a rapidly changing world.

The psychological branches of *abhidharma,* or Buddhist psychology, as well as yogic and Sufi psychologies, developed and evolved over thousands of years. The true psychology of the Western world is still in a period of inception, and it will require the passionate participation of intelligent individuals who understand the importance of embodied psychospiritual transformation for it to grow into its true possibility.

This chapter offers a vision of the union between psychology and spirituality, a vision that offers a possibility for human integration that addresses all levels of our experience. It envisions a new psychology that is fully integrated with, and informed by, spiritual wisdom and that denies no aspect of our human experience. To practice this new psychology requires the cultivation of refined discernment and a willingness to continue to deepen that discernment throughout our lives as we pass through subsequent stages of spiritual development and integration.

Psychology and Spirituality: One Path or Two?

The impersonal is a truth, the personal too is a truth; they are the same truth seen from two sides of our psychological activity; neither by itself gives the total account of Reality, and yet by either we can approach it.

—SRI AUROBINDO, *"The Divine Personality"*

There is great debate, and in many cases a sharp divide, between practitioners of psychology and those of spirituality. On one end of the spectrum, most of mainstream psychology does not concern itself with issues of consciousness and spirit, and rejects what is not scientifically quantifiable. On the other end, many contemporary spiritual traditions view the psyche as an unreal construct and believe that psychological work is an indulgent reinforcement of the story of the false self. In between these poles lie a variety of approaches that take into account both the personal and impersonal aspects of our experience, validating that some aspects of our experience can be empirically confirmed while others remain mysterious but equally "real." Meanwhile, many mainstream psychotherapists and their clients continue to miss out on the benefits of spiritual wisdom, and many teachers and students of Western spirituality make grave errors by rejecting the psychological domain and thus not cultivating skills and practices to work with it effectively.

Ultimately, psychology and spirituality do not need to be distinct, but it can be helpful to make distinctions between them in order to understand the primary function of each in relation to the other. We can then discover how these approaches complement and support one another, together forming a more complete approach to human understanding than either one alone can provide. John Welwood, one of the leading contemporary synthesizers of psychology and spirituality, says that the task at hand involves

> *the integration between liberation—the capacity to step beyond the individual psyche into the larger, nonpersonal space of pure awareness—and personal transformation—the capacity to bring that larger awareness to bear on all one's conditioned psychological structures, so that they become fully metabolized, freeing the energy and intelligence frozen inside them, thereby fueling the development of a fuller, richer human presence that could fulfill the still unrealized potential of life on this earth.*[2]

Spiritual understanding comes from a direct perception of a greater intelligence, force, or power. Some people call it non-duality; others call it Christ, Allah, spirit, or God. Spiritual technologies help us access an experience of consciousness itself, and sustained spiritual practice supports us in learning to anchor ourselves in a more abiding sense of that greater reality. Meanwhile, psychological work helps unravel the complex strands that constitute our personal psyche—patterns and wounds that, if not tended to, can impede our growth and block our perception of spiritual realities.

In 1994 I lived and studied in India for a year, and during that time I rented a room from a Dutch man named Hamsa. As a child during World War II, Hamsa spent several years imprisoned in Japanese concentration camps, during which time he experienced extreme trauma produced by torture and separation from his family. As a young adult he set out for India, and by the time I met him he had lived there for more than four decades. By intellectual standards, Hamsa was a genius. Highly intelligent by nature, he had also become a great scholar of Hindu religion. He was a warrior practitioner, engaging demanding spiritual disciplines and austerities over sustained periods of time, and he had experienced repeated high states of mysticism.

When I met Hamsa, near the end of his life, he carried with him a deep sorrow at his failure to realize his spiritual aspirations, accompanied by an unspoken sense of having been betrayed by God because he had given everything to the spiritual path but had not accomplished his goals. From the outside, however, it was quickly apparent to those who knew him well that he was a man who had been unable to face and digest the impact of his childhood trauma. He continually attempted to suffocate his pain by increasing the intensity of his spiritual practices and austerities, resulting in severe narcissism and pathological spiritual bypassing. While he dazzled those around him with esoteric rituals and encyclopedic knowledge of Vedic ritual and Hindu mythology, I longed to take him into my arms and let the child within him cry until the ocean of tears wore down the stone walls that kept his tender heart from letting human and divine love penetrate him. "Here is where psychological work might serve as an ally to spiritual practice," writes John Welwood, "by helping to shine the light of awareness into all the hidden nooks and crannies of our conditioned personality, so that it becomes more porous, more permeable to the larger being that is its ground."[3]

It is very important to understand that our psychological blocks can actually impede our capacity to open to spiritual understanding and experience. Trauma and a sense of betrayal in childhood, which many have experienced to some degree, can result in a failure to trust the Divine and life itself and in great difficulty in surrendering to the unknown. Many of us learned from a very young age that the world was not a safe place, and that whatever "God" existed was not a God who would protect us from child abuse. Feelings of abandonment and isolation in childhood can make it much more challenging to encounter and open to the experience of spaciousness that meditation offers, as it can be difficult to distinguish between nondual emptiness and the experience of profound lack and psychological emptiness. Disappointment in childhood authorities, teachers, and religious leaders can make it very difficult to trust spiritual teachers, teachings, and even the Divine itself. Undigested emotions from our past profoundly color our relationship to spiritual concepts, practices, and experiences.

On the other hand, we can get so wrapped up in psychological processing that it becomes a kind of narcissistic self-involvement, leaving us trapped in a cul-de-sac that neither brings about the powerful capacity for compassion and wisdom that can be discovered through spiritual practice, nor produces the sense of social responsibility that Hillman claims the field of psychology has failed to pay attention to. Many schools of mainstream psychology have routinely failed to take into account a broader spiritual perspective, frequently reducing profound spiritual insights to neurotic fantasies, infantile regressions, and idealized projections. For example, I once consulted with a psychologist in her late thirties who was experiencing tremendous confusion about her spiritual life because her therapist had convinced her that her relationship with her spiritual teacher was purely a romanticized projection based on unmet childhood needs and a failure to individuate from her father.

One helpful framework by which to understand the differing functions of psychology and spirituality is to consider the distinction between the content and the context of consciousness. Psychology addresses the content of our consciousness. It helps us understand the familial and even ancestral or karmic forces that inform our egoic, or personality, structure. It looks at the stories, relationships, patterns, and perceptions that make up the life of the unconscious—the powerful unconscious decisions we made so long ago that we no longer remember them, yet they continue to run our lives. Spirituality addresses the context of consciousness. It helps us access and experience the field of consciousness from which all manifestations arise. This is a very important distinction.

Psychology addresses our personal, individual makeup. It helps us understand the unconscious "stories" that live within us and repeat themselves in limiting and sometimes self-destructive patterns. It assists us in unraveling the defensive structures we formed in childhood that once kept us safe and helped us survive emotionally in our environment but that now block us from further development or from opening to our deeper potential. Spirituality, on the other hand, helps us discover the nature of mind itself—what Hindu and Buddhist traditions refer to as nonduality. It allows us to access something that is larger than our own story—to open to the perennial truths that mystics from all traditions have always known.

Integral philosopher Ken Wilber makes a distinction between what he calls "translation" and "transformation." The domain of translative spirituality includes a wide variety of practices, rituals, and belief systems that reorganize the psyche and create meaning and understanding for the separate self. Transformative spiritual practices undermine the very notion of the separate self, often leading to painful experiences of annihilation and disillusionment accompanied by powerful physiological processes.

Many people do a great deal of psychological work, and the resulting insights and changes are so profound they assume this is what spiritual transformation is about: they have never had experiential contact with nondual reality and thus remain unaware of deeper spiritual possibilities. On the other end of the spectrum are those who do a lot of meditation and spiritual practice and assume they have transcended their psychological dynamics—at least until repeated failures in relationships, parenting, and working with their own emotions remind them that they have not.

A chain is only as strong as its weakest link, and I am convinced that most spiritual scandals are the result of spiritual teachers who have significant areas of psychological blindness. They assume their great spiritual insight has taken care of their psychological wounds when it has not. This form of spiritual bypassing seems to be particularly common among

Western teachers and practitioners of Eastern spiritual traditions, since in the process of transplanting these traditions into the Western world they are removed from their original cultural context and do not necessarily take into account the psychological variables involved in the culture into which they are being imported. Even what appears to be insight into "objective truths" incurs this risk.

A Mutually Enhancing Process

Tantric tradition suggests that relative reality and ultimate reality are two expressions of the same truth. They co-emerge, or arise simultaneously, and each carries powerful reflections of the other. As two facets of the same diamond, they have distinct properties, functions, and expressions, yet if we aspire to psychospiritual integration, we see that they need each other. If we enter the path of self-knowledge through the psychological, to fulfill our quest we must eventually learn to access and experience nondual, or ultimate, truth. If we enter our spiritual process through nondual experience, our understanding must eventually integrate its way through the dual, or personal, aspects of our experience.

Human beings seem to evolve in a spiral-like pattern—a "departure and return to higher integration," in the words of transpersonal psychologist Michael Washburn. At some junctures, and within some spirals, unlocking a particular psychological structure can be the very thing that propels us powerfully forward into another layer of spiritual understanding. At other times it is the opening that arises from our spiritual understanding that gives us courage to move into and through the next level of psychological work.

A powerful example of how this works can be seen in the life of my friend Kenny Johnson (whose experience I reflected on in Chapter 7) who runs a prison project called This Sacred Space. The program helps prisoners access their spiritual wholeness, awaken their conscience, and begin a healing process in order to find their way out of their interior as well as exterior prison. Kenny is an ex-convict, and he describes himself as having lost a sense of conscience in his early life. He gradually began studying spiritual texts and meditating. Then, as the result of an encounter with a spiritual teacher who was giving a program in the prison where he was incarcerated, he had a profound spiritual awakening. The conscience that awakened within him gave him the necessary courage to begin the journey within to unpack his psychology and learn to feel and face his feelings. As he engaged his own psychology, he began to rediscover himself, and his sense of spiritual understanding deepened. He continues to explore and grow in this way to this day, and he inspires other prisoners through his teachings and example.

I've found that something very powerful happens with clients when the therapist engages psychological work with them from a spiritual context. The word *spirituality* may never even be mentioned in the therapy room, but the therapist's own understanding of ego, karma, and consciousness deeply informs the quality of therapy. Clients inevitably discover from within themselves their own spiritual insights about the nature of the mind and the unconscious. This sense of spaciousness and insight into the impersonal nature of our conditioning gives them courage to travel more deeply into their own unconscious, and as they heal different levels of psychological wounding they are freed to experience deeper levels of spiritual truths. As this subtle process continues, spirituality and psychology begin to merge. There arises a deepening form of embodied inquiry that could not be said to be strictly spiritual in the traditional sense, yet it goes far beyond the confines of traditional "psychology." Carl Jung wrote:

> *The main interest of my work is not concerned with the treatment of neuroses but rather with the approach to the numinous [a sense of the holy]. But the fact is that the approach to the numinous is the real therapy and inasmuch as you attain to the numinous experiences you are released from the curse of pathology.*[4]

You may recall our discussion of the koshas in Chapter 4. This model suggests that the body is made up of five sheaths, or koshas, some visible and others invisible. The outermost sheath is the physiological sheath, proceeding to the energy sheath, mind sheath, wisdom sheath, and bliss sheath. Psychological work generally involves the first three of these sheaths, and spirituality the second two and the knowledge that emerges beyond this. But because these levels are highly interconnected, blocks in one of the areas, particularly the lower sheaths, frequently block the development of the higher sheaths and do not allow for higher integration. Similarly, work with the higher sheaths helps balance the lower sheaths.

When spirituality and psychology come together, there emerges a more holistic vision of life. When a person simultaneously does deep psychological work and spiritual practice, the insights gained from one help him or her go deeper into the other. I believe that, particularly for Westerners, psychology and spirituality need each other. Ultimately, there is a union between the two, but they do not replace each other.

Toward a New Psychology

The possibility of a new psychology is not actually that new, although it is still in its inception. Since the beginning of

Western psychology there have been visionaries who possessed a vast and integral vision of the potential of the human psyche. Sigmund Freud, the founder of psychoanalysis, who is widely critiqued for the weaknesses in his theory and person, said: "I want to entrust [psychoanalysis] to a profession that doesn't yet exist, a profession of secular ministers of souls, who don't have to be physicians and must not be priests."

Jung was a gifted mystic who dedicated his life to a courageous and ruthless exploration of the psyche—his own as well as that of his many patients—and suggested that psychology is incomplete and also fundamentally misconceived unless it seeks to understand spiritual possibilities. Roberto Assagioli, referred to in the introduction, was an Italian psychiatrist who founded psychosynthesis; he stressed that psychotherapy must not only treat psychopathology but must also foster spiritual awakening and deal intelligently with the challenges such an awakening brings, including such phenomena as spiritual pride, ego inflation, or the heightened capacity to experience the depth of our core wounding and the intensity of meeting and digesting this experience. Wilhelm Reich emphasized the importance of the mind-body connection in psychological transformation and conceptualized the notion of "body armor." Abraham Maslow introduced the concept of peak experiences into modern psychology and suggested that beyond the first three forces of psychology, which he considered to be behaviorist, psychoanalytic, and humanistic, there would be a fourth force of psychology that was transpersonal and focused on self-actualization.

In the East, in addition to the ongoing yogic, Buddhist, and Sufi psychologies, the twentieth-century revolutionary saint Sri Aurobindo proposed an integral yoga whose aim is "an inner self-development by which each one who follows it can in time discover the One Self in all and evolve a higher consciousness than the mental, a spiritual and supramental consciousness which will transform and divinise human nature."[5] His volumes of work have been very influential in the thinking of many of the Western world's transpersonal psychologists.

In contemporary times, there are a number of emerging disciplines that are working toward a new psychology—including transpersonal psychology, integral psychology, and nondual psychology—in addition to a number of independent schools that work with psychospiritual transformation. These approaches share the acknowledgement that human beings develop along what Ken Wilber calls a "spectrum of consciousness" of infinite possibility. Further, they agree that a comprehensive psychology must work toward increasing wholeness and psychospiritual integration rather than simply try to "fix" people so they comply with a socially agreed upon norm for mental health that is profoundly limited in its conception of what is possible for a human being.

Although transpersonal psychology is relatively new as a formal discipline, beginning with the publication of *The Journal of Transpersonal Psychology* in 1969 and the founding of the Association for Transpersonal Psychology in 1971, it draws upon ancient mystical knowledge that comes from multiple traditions. Transpersonal psychologists attempt to integrate timeless wisdom with modern Western psychology and translate spiritual principles into scientifically grounded, contemporary language. Transpersonal psychology addresses the full spectrum of human psychospiritual development—from our deepest wounds and needs, to the existential crisis of the human being, to the most transcendent capacities of our consciousness.

There have been numerous prominent theorists and practitioners in the field: Stanislav Grof, who founded holotropic breathwork and later, with Christina Grof, formed the Spiritual Emergence Network; Roger Walsh, who spearheaded work in transpersonal psychiatry and, with Frances Vaughan, published a number of groundbreaking books on psychospiritual integration; Michael Washburn, referenced numerous times throughout this book, who brought forth a theory of spiral dynamics; Hameed Ali, also known as A. H. Almaas, who formed the Diamond Heart School. Philosopher Ken Wilber has published hundreds of writings that have been very influential in the development of transpersonal psychology and created the field of integral studies, which includes a branch of integral psychology that endeavors to "honor and embrace every legitimate aspect of human consciousness."[6] Graduate schools, which include the California Institute of Integral Studies and the Institute of Transpersonal Psychology, have formed accredited programs to teach these approaches, and the number of universities across the world that offer courses in transpersonal psychology is increasing dramatically.

Michael Washburn describes transpersonal theory as "a project that involves a thorough rethinking of each of these perspectives in terms of the other." Transpersonal psychologists are committed to developing a comprehensive psychology that covers the full range of human experience, from psychosis to transcendence. Practical applications of transpersonal theory include incorporating a transpersonal context into therapeutic practice, as well as integrating this perspective with ethics, ecology, social justice, gender issues, and community-building.

Regardless of the label or discipline under which these new methodologies fall, it seems clear that there is emerging a field of nondual psychology. This psychology contextualizes the dynamics of the human mind from the perspective of nondual experience, which alters one's whole perspective on the mind and changes the focus of therapy from "fixing" someone who is "broken" to a process of integration and endless self-discovery. The psychology of mind becomes transformed into the psychology of truth. I believe that modern psychology will reach its peak when it merges with spirituality in this way, teaching us how to open up to, and become one with, all of life.

It is important to note that in the union of psychology and spirituality the nondual, or transpersonal, has primacy. The nondual is the base from which all psychology arises. In Hindu philosophy Shiva represents the masculine principle of formlessness, from which the feminine principle of Shakti, or manifestation, arises. Michael Washburn explains:

> Although transpersonal theory aims at a genuine synthesis of spiritual and psychological perspectives, it nonetheless gives the spiritual perspective a theoretical priority. Transpersonal theory assumes that human development aims ultimately at a spiritual fulfillment and, therefore, that human nature can be properly understood only from a spiritual standpoint. Transpersonal theory, that is, holds that spirituality . . . should play the role of guiding principle in a unified understanding of the human psyche.[7]

As mentioned in Chapter 4, when European students first began to visit Swami Prajnanpad in the 1920s, he recognized that the Western psyche comprised distinct elements that nondual spirituality alone did not address, and so he read and digested Freud's theory and developed a psychotherapy for his disciples. He situated Freud's psychoanalytic theory into a nondual context and taught his students that they must learn to be "at one with" all experience, regardless of its nature; that this oneness was not to be found by transcending, or rising above, their psyche, but by meeting each element of their experience with the intention to become one with it. It is through clear discernment of one's experience, and being at one with what is discerned, that nondual awareness is discovered.

Gilles Farcet, a teacher in the lineage of Swami Prajnanpad, explains that when the Swami worked with people spiritually he dealt directly with their relationships with intimates, friends, money, love, and sex. Each circumstance would be approached from the perspective of learning "to be one with" the experience, digest it fully, and see it clearly for what it was. Although the Swami himself was a renunciate and was not personally involved in the world of money, sex, and intimate relationship, he approached his students' work on each of these with the view of helping them free themselves of their neurotic relationship to them. He believed that you could not be free of what you do not know, and to be free of something you must experience the *bhoga*, or deliberate, full, and conscious experience of that aspect of life. "We try to be free before knowing sufficiently well our slavery," explains Arnaud Desjardins.

One aspect of nondual psychology is that it is a psychology of complete acceptance. Swami Prajnanpad taught his students to "accept what is, as it is, here and now, without judgment." It is this capacity to accept—to be fully "at one with"—that introduces an element of alchemy to the transformational process and distinguishes it from dualistic approaches. Rumi tells us that the moment we accept our troubles the door will open.

There is an element of service and social responsibility that becomes the apparent next step—an "obligation of love" that arises from integrated states of spiritual understanding. Contemporary spiritual traditions increasingly emphasize the aspect of spiritual maturation that involves not only developing oneself but contributing in some way to the greater world.

People engage their service and social responsibility at different levels. Some do social activism; others mother their children in a way that demonstrates to the child that he or she is truly loved and supported in the world. Some people offer a life of prayer and renunciation, while others make their contribution by running a business or teaching school with commitment and integrity. Regardless of how it is expressed, the context of one's life becomes service, and one is aware of the need to discover how he or she can best contribute. The perspectives and contributions of innovators of transpersonal, integral, and nondual psychologies represent an evolutionary trend in the development of Western psychology.

Enlightened Duality

Spiritual teacher Lee Lozowick coined the term *enlightened duality* to refer to "the realization of nonduality as expressed in and through the body and the full expression of all of life, experiencing and enjoying it as it is, without identification." The context of enlightened duality is nondual awareness, while its content is duality.

It is easy to imagine that enlightenment is the end of the path rather than the beginning. If enlightenment is our true nature, as we intuitively understand when we find ourselves in enlightened awareness, we are never far from its perception. And still, regardless of how many "experiences" we have had of our essential enlightened nature, there remains a lifelong process of integrating understanding into the body on a cellular level, into the deep grooves of psychological conditioning, and into all aspects of daily life. Most of us have trouble accepting the fact that as awe-inspiring and life-changing as moments of enlightened experience are, they are merely the beginning of the spiritual journey rather than its completion, for it will not be complete until we have embodied our nondual insight into every microfiber of dualistic expression.

Author and psychologist John Prendergast has been working to develop a nondual approach to psychotherapy that facilitates the discovery of embodied nonduality. "Most major Eastern nondual spiritual traditions recognize that awakening is the beginning rather than the end of an open-ended process of spiritual transformation," writes Prendergast and his colleague Kenneth Bradford. "It is one thing to thoroughly wake up to one's true nature as the formless ground of being or no-self; it is another to actualize or embody this awareness in one's daily life in the body and in relationship and to transpose these changes to collective, societal structures."[8]

From the perspective of enlightened duality, the key to effectively working with all the "stuff" of this world without getting caught in the mire of it is found through cultivating an abiding awareness of the nondual nature of all manifest phenomena. Maybe we are not experientially aware of the nondual context at all times, but we have glimpsed it powerfully enough that we are able to make useful distinctions and intelligent and caring choices in any given moment based on the context of what we have understood. Over time, the enlightened perception becomes more grounded and stabilized, while at the same time it gives way to endless growth. As the practitioner of enlightened duality goes about her or his day, the world of duality and manifestation is engaged fully, including whatever emotion, neurosis, effort, struggle, or joy arises. Nothing is denied as illusory, prematurely transcended, or "spiritualized" away, and at the same time, there is a consistent attention to bringing nondual awareness to each circumstance. Enlightened duality engages all the gritty, neurotic, profane, and imagined "unspiritual" aspects of our experience, yet views all experience from the context of oneness.

Eventually, enlightened duality extends beyond one's self and into the commitment to serve a greater whole. In a world of enlightened duality, the context of enlightenment would transform all aspects and structures of society—from architecture to education, politics, ethics, and our collective relationship to ecology and the earth. Speaking to this vision, the Indian sage Sri Aurobindo wrote:

> *The yoga we practice is not for ourselves alone, but for the Divine; its aim is to work out the will of the Divine in the world, to effect a spiritual transformation and to bring down a divine nature and a divine life into the mental, vital and physical nature and life of humanity.*[9]

Enlightened duality represents a fulfilled expression of the union between psychology and spirituality and the maturation of our capacity to spiritually discern. The vision of such a possibility should guide spiritual and psychological traditions, as they, and we, attempt to evolve, deepen, and become more integrated human beings. As our vision of a discerning, human integration begins to emerge, it is time to address the question of the role of the spiritual teacher. The next chapter, "The Question of the Teacher," looks at some of the primary areas of discernment to consider when contemplating the complex subject of the function of the teacher in spiritual transformation.

Chapter 11

~

The Question
of the Teacher

*To get to an unknown land by unknown roads, a traveler
cannot allow himself to be guided by his old experience.
He has to doubt himself and seek the guidance of others.
There is no way he can reach new territory and know it truly
unless he abandons familiar roads.*

—MIRABAI STARR, *The Dark Night of the Soul* [1]

The subject of the spiritual teacher—sometimes referred to as guru, sheikh, roshi, lama, or mentor—is one of the most complex issues in contemporary Western spirituality. In essence, there are two powerful, and often contradictory, forces at work with respect to the function of the teacher: (1) the power of the teacher to transmit and support the student in a process of profound transformation, and (2) the power of the unripened teacher to unintentionally and unconsciously thwart students' growth due to the teacher's incomplete development and unintegrated psychological material. The potential advantages of having a spiritual teacher are immense and unique, yet the pitfalls that arise are painfully common. As sincere and dedicated practitioners of spirituality who aspire to cultivate clear discernment in our lives, it is critical that we educate ourselves on this subject so that we can discern whether or not we need or want a teacher, distinguish between more and less effective teachers, and make good use of the teachers we do have in our lives.

Not everyone will have a spiritual teacher. Every path is distinct. Some people are disciplined and grounded, and their practice is well-rounded enough that they can stand on their own. Others want to grow spiritually, but do not feel the need to develop in the ways that a spiritual teacher provides. Still others have a deep and direct connection with a clear and reliable inner source of guidance. It is not everybody's karmic destiny to have a teacher. Regardless of where we fall on this spectrum, it is wise to educate ourselves on the subject of the teacher so we are not swayed by our unconscious reactions to authority and can represent a discerning approach to spiritual transformation.

Among those who have teachers, some have very distant ones (such as some of the great Hindu gurus) whom they see rarely or may never meet. Others have more intimate, personal contact with their teachers. My experience in surveying a variety of spiritual traditions over many years is that when possible, students generally benefit from at least some regular contact with their teacher, or at least with a senior student who is supported by the teacher to help other students.

This chapter considers the benefits and difficulties of having a spiritual teacher and the complex questions and psychological challenges that surround this relationship.

The Spiritual Possibilities of Having a Teacher

Among the many benefits of having a spiritual teacher, perhaps the most important is transmission—passing on the experience of living truth from one human being to another. Some teachers have the gifted capacity to powerfully invoke a direct experience of Truth, or the Divine, in their students. The experience is almost always temporary, yet it ignites the transformational fire within the student, which is often the pivotal moment in his or her journey on the spiritual path. In the same way that the description of a kiss is not the same as an actual kiss, reading ideas about spiritual experience or understanding is very different from the direct experience of it through the transmission of a spiritual teacher. *"Jyota se jyota jagaavo, sadaguru jyota se jyota jagavo,"* says the *Sri-Skanda Purana*. "Light my lamp from your lamp, O Satguru, remove the darkness covering my heart."

Another function of the teacher is to convey the great body of teachings, or dharma, to the student. The effective teacher has studied and practiced the dharma for many years and has assimilated it in such a way that it is accessible to students. The skilled teacher can help the student learn to integrate dharmic principles in a way that is both culturally and developmentally appropriate to his or her level of understanding and spiritual needs at a given time.

When the teacher is physically accessible, another valuable function he or she can provide is to offer direct observations to students with respect to their spiritual practice. It is true that a teacher who is deceased can offer subtle feedback, but the student must be a very seasoned practitioner to interpret it correctly. The living teacher may, at times, offer important modeling of spiritual qualities, including wisdom, dignity, and warriorship. Some teachers can help the student envision a unique possibility for his or her life that the student was unable to perceive. Others may simply embody a certain radiance of being. Each teacher is unique in his or her gifts, and each has at least some flaw. As we mature along the spiritual path, we are able to increasingly perceive the teacher with more objectivity with respect to his or her divine as well as human aspects.

Above all, we must understand that the teacher's function involves a differentiation in roles among equals for the purpose of transformation. I remember a time in 1994 when I lived in close proximity to a great saint, Yogi Ramsuratkumar, in southern India. He was unlike anyone I have ever met before or since in his power, radiance, and capacity to transmit enormous blessings to all those who sought his help. He lived and traveled with a small group of disciples who were also truly admirable exemplars of spiritual devotion, attention, and service. The sublime atmosphere around the saint was palpable; the mysticism could be tasted with each breath. As I sat on the floor among the disciples, opening to this unprecedented experience in my life, the essential equality among us all revealed itself with great clarity. The role each of us assumed was a matter of function among equals for the purpose of evoking spiritual transmission. The student-teacher relationship is a construct used to transmit spiritual truth, and we must be careful not to get lost in our psychological projections about who the teacher is or who we are in relationship to him or her.

Sufi sheikh Llewellyn Vaughan-Lee explains that there are twelve levels of spiritual initiation a human being passes through in the soul's journey through life.[2] He explains that a seeker and lover of truth can progress through the first six without a teacher, but to move through and navigate the seventh layer and beyond we need a teacher's help, whether or not we live in physical proximity to him or her. There are certain aspects of transformation that need some type of intervention from outside the egoic mechanism. Sometimes a shock, a powerful experience of grace, a loss, or disciplined spiritual practice can help us to make the leap, but the presence of a wise teacher is one of the most effective transformative influences in the course of our spiritual journey.

There is an important distinction to be made between relative spiritual authorities and absolute authorities. Most spiritual teachers, even very good ones, are relative spiritual authorities. These individuals have gained deep understanding and can tremendously help others. They transmit the dharma, exemplify many important principles, and are skillful in helping their students deepen their inner wisdom. Though some relative authorities give powerful spiritual transmissions, they also suffer many of the same challenges as other human beings, including divorce, depression, illness, death of loved ones, and aging. Such teachers, and they are in the majority, will have human flaws that impact the quality of their transmission and teachings.

More rare are absolute authorities who embody what they teach to an exemplary degree and have fully integrated the higher knowledge they have accessed. They are powerful people capable of strong transmission. Yet even if we should be lucky enough, or blessed enough, to encounter such rare individuals, we must still learn to be in healthy relationship with them, as even absolute spiritual authorities are still human. To learn to hold the polarity of the human and divine aspects of the teacher is one of the most important aspects of empowered discipleship.

Regardless of whether we are with relative or absolute spiritual authorities, even in the best of relationships there will be a psychological dynamic between the student and the teacher, "fueled" by either the teacher's or the student's projections. It is important to be aware of the psychological challenges that one is likely to encounter when relating to a spiritual teacher.

The Psychological Challenges of
Having a Teacher

Along with the benefits of having a spiritual teacher, even a good one, come the psychological challenges inherent in the student-teacher relationship. To navigate it with discernment, we need to be aware of the psychological challenges we are likely to encounter. When not attended to, they become detrimental both to the student's development and to the relationship itself. Other important qualities of the relationship with one's teacher—including surrender, trust, and obedience—are compromised when the psychological relationship with the teacher is immature and unconscious.

The task required of the spiritual student is to become psychologically mature in relationship to the teacher. It is the nature of the human mind to project, and due to many people's challenging childhoods, the tendency to recreate complex psychological relationships from childhood in relationship to the teacher is quite common.

Psychologically differentiating from the teacher requires that we understand our own unhealthy psychological dynamics from childhood thoroughly enough to continually check that we are not reenacting these dynamics with the teacher or a community of spiritual practitioners. For most people, psychological maturity in relationship to the spiritual teacher either comes from a rare childhood in which there was little psychological wounding or, more commonly, from extensive psychological work on oneself over an extended period of time, often in the form of psychotherapy.

Mutual complicity is the term used to describe a relationship in which the student and teacher reciprocally and unconsciously support a distorted psychological dynamic between them. This unwholesome dynamic often extends into our relationships with the hierarchies that encircle the teacher, whether we are in a position of power and control within them or we are relating to the spiritual teacher and teachings through them.

We must understand that in relation to anyone in a position of authority—no matter how divine that individual is—we will bring to that circumstance a certain degree of psychological projection that results from our relationships with parents and other significant authorities in our lives. We will also inevitably experience, and need to take into account, the teacher's own psychological dynamic.

Many spiritual traditions work within a system where there is a root guru, lama, or teacher and many other teachers who help the student with certain aspects of their development along the way. This model respects the likelihood that the teacher cannot provide everything for his or her students.

The Psychological Challenge of Being a Teacher

The teacher faces his or her own set of psychological challenges. My work in this field for the past fifteen years has given me a close-up view of the lives of countless individuals in positions of spiritual authority and an opportunity to track their lives over time. I am convinced that there are simultaneous processes of spiritual and psychological development at play in those who find themselves functioning as a teacher, a student, or both. It is neither right nor wrong that these processes arise; they simply do, so the individual must take responsibility for attending to the dynamics that accompany them.

It is difficult for many teachers to accept that their spiritual realization does not exempt them from the need for an ongoing investigation into their own psychological makeup, and it is surprisingly hard for many spiritual teachers to self-reflect on this subject. It is as if the teacher fears that acknowledging his or her psychological weaknesses will diminish his or her spiritual authority, whereas I believe the opposite is true: to take responsibility for knowing and tending to one's psychological weaknesses and idiosyncrasies is a way of protecting one's students from falling into unconscious traps of projection and mutual complicity.

Countertransference is the psychological term that refers to the psychologist's own internal response to what the client says and projects. In similar fashion, the spiritual teacher will have an internal response to the ideas and projections cast upon him or her. It will evoke any latent tendencies toward narcissism, power, fame, and inappropriate seduction. All of these arise from a distorted and inflated sense of self that results from mistaking one's egoic personality for one's true self and believing that the projections cast by one's students are actually true of oneself. Although the students' projections are essentially impersonal, it is easy for both student and teacher to take them personally. Psychologist Jennifer Welwood explains:

> *Unacknowledged inflation eventually ripens into abuse of power, and unacknowledged abuse of power eventually ripens into corruption. Even if this corruption is not acted out externally, it remains an inner condition that has not been remedied. All of us in human form must grapple with our unconscious tendencies. Even when we have cultivated the capacity to recognize our awake nature, significant areas of our mindstream remain unawakened, and unintegrated with our awakening, with tremendous residual momentum toward habitual tendencies. We are either consciously grappling with this or unconsciously enacting it, and those are the only*

two choices. Few are exempt from this human predica-
ment and the arduous evolutionary work that goes with
it, even among those who claim to be spiritually realized,
radically awakened satgurus.[3]

Nondual awakening coexists with the laws of duality, the
process of karma, and human psychology. If a teacher does
not tend to his or her dual, human experience as well as to
nondual awareness, the teacher's disciples will pay the price,
and he or she will also suffer the karmic consequences of premature assumptions of spiritual enlightenment or awakening.
Psychologist and Sufi sheikh Robert Frager says Sufism teaches
that when we are in a spiritual teaching function and we
make a mistake, the karmic consequences are doubled. When
someone we teach then goes on to teach others and makes
a mistake, our karmic consequences are quadrupled, and so
forth. It is a lesson about being very humble with respect to
the responsibility inherent in spiritual teaching and about how
few people are destined for this role in a traditional way.

A further distinction to make is that spiritual realization
does not necessarily mean that one has developed the skill
to convey that realization to others. Many people mistakenly
believe that a teacher is qualified to teach simply by virtue of
his or her own realization. The reality, however, is that there
are probably thousands, if not tens of thousands, of individuals who experience deep spiritual realization but who do not
possess the set of skills required to convey it. Teaching requires
skillful means—the ability to perceive, work with, and effectively communicate with students according to their stage of
spiritual development as well as their particular psychological
structure. Such teachers are rare.

Carl Jung coined the term *gnostic intermediary* to refer to
an individual who possesses the extremely skillful means to

be able to translate living spiritual wisdom from one culture to another—and even within subcultures of a given culture. Roger Walsh, the founder of transpersonal psychiatry, describes this in depth: Gnostic intermediaries are people who personally incorporate the wisdom of a tradition and can then speak directly from their own experience and translate this experience and understanding into the language and concepts of the culture to which they wish to communicate. [4]

Walsh goes on to explain that becoming a gnostic intermediary requires three processes: (1) becoming wise (as opposed to the mere acquisition of knowledge); (2) learning the language and systems of the culture one wishes to communicate to; and (3) translating experience into the language and concepts of the new culture so that the recipient of the wisdom feels an "aha!" experience.

In some way, everyone on the spiritual path is a gnostic intermediary, whether we see ourselves as teachers or students. We are trying to grow spiritually and to share with others the fruits of our growth. Regardless of our function, we are all asked to integrate this knowledge and express it through our lives, so we can serve others and the healing of life on the planet at progressively deeper levels.

"The purity of the teacher is secondary to the purity of the student," said Arnaud Desjardins. At the end of the day, the question of the student is more relevant to us than the question of the teacher, since for most of us, our primary consideration on the spiritual path is how to become effective practitioners rather than how to become spiritual teachers. Furthermore, it is always the best students who become the greatest teachers. To place our attention on being a lifelong spiritual student is a far healthier attitude than aspiring to be a spiritual teacher. It is our studenthood that keeps us in integrity, and sometimes it is the good students who help sincere teachers become better ones by empowering them as teachers and helping them grow. "The last thing the world needs is another yoga teacher," my yoga teacher Bhavani used to tell us. "What the world needs is a dedicated yoga student."

Once again, it is the cultivation of keen discernment that helps us navigate the labyrinth of the teacher-student relationship with efficiency, respect, intelligence, and love. It is our responsibility to become knowledgeable, conscious, discerning students of the spiritual path so that we will not miss out on the unique possibilities that can be gained from relating to spiritual teachers—and so that we avoid falling into the traps that many sincere spiritual practitioners have encountered. Above all, it is our spiritual maturity and capacity to make important distinctions within our own experience that will be our greatest protection and asset on the path.

Chapter 12

~

Om Mani Padme Grow Up!

Raising yourself is enough,
without worrying about the dead!
—LEE LOZOWICK

O*m mani padme hum* is the great Tibetan mantra of compassion which is said to contain all of the Buddha's teachings. In contemporary times, when psychological, sociological, economic, political, and spiritual confusion prevails, one of the most compassionate, life-affirming intentions we can evoke for our lives on the spiritual path is *Om mani padme grow up!*

It is very easy to go through life—even if one has become a parent, an executive, a senior citizen—and never really grow up, even psychologically. Becoming a spiritually mature and integrated human being is a still more challenging task, and it does not happen without great effort and wise discernment. To grow up spiritually requires refinement of one's discernment, and expresses itself through a spiritual maturity that includes self-responsibility, spiritual practice, and gratitude.

Spiritual teacher Arnaud Desjardins was once asked by one of his students what he should do for his fortieth birthday. He answered, "Act like a forty-year-old man!" Psychologist and mystic Carl Jung suggested that the many important problems of life cannot be solved but only outgrown. We outgrow our problems by growing up in relation to them, and we transform spiritual immaturity by cultivating a capacity for discernment that is powerful enough to pierce through ignorance and confusion on every level of our experience.

Fleet Maull, Buddhist teacher and the founder of the Prison Dharma Network, learned the lessons of growing up the hard way. While serving as a personal attendant to his teacher, Chögyam Trungpa Rinpoche, Maull was simultaneously running drugs in South America. He was caught and imprisoned for fourteen years, during which time he had to leave his son and his teacher, who subsequently died while he was still in prison. Although Maull had been a long-time Buddhist practitioner prior to his imprisonment, his losses gave him a whole new perspective on the importance of self-responsibility, the irreplaceable value of spiritual practice, and the need to grow up psychologically and spiritually. His losses taught him how to discern.

While listening to Maull talk about his experience, a young man in the room who was a very serious spiritual practitioner asked him, "Do you have any advice for us on what we might do in order to understand this urgency, this necessity, to wake up and grow up without having to get ourselves into the kind of trouble you did?" "That's the million-dollar question," Maull responded.

Growing up is a fundamental task of spiritual discernment and means that we take full responsibility for our existence here on earth. It means we must find a way to help make the world a better place and fulfill that calling. If what many of the world's great psychologists and spiritual masters have suggested is true—that we are 90 percent unconscious and 10 percent conscious—then those of us who are deeply committed to spiritual life face a monumental task: first to learn what it is that is unconsciously running us, and then to learn how to discern clearly in relationship to that. To become conscious of what is unconscious means giving up the victim position that characterizes psychological immaturity and taking responsibility for our own psychological healing and our impact on others.

Growing up spiritually is a still higher calling—and can only happen as a result of clear discernment. Most spiritual practitioners, including teachers, embark on the path as spiritual "children." We do not know ourselves, and as we find the path (or it finds us), we may be blessed with a period of profound insight and experience that lasts for many months or even years. The temporary insight into enlightenment often provides a sense of all-knowing and invincibility that is deceiving. We think we know more than we do and are often self-righteous in our "knowing." As time goes on, life itself tests these insights and, if we are self-observant and willing to grow, opens our eyes to our spiritual naïveté. Many spiritual teachers report being surprised to realize, in retrospect, how little discernment they had in the early years of their professed enlightenment and teaching careers, and how childish many of their actions were.

"Enlightenment" itself has progressive levels of maturity (outlined in Chapter 1). When people have profound nondual insight, even when it begins to stabilize, there is still a deeper process to unfold. Whereas many realizers suggest that there is one nondual state that cannot change, grow, be diminished, or be deepened, yoga philosophy and other esoteric traditions suggest otherwise—that there are many levels and stages of enlightenment, and that very few people have ever reached its heights. It requires discernment to see our own spiritual development in this respect and to appreciate that there is literally no limit to our deepening process. We are called to continue to discern and grow spiritually as long as we live.

In my own work as a spiritual journalist, which now spans many years, I have interviewed more than a hundred teachers who are considered to be, and consider themselves to be, enlightened. Although there is some general agreement among these individuals about the nature of the nondual experience, there are clear differences in the level and caliber of their teaching in terms of both their psychological and spiritual maturity. It can be difficult to perceive these distinctions if one has not known many teachers and does not know what questions to ask and what criteria to consider when meeting them.

The fact is that fully enlightened beings on the planet are rare. Instead, most of us are on a continuum, moving from spiritual childishness through spiritual adolescence and into spiritual maturity. Although in deeper stages of spiritual realization, a teacher might exemplify many childlike qualities of innocence, openness, and unboundedness, this child*like*ness is distinct from child*ish*ness, or immaturity, which usually points to a lack of psychological integration.

Learning to discern these levels and layers is an ongoing and shared task for spiritual practitioners and teachers alike, and it is yet another reason we must prioritize a commitment to cultivating discernment within ourselves. Chinese Taoist philosopher Lao Tzu said: "Give a man a fish and you feed him for a day; teach him how to fish and you feed him for a lifetime." To learn to discern grows us spiritually and nourishes our spiritual path for a lifetime.

Self-Responsibility

Every life is an unanswered question and an uncharted possibility. There are questions of the soul that no guru, dharma, book, therapist, or wise friend can answer for us. At the metaphorical pearly gates of heaven, there will be no one there to say, "You were a good Christian (or Buddhist, or disciple, or yogi). Now run along to paradise." Instead, we will stand alone in the presence of the mystery, with the sum total of all the moments of our lives and the degree of awakening, understanding, and compassion we have brought to bear on these moments. We will need to turn deeply within and surrender.

There is a certain aloneness inherent in every life that no other human being—divine or otherwise—can fill. We are continually making choices, there is a consequence for every decision, and we encounter crossroads throughout our lives. Discernment is required at every turn of life and at every juncture of spiritual development. The degree to which we are awake, conscious, and discerning in our experience and choices is the extent to which we can consciously participate in our soul's unfolding.

After many years of harrowing practice and deep purification under the guidance of her teacher, the great Sufi mystic Irina Tweedie wrote:

> *The realization that every act, every word, every thought of ours not only influences our environment but for some mysterious reason forms an integral and important part of the Universe, fits into it as if by necessity so to say, in the very moment we do, or say, or think it—is an overwhelming and even shattering experience. The tremendous responsibility of it is terrifying. If all of us only*

knew that the smallest act of ours, or a tiny thought, has such far-reaching effects as to set in motion forces which perhaps could shatter a galaxy. . . . If we know it deeply and absolutely, if this realization becomes engraved permanently on our hearts, on our minds, how careful we would act and speak and think. How precious life would become in its integral oneness. And this, I think, is as far as the human mind and heart can go.[1]

To take full responsibility for ourselves is to discern the impact of our experience on all of life. The discovery of the truth about ourselves is not gained easily or cheaply. There is a price for growing up spiritually, and that is to discern clearly and take full responsibility for our own internal and external world, both that which is conscious and that which is unconscious within us, particularly the aspects of our experience that we choose to leave just beneath consciousness. We must be willing to face illusions and limited ideas upon which we have hung our whole identity, to look at the many things within ourselves we would rather not see, to make consistent efforts, and to lose face and suffer the loss of our identities and dreams to whatever degree is required by the path. These great internal tasks can only be achieved through clear discernment with relationship to all aspects of our experience.

We can pay people to clean our house, do our taxes, teach us piano, and fix broken bones, but nobody can do our inner work for us. Nobody. To truly take responsibility for ourselves, we must grow up psychologically and spiritually, so we can respond to life as mature and authentic men and women. Jeanne de Salzmann, a teacher in the lineage of G. I. Gurdjieff, refers to this decision to take full responsibility for oneself in her essay "First Initiation." She writes:

EYES WIDE OPEN

You will see that in life you receive exactly what you give. Your life is the mirror of what you are. It is in your image. . . . The first requirement, the first condition, the first test for one who wishes to work on himself is to . . . see things in himself which he has never seen before, see them actually. . . . And in order to see, he must learn to see; this is the first initiation of man into self-knowledge. . . . But you will see that it is not easy. And it is not cheap. You must pay dearly. . . . You must pay, pay a lot, and pay immediately, pay in advance. Pay with yourself. By sincere, conscientious, disinterested efforts. The more you are prepared to pay without economizing, without cheating, without any falsification, the more you will receive.[2]

The Intrinsic Value of Practice

Without preparing ourselves through preliminary practices, the only answer to the question, "Who am I?" is "The same old fool."

—SWAMI SIVANANDA

There is a great philosophical debate in the world of contemporary spirituality about the value of spiritual practice. Some say that practice has nothing to do with enlightenment and that the very act of practicing implies a striving that is actually an impediment to true realization. Proponents of this viewpoint say that the "effort" and "doing" of spiritual practice actually take us away from the experience of enlightenment that is always present as our natural state. On the other end of the spectrum, those who advocate a practice perspective say that disciplined spiritual practice is utterly necessary and that it is almost impossible to grow and mature spiritually without it. Cultivating discernment allows us to see clearly and take full responsibility for our perspective and relationship to spiritual practice.

It is true that when we experience awakened consciousness there seems to be no direct correlation to a life of practice, yet every mystical tradition throughout the centuries has agreed upon the necessity of some form of disciplined practice. If we explore the biographies of the great realizers—even the ones who tell us that practice is not a requisite for enlightenment—we see that each of them devoted extended periods of their lives to arduous searching and disciplined practice. For example, Ramana Maharshi, a great southern India saint whose spiritual realization is almost universally agreed upon, discovered the truth about the nature of his existence at the age of seventeen. He then did more than thirty years of spiritual practice and integration before he was willing to share his teachings on a wider scale and allow an ashram to be built.

Although spiritual practice and the experience of enlightenment are not connected in a linear, causal manner—that is, practice does not *produce* enlightenment—they nonetheless have an intimate relationship to each other. "Enlightenment is an accident," says Buddhist teacher Jack Kornfield, "but spiritual practice makes you accident-prone."

Paradoxically, it is the effort of practice that seems to allow progressive surrender to occur. We cannot make an effort to surrender, as surrender is letting go; nonetheless, practice places us in a stream, or context, in which we are more available to receive and rest in the states of surrender that inevitably arise in a life dedicated to awakening. Practice exercises an invisible subtle "muscle" that builds an unseen but powerful matrix in the body. This matrix helps us integrate and stabilize the powerful insights and experiences that arise in our lives on the path. Spiritual practice is called *sadhana* in Sanskrit, which means "process." To enter the stream of practice is to place oneself in a process and remain there until its usefulness is complete. It is the process itself that gradually brings about our spiritual discernment and maturation.

I remember a period of time, after ten years of rigorous, disciplined meditation and dietary practices, when I felt the need to test the importance of this notion of practice. I was curious about the philosophical arguments against practice, and it had also become apparent to me that much of my motivation for such intense practice was the deeply engrained belief that if I practiced hard enough, *I* would be enough. I had uncovered deep psychological projections not only onto my teacher but also onto the notion of spiritual practice itself, as well as onto my ideas of God and the Divine. And so for a period of time, I stopped practicing altogether.

The first thing I understood was that nothing bad was going to happen to me if I stopped practicing—I did not lose favor with the Divine or with my teacher. I also realized that there was no promise of getting what I desired simply because I practiced. Why then, I wondered, should I resume practice? And then I considered: if I were to be a fully mature woman on the path of life itself, which is inherently spiritual, how would I live my life? And I realized that I would *choose* to do the very things I had once called "practice" anyway because it made sense to do so. I would try to spend time daily in meditation or contemplation and in study. I would eat well, in a way that gave good energy to my body, and I would exercise my body because I knew it was a fleeting gift, and I wanted to remain strong and healthy. I would try to live with integrity, strengthen my conscience and self-knowledge, continue to study, and make my life one of service. In other words, the practices I had been doing for so many years were not just a means to an end, but an expression of that end itself.

The problems we might encounter with practice are therefore not inherent in the act of disciplined practice itself, but rather in the attachment to a specific outcome of practice, which can create a kind of striving and lack of acceptance of one's present reality. If a practice is steady and carried forth in the context of a community of spiritual practitioners and with reliable sources of spiritual guidance and feedback, it will eventually reveal to us our confused motivations for practice, and it will clarify and strengthen our mature motivations. The practice itself bears the fruits of discernment.

Practice is not only something engaged to direct us toward a positive transformation; it is an organic expression of spiritual wisdom. Practice becomes the beginning, middle, and end result of the path. It is said that when the disciples said to Jesus, "Tell us what our end will be," Jesus replied, "If you haven't found the beginning, why ask about the end? For where the beginning is, the end is also. Blessed are those who stand at the beginning, for they will know the end, and they will not taste death."

Give Thanks and Praise

Before you ask God for what you want, first thank God for what you have.

—TALMUD

"For only in praising is my heart still mine," wrote Rainer Maria Rilke, although he experienced tremendous personal and existential suffering in his life. There is an aspect of growing up on the spiritual path where we learn to give thanks and praise not because we like everything the way it is, but as an expression of gratitude for the gift and mystery of life itself: for the fleeting hours and years of incarnation that are given to us, for the opportunity for self-knowledge and awakening, for what Buddhists call "this precious human birth." We are not blind to the pain and suffering outside or within ourselves, yet we are able to perceive life through a discerning heart and mind in such a way that we can recognize something greater and more vast from which it all arises. Whether we call this God, emptiness, or something in between, the clarity of our discerning vision leads us to praise.

Native American poet Sherman Alexie powerfully expresses the discernment of gratitude even in the midst of great suffering in his poem "Praise the Opera." He recounts the tragedies that continue to befall his reservation and his family—the broken homes, the child molestation, the runaways and missing children—as well as his own anger and suffering, and yet he has developed the capacity to praise, even in hell, and instructs us to do the same.

Spiritual maturity is not a function of age, or of years on the path, but of a powerful and discerning choice from within to cultivate gratitude as a way of being in the world. In 1944, while hiding from the Nazis, fifteen-year-old Anne Frank wrote in her famous diaries, "We have many reasons to hope for great happiness, but . . . we have to earn it. And that's something you can't achieve by taking the easy way out."

I asked my friend Marina, a psychologist from Spain, why the Spanish people seem so much happier overall than Americans. "Because in America everybody is waiting until they have figured themselves out before they can really enjoy life, and in Spain the people choose to celebrate life while figuring out who they are," she replied.

We give thanks and praise through the conscious cultivation of gratitude. Like contentment, gratitude arises from learning to discern clearly. To praise is to choose gratitude even in hell. When Kenny Johnson had a spiritual awakening while he was in prison, he chose to express gratitude and praise even in that environment. The Bauls of Bengal, celebrated by the mystical poet Rabindranath Tagore, are renunciate beggars who travel the land singing praises of "love in hell" and sharing the ecstatic teachings of tantra through musical celebration and song. Spiritual teacher Robert Ennis, while dying a painful death of AIDS and having fallen into a coma, suddenly opened his eyes and said, "Thank you," to those around him, before lapsing back into his final sleep. To be able to see clearly amid suffering and difficulty is a powerful fruit of discernment and an expression of spiritual maturity.

The name of Patañjali, who was the compiler of the *Yoga Sūtras,* means "one who falls into open hands." We practice learning to open and say "thank you" to each experience we have in life, no matter what it is—what the poet Rumi calls "joy at sudden disappointment." This is not an easy thing to do, of course, but it is worth aspiring to, for if we learn to praise even in the darkest of times, we discover an unshakable inner strength.

One description of the Sanskrit term *shraddā,* often translated as "faith," is "love of the unknown." Shraddā says: "I am given everything I need, even if it is not what I imagine that I want. The situation in front of me *is* a blessing in disguise, even if I do not experience it that way." Faith says, "I choose the life I am given."

Unless we are one of the lucky ones who happen to be born with unshakable trust in life, faith must be cultivated. It is an act of will, a discipline of mind, and a discerning choice that we make again and again until one day it arises of its own accord. We release our need to control life, and let life itself instruct us.

One of the great expressions of gratitude and praise is a commitment to a life of service. Our discernment has led us to want to serve others and for our lives in general to be of service. The deep desire to serve arises from the acknowledgment that our lives are given not only for the taking and for our own pleasure and enjoyment, but to serve something greater than ourselves. "I do not know what your destiny will be," wrote theologian and musician Albert Schweitzer, "but one thing I do know: the only ones among you who will be really happy are those who have sought and found how to serve."

To place others first and serve them is one of the most practical expressions of thanks and praise we can offer to life. Even when we do not feel grateful, we act grateful. Service is not expressed in any one way, nor is it necessarily conveyed in grand gestures that all the world can see. Our service may come through the quality of our parenting or consistent small acts of kindness toward others or living an ecologically conscious life. Some serve through a life of prayer, others through social activism or transformative art. What lies beneath these acts of service is the decision to live our lives dedicated to something greater than ourselves. Indian saint Yogi Ramsuratkumar, who slept and ate little and gave his whole life to the healing and service of others, said, "If I have served one person, my life is worthwhile."

Indian spiritual teacher Swami Prajnanpad said that the spiritual development and maturation of human beings is a fourfold process that moves progressively from self-centeredness to other-centeredness. Initially, our lives revolve only around "myself." In the next stage, it is "myself and the other." As we further develop, this shifts into "the other and myself," and finally, simply, "the other." Growing up spiritually means we gradually move from self-centeredness toward other-centeredness as our discernment and spiritual maturity guide us to embody authentic spiritual wisdom.

A Love Letter from the Divine

To grow up on the spiritual path is to be whole in oneself and a radiant exemplar of spiritual wisdom in a world full of suffering. *Sūtra,* in Sanskrit, means thread, and we create a thread of discernment to connect and guide us through the challenges of the spiritual path. As we thread discernment throughout the whole of the spiritual journey, we become increasingly radiant and intelligent with respect to the totality of our lives. The "crowning wisdom" of viveka khyātir becomes an abiding capacity that brings us great well-being, as it leads us to make wise choices such that we can die without regret and feeling that we have lived well and fully.

In 2001, I traveled twenty-four hours on planes, buses, and trains to a little town in the mountains of northern India because I had heard there was an enlightened woman who lived there. I was deeply interested in witnessing the expression of enlightenment through a female body. There I met Vimala Thakar, the unofficial successor of the late and great J. Krishnamurti. Over the course of three days, I had two one-hour interviews with her. Toward the end of the second meeting, having learned of her life of ceaseless practice and overcoming challenges and adversity against all odds, I asked her how she had found the courage to live so boldly. Upon hearing her answer, I knew immediately that I had traveled far and wide just to hear her message—a message that speaks to the whole of this book. With the voice of a woman who had lived without compromise, a true warrior of the spirit, a compassionate mother of the world, she answered:

> *My love of life and the urge to discover the truth first-hand sustained me. I had read so much, but I could not be satisfied in borrowing anyone's version of truth. I*

*would probe and probe until the light dawned on me.
Living here in India, a woman unmarried—it was
not a path of roses. There were many difficulties and
handicaps. But a revolutionary cannot have the luxury
of defeat—pessimism, negativity. Never. Difficulties can
be converted into opportunities, challenges into the call
for more creativity. Everything in life has two aspects: if
you know how to use it, it becomes an advantage, and if
you don't know how to use it, it becomes a disadvantage.
That's what I have done, my dear. For every challenge
I received, I would say, "This is a love letter from the
Divine, and I must find an answer from within."*

The Divine has sent you a love letter, written in the form of
your life. Will you receive it? How will you respond?

Notes

Introduction

1 Iyengar, B. K. S., *Light on the Yoga Sūtras of Patañjali.* New Delhi, India: HarperCollins Publishers India, 2005 (first edition, 1993), p. 132.

2 Rilke, Rainer Maria. *Letters to a Young Poet.* Revised paperback. New York: W. W. Norton & Company, 1993, p. 35.

3 Llewellyn Vaughan-Lee, personal interview, February 2008.

Chapter 1

1 Keegan, Paul. "Yogis Behaving Badly" *Business2 Magazine,* September 2002.

2 Caplan, Mariana. *Halfway Up the Mountain.* Prescott, AZ: Hohm Press, 1999, p. 474.

3 One such exception is Adyashanti, a teacher who represents this movement yet advocates intensive meditation and a rigorous and integrated process of psychological and spiritual inquiry.

4 Iyengar, B. K. S., *Light on the Yoga Sūtras of Patañjali.* New Delhi, India: HarperCollins Publishers India, 2005 (first edition, 1993), pp. 64–5.

5 Ibid., pp. 71–73.

6 Aurobindo. *The Synthesis of Yoga.* Twin Lakes, WI: Lotus Press, 1996, pp. 47–8.

Chapter 2

1 Chesson, H. W., et al. "The Estimated Direct Medical Cost of STDs among American Youth, 2000." 2004

National STD Prevention Conference, Philadelphia, PA, March 8–11, 2004. Abstract P075.

2 Smith, J., and J. Robinson. "Age-Specific Prevalence of Infection with Herpes Simplex Virus Types 2 and 1: A Global Review." *The Journal of Infectious Diseases,* 186 (2002): S3–28

3 Chapter 3 in *Halfway Up the Mountain* considers these motivations in depth.

4 *Satori,* a term often used in Zen Buddhism, refers to a state of sudden enlightenment.

5 A full account of this phenomenon can be found in the article, "Adventures of a New Age Traveler," by Mariana Caplan, in Stephen Dinan, ed., *Radical Spirit: Spiritual Writings from the Voices of Tomorrow.* (Novato, CA: New World Library, 2002).

6 Desikachar, T. K. V. *The Heart of Yoga: Developing a Personal Practice.* Rochester, VT: Inner Traditions International, 1995, p. 127.

7 Desikachar, T. K. V. *The Heart of Yoga: Developing a Personal Practice.* Rochester, VT: Inner Traditions International, 1995, p. 126.

Chapter 3

1 Iyengar, B. K. S., *Light on the Yoga Sūtras of Patañjali.* New Delhi, India: HarperCollins Publishers India, 2005 (first edition, 1993), p. 69.

2 de Salzmann, Jeanne. "First Initiaton." In *Gurdjieff: Essays and Reflections on the Man and His Teaching,* edited by Jacob Needleman and George Baker. New York: Continuum, 1996.

Chapter 4

1 Svoboda, Robert. *The Greatness of Saturn*. Twin Lakes, WI: Lotus Press, 1997, p. 4.

2 Welwood, John. *Toward a Psychology of Awakening*. Boston: Shambhala Publications, 2000, p. 42.

3 Jacques Castermanne, personal interview, July 2005.

4 Some discussions of the sheaths of the body include two additional levels—*cittamayakosha*, the sheath of consciousness, and *ātmamayakosha*, the sheath of the individuated soul.

5 Gilles Farcet. personal interview, July 2007.

6 Iyengar, B. K. S., *Light on the Yoga Sūtras of Patañjali*. New Delhi, India: HarperCollins Publishers India, 2005 (first edition, 1993), p. 112.

7 Ibid., p. 116.

8 Ibid., pp. 116–7.

Chapter 5

1 Trungpa, Chögyam. *Cutting Through Spiritual Materialism*. Boston: Shambhala, 1973, p. 13.

2 Ibid., p. 3.

3 Welwood, John. *Toward a Psychology of Awakening*. Boston: Shambhala, 2000, p. 207.

4 Judith Lief. personal interview, September 1998.

5 "Zen Boyfriends" premiered as a musical comedy in San Francisco in March 2009. For more information, see zenboyfriends.com.

6 Wilber, Ken. *The Collected Works of Ken Wilber,* volume 4. Boston: Shambhala, 1999, p. 460.

Chapter 6

1   Walsh, Roger. *The World of Shamanism: New Views on an Ancient Tradition.* Woodbury, MN: Llewellyn Publications, 2007, pp. 108–9.

2   Kessler, R. C., et al. "Prevalence, Severity, and Comorbidity of Twelve-Month DSM-IV Disorders in the National Comorbidity Survey Replication (NCS-R)." *Archives of General Psychiatry* 62, no. 6 (2005): 617–27.

3   "The Numbers Count: Mental Illness in America," Science on Our Minds Fact Sheet Series.

4   Walsh, Roger, Bruce Victor, Robin Bitner and Lorena Hillman. "Optimal Healing: What Do We Know about Integrating Meditation, Medication, and Psychotherapy." *Buddhadharma,* in press.

5   Grof, Stanislav, and Christina Grof. *The Stormy Search for the Self.* New York: Tarcher/Putnam, 1990, p. 34.

6   Grof, Stanislav, and Christina Grof. *The Stormy Search for the Self.* New York: Tarcher/Putnam, 1990, p. 36.

7   Saint John of the Cross. *Dark Night of the Soul.* 3rd ed. Edited by E. Allison Peers. New York: Image Books, 1959, p. 34.

8   An overview of Michael Washburn's developmental theory can be found in: Washburn, Michael. *The Ego and the Dynamic Ground.* New York: State University of New York Press (SUNY), 1995.

9   Mother Teresa. *Mother Teresa: Come Be My Light: The Private Writings of the Saint of Calcutta.* New York: Doubleday, 2007, pp. 1–2.

10 Tweedie, Irina. *Daughter of Fire.* Nevada City, CA: Blue Dolphin Publishing, 1986, p. 109.

11 Starr, Mirabai. *The Dark Night of the Soul*. New York: Riverhead Books, 2002, p. 103.

12 Lama Palden Drolma, personal interview, December 2007.

13 Khyentse, Dzongsar Jamyang. *What Makes You Not a Buddhist?* Boston: Shambhala, 2007, p. 27.

14 Ibid., p. 120.

15 Desikachar, T. K. V. *The Heart of Yoga: Developing a Personal Practice*. Rochester, VT: Inner Traditions International, 1995, p. 126.

Chapter 7

1 Ngakpa Chögyam, personal interview, 2002.

2 Chögyam, Ngakpa. *Wearing the Body of Visions*. Ramsey, NJ: Aro Books, 1995, p. 172.

3 Prendergast, John, Peter Fenner, and Sheila Krystal, eds., *The Sacred Mirror*. New York: Omega Book, 2003, p. 154.

4 The exception to this in recent times has been a counter-trend in Western Buddhist groups to demonstrate social involvement as an ethic.

5 Desjardins, Arnaud. *The Jump into Life: Moving Beyond Fear*. Prescott, AZ: Hohm Press, 1994, p. 73.

6 Ibid., p. 60.

7 Feuerstein, Georg. *Tantra: The Path of Ecstasy*. Boston: Shambhala, 1998, p. 139.

8 Welwood, John. *Toward a Psychology of Awakening*. Boston: Shambhala, 2000, p. 29.

9 Osho. *The Book of Secrets*. New York: St. Martin's Griffin, 1974, p. 644.

10 Desjardins, Arnaud. *The Jump into Life: Moving Beyond Fear*. Prescott, AZ: Hohm Press, 1994, p. 54.

11 For more information on Kenny Johnson's work, see thissacredspace.org.

12 Simmer-Brown, Judith. *Dakini's Warm Breath: The Feminine Principle in Tibetan Buddhism.* Boston: Shambhala, 2002, p. 217.

Chapter 8

1 Jung, Carl Gustav. *Collected Works of C. G. Jung, Volume 11: Psychology and Religion: West and East.* Princeton, NJ: Princeton University Press, 1975, p. 131.

2 Rilke, Rainer Maria. "Turning." *Uncollected Poems.* New York: North Point Press, 1996, p. 93.

3 Jung, Carl Gustav. "The Stages of Life." *Collected Works of C. G. Jung, Volume 8: The Structure and Dynamics of the Psyche.* Princeton, NJ: Princeton University Press, 1976, p. 752.

4 Claudio Naranjo, personal interview, January 1999.

5 Washburn, Michael. *The Ego and the Dynamic Ground.* New York: State University of New York Press (SUNY), 1995, p. 75.

6 Ibid. p. 76.

Chapter 9

1 Ferrer, Jorge. "Embodied Spirituality, Now and Then." *Tikkun*, May/June 2006, p. 43.

2 Summaries of research done by the Heartmath Institute can be found at heartmath.org.

3 Iyengar, B. K. S. *Light on the Yoga Sūtras of Patañjali.* New Delhi, India; HaperCollins, 1993, p. 55.

4 Steiner, Rudolph. *How to Know Higher Worlds.* Herndon, VA: Steinerbooks, 1994, p. 36.

5   Walsh, Roger, Bruce Victor, Robin Bitner, and Lorena Hillman. "Optimal Healing: What Do We Know about Integrating Meditation, Medication, and Psychotherapy." *Buddhadharma*, in press.

6   Jodorowsky, Alejandro. *The Spiritual Journey of Alejandro Jodorowsky.* Rochester, VT: Park Street Press, 2008, p. 46.

Chapter 10

1   Desjardins, Arnaud. *The Jump into Life: Moving Beyond Fear.* Prescott, AZ: Hohm Press, 1994, p. 16.

2   Welwood, John. *Toward a Psychology of Awakening.* Boston: Shambhala, 2000, p. 197.

3   Ibid., p. 197.

4   Jacobi, Jolande, and Ralph Manheim. *The Psychology of C. G. Jung.* New Haven, CT: Yale University Press, 1973, p. 377.

5   Aurobindo. *Sri Aurobindo on Himself.* Pondicherry, India: Sri Aurobindo Ashram Trust, 1972, pp. 95–97.

6   Wilber, Ken. *Integral Psychology.* Boston: Shambhala, 2000, p. 2.

7   Washburn, Michael. *The Ego and the Dynamic Ground.* New York: State University of New York Press (SUNY), 1995, p. 1.

8   Prendergast, John, and Kenneth Bradford, eds. *Listening from the Heart of Silence.* St. Paul, MN: Paragon House, 2007, p. 12.

9   Aurobindo. *The Yoga and Its Objects.* Calcutta, India: Arya Publishing House, 1938.

Chapter 11

1   Starr, Mirabai. *The Dark Night of the Soul.* New York: Riverhead Books, 2002, p. 149.

2   An audio recording of a talk entitled "The Twelve Levels of Initiation" by Llewellyn Vaughan-Lee that elaborates on these levels can be found at goldensufi.org/audioarchives.html.

3   Jennifer Welwood, MFT, personal correspondence.

4   Walsh, Roger, "The Search for Synthesis," *Journal of Transpersonal Psychology* 32, no. 1: 19–45.

Chapter 12

1   Tweedie, Irina. *Daughter of Fire.* Nevada City, CA: Blue Dolphin Publishing, 1986, p. 812.

2   de Salzmann, Jeanne. "First Initiation." In *Gurdjieff: Essays and Reflections on the Man and His Teaching.* edited by Jacob Needleman and George Baker. New York: Continuum, 1996.

Glossary

abhidharma (Sanskrit): Buddhist psychology

acharya (Sanskrit): a religious teacher or scholar

Advaita-Vedanta (Sanskrit): a school of Vedanta (literally the end or goal of the Vedas) in Hindu philosophy.

ahamkāra (Sanskrit): the utterance of "I" or creation of an identity we believe ourselves to be

alabdhūmikatva (Sanskrit): the realization that we are not as far along the spiritual path as we believed ourselves to be, accompanied by disappointment and frustration

ānandamayakosha (Sanskrit): the sheath of bliss, or pure being, that surrounds pure consciousness; causal body

ānanda (Sanskrit): bliss; a powerful state of realization often mistaken for enlightenment

annamayakosha (Sanskrit): the sheath of human experience that includes the physical body, including physiological functions

asamprajñātā sāmadhi (Sanskrit): a state in which consciousness merges into a mindless, beginningless, and endless state of being

āsana (Sanskrit): seat; position assumed in the practice of yoga

asmitā (Sanskrit): a state of realization in which the individual dwells in his or her true Self

atha (Sanskrit): frequently translated into English as "now"; also refers to every moment we begin again

ātmamayakosha (Sanskrit): the sheath of the individuated soul

atman (Sanskrit): individuated pure consciousness

bhoga (Sanskrit): deliberate, full, conscious experience of an aspect of life *brahmacharya* (Sanskrit): someone whose life is devoted to the realization of Brahma or God. In a traditional yogic sense, a brahmacharya practices sexual celibacy for the purpose of redirecting sexual energy to support spiritual realization.

chi (or qi) (Chinese): life-force energy

cittamayakosha (Sanskrit): the sheath of consciousness

dharma (Sanskrit): the "virtuous path" available to everyone who lives life directed toward the highest possibility. To act in accordance with dharma is to take actions resonant with divine order or objective truth (rather than being moved by the unconscious forces of karma).

guru (Sanskrit): a Hindu spiritual teacher or leader; "heavy weight"

Jangalykayamane (Sanskrit): "the jungle physician"; or inner healer, in yogic philosophy

karma (Sanskrit): act, action; that which causes the entire cycle of cause and effect. The soul incarnates again and again to complete various tasks and lessons; also refers to the universal law of cause and effect.

kāyā sadhana (Sanskrit): the practice of ultimate realization in the body in this lifetime

kosha (Sanskrit): a subtle level of our bodies and energy systems

lama (Tibetan): a respectful title for a Tibetan Buddhist spiritual teacher; or an honorific title for an advanced nun, monk, or practitioner

lingam (Sanskrit): a phallic symbol that represents Lord Shiva, the masculine principle of formless truth

madhyamā-pratipa (Sanskrit): the middle way

manomayakosha (Sanskrit): the level, or sheath, of the mind, including the processing of thoughts and emotions

mast (Sanskrit): an individual stuck in a high state of spiritual attainment; someone who is nonfunctional due to spiritual "intoxication"

maya (Sanskrit): illusion; refers to an illusory relationship to nondual reality

neo-Advaita: a contemporary Western spiritual movement loosely based on certain aspects of traditional Indian Advaita-Vedanta.

nirbīja samādhi (Sanskrit): where consciousness merges into a mindless, beginningless, and endless state of being

nirodha (Sanskrit): the fifth stage of emotional progression, characterized by fluid peacefulness in relationship to one's inner and outer life

Om mani padme hum (Sanskrit): six-syllable mantra of compassion chanted by Tibetan Buddhists

prānamāyakosha (Sanskrit): the sheath of prana, the force that vitalizes and holds together the body and the mind

prana (Sanskrit): life-force energy

prasupta (Sanskrit): the first stage in emotional integration in which the emotions are repressed

purusha (Sanskrit): a nondual, formless source at the core of all experience

rinpoche (Tibetan): an honorary title (literally "precious one") used in Tibetan Buddhism to address spiritual masters

roshi (Japanese): a spiritual teacher in the Zen Buddhist tradition

sadhana (Sanskrit): the process of spiritual practice

sadhu (Sanskrit): a holy man or woman in India who takes a vow of renunciation of worldly life in order to pursue mystical understanding

samādhi (Sanskrit): a state of singular concentration in which the consciousness of the experiencing subject becomes one with the experienced object; integration

samskaras (Sanskrit): deep patterns of conditioning; unconscious imprints or impressions

santosha (Sanskrit): contentment

satguru (Sanskrit): a title bestowed on an enlightened guru whose life purpose is guiding others along the spiritual path

satori (Japanese): Zen Buddhist term for a state of sudden enlightenment

satsang (Sanskrit): literally "being together in truth"; usually refers to a gathering of spiritual practitioners for the purpose of studying truth

sesshin (Japanese): a period of especially intensive Zen practice

sheikh (Arabic): a spiritual instructor in the Sufi tradition

shraddā (Sanskrit): faith or love of the unknown

sri (Sanskrit): honorific prefix to the name of a deity or venerated person

sūtra (Sanskrit): "thread"; refers to the 195 aphorisms expounded by Patañjali that characterize classical yoga

swami (Sanskrit): respectful title for a Hindu religious teacher

svādyāya (Sanskrit): self-study; the process of soul-searching needed to understand one's own nature

tantra (Sanskrit): the practice of weaving the totality of experience into one continuous fabric of awakened awareness

tanu (Sanskrit): "thinning"; the fourth stage of emotional progression in which we navigate feelings and learn the potent energies of the external environment and our own unconscious

tapas (Sanskrit): "heat"; the internal fire of transformation, or "essential energy," that burns away all obstacles separating us from who we really are

thangka (Tibetan): a Buddhist painting depicting spiritual deities, gods, or spiritual processes

trimurti (Sanskrit): the Hindu trinity of three principle deities: Brahma, the creator, Vishnu, the sustainer, and Shiva, the destroyer

tulku (Tibetan): Buddhist spiritual teacher

udāra (Sanskrit): second stage of emotional progression—characterized by moodiness—in which repression lifts and unconscious emotions break through, often explosively

vicāra (Sanskrit): a subtle understanding of truth attained through personal investigation, in which the mind becomes still and acuteness of perception is revealed

viccina (Sanskrit): a stage of emotional progression characterized by emotional fluctuation

vijñānamayakosha (Sanskrit): the wisdom body, or sheath, that surpasses the knowledge of mind and is endowed with the function of knowledge

vikalpa (Sanskrit): verbal or intellectual knowledge that's devoid of substance and not integrated or embodied

vitarka (Sanskrit): an intellectual grasp of knowledge or truth derived from thinking and study

viveka khyātir or ***viveka-khyāti*** (Sanskrit): spiritual discernment; "the crowning wisdom" on the spiritual path

Yoga Sūtras of Patañjali (Sanskrit): a text dating at least two thousand years that outlines the path of classical yoga; written by Patañjali, an Indian mystic

yoni (Sanskrit): female symbol shaped like a vagina that represents Shakti, or the feminine principle of manifestation

Bibliography

Aurobindo. *Sri Aurobindo on Himself.* Pondicherry, India: Sri Aurobindo Ashram Trust, 1972.

Aurobindo. *The Life Divine* (vol. 1). Pondicherry, India: Sri Aurobindo Ashram, 1977.

Aurobindo. *The Synthesis of Yoga.* Twin Lakes, WI: Lotus Press, 1996.

Bache, Christopher. *Dark Night, Early Dawn: Steps to a Deep Ecology of Mind.* Albany: State University of New York Press, 2002.

Barks, Coleman, ed. *The Essential Rumi.* San Francisco: HarperSanFrancisco, 1995.

Campbell, Joseph, ed. *The Portable Jung.* New York: Penguin Books, 1972.

Caplan, Mariana. "Adventures of a New Age Traveler." In *Radical Spirit: Spiritual Writings from the Voices of Tomorrow,* edited by Stephen Dinan. Novato, CA: New World Library, 2002.

———. "Death Don't Have No Mercy." In *The Best Buddhist Writing* 2006, (edited by Malvin McLeod. Boston: Shambhala Publications, 2006.

———. *Do You Need a Guru? Understanding the Student-Teacher Relationship in an Era of False Prophets.* London: 2002.

———. *Halfway Up the Mountain: The Error of Premature Claims to Enlightenment.* Prescott, AZ: Hohm Press, 1999.

———. *To Touch Is to Live.* Prescott, AZ: Hohm Press, 2002.

———. *The Way of Failure: Winning through Losing.* Prescott, AZ: Hohm Press, 2001.

————. *When Sons and Daughters Choose Alternative Lifestyles.* Prescott, AZ: Hohm Press, 1996.

Chilton Pearce, Joseph. *The Biology of Transcendence: A Blueprint of the Human Spirit.* Rochester, VT: Inner Traditions, 2004.

————. *The Death of Religion and the Rebirth of Spirit: A Return to the Intelligence of the Heart.* Rochester, VT: Inner Traditions, 2007.

Chödrön, Pema. *When Things Fall Apart: Heartfelt Advice for Difficult Times.* Boston: Shambhala, 2000.

Chögyam, Ngakpa. *Wearing the Body of Visions.* Ramsey, NJ: Aro Books, 1995.

Cohen, Leonard. *Book of Mercy.* Toronto, ON: McClelland & Stewart, 1984.

Deida, David. *The Way of the Superior Man.* Boulder, CO: Sounds True, 2004.

Desjardins, Arnaud. *The Jump into Life: Moving Beyond Fear.* Prescott, AZ: Hohm Press, 1994.

Desikachar, T. K. V. *The Heart of Yoga: Developing a Personal Practice.* Rochester, VT: Inner Traditions International, 1995.

Diener, Michael S., Erhard Franz-Karl, and Ingrid Fischer-Schreiber. *The Shambhala Dictionary of Buddhism and Zen.* Boston: Shambhala, 1991.

Eliade, Mircea. *Yoga: Immortality and Freedom.* Princeton, NJ: Princeton University Press, 1970.

Farcet, Gilles. *The Anti-Wisdom Manual: A Practical Guide for Spiritual Bankruptcy.* Prescott, AZ: Hohm Press, 2005.

Ferrer, Jorge. *Revisioning Transpersonal Theory.* Albany: State University of New York Press, 2002.

Feuerstein, Georg. *Tantra: The Path of Ecstasy*. Boston: Shambhala, 1998.

———. *The Philosophy of Classical Yoga*. Rochester, VT: Inner Traditions International, 1996.

———. *The Yoga Tradition*. Prescott, AZ: Hohm Press, 1998.

Fields, Rick. *How the Swans Came to the Lake: A Narrative History of Buddhism in America*. Boston: Shambhala, 1981.

Forsthoefel, Thomas, and Cynthia Ann Humes. *Gurus in America*. Albany: State University of New York Press, 2005.

Frager, Robert. *Heart, Self, and Soul: The Sufi Psychology of Growth, Balance, and Harmony*. Wheaton, IL: The Theosophical Publishing House, 1999.

Grof, Christina, and Stanislav Grof. *Spiritual Emergency: When Personal Transformation Becomes a Crisis*. Los Angeles: Jeremy Tarcher, 1989.

Grof, Stanislav. *Beyond the Brain: Birth, Death, and Transcendence in Psychotherapy*. Albany: State University of New York Press, 1985.

Grof, Stanislav, and Christina Grof. *The Stormy Search for the Self*. New York: Tarcher/Putnam, 1990.

Iyengar, B. K. S., *Light on the Yoga Sūtras of Patañjali*. New Delhi, India: HarperCollins Publishers India, 2005 (first edition, 1993).

Jacobi, Jolande, and Ralph Manheim. *The Psychology of C. G. Jung*. New Haven, CT: Yale University Press, 1973.

Jodorowsky, Alejandro. *The Spiritual Journey of Alejandro Jodorowsky*. Rochester, VT: Park Street Press, 2008.

Jung, Carl Gustav. *Collected Works of C. G. Jung, Volume 8: The Structure and Dynamics of the Psyche*. Princeton, NJ: Princeton University Press, 1976.

————. *Collected Works of C. G. Jung, Volume 11: Psychology and Religion: West and East.* Princeton, NJ: Princeton University Press, 1975.

Khytense, Dzongsar Jamyang. *What Makes You Not a Buddhist?* Boston: Shambhala, 2007.

Ladinsky, Daniel. *The Gift: Poems by Hafiz the Great Sufi Master.* New York: Penguin Arkana, 1999.

————. *I Heard God Laughing.* Oakland, CA: Mobius Press, 1996.

————. *The Subject Tonight Is Love: 60 Wild and Sweet Poems of Hafiz.* Myrtle Beach, SC: 1996. Berkeley, CA: North Atlantic Books. 1997.

Levine, Peter. *Waking the Tiger: Healing Trauma.* Berkeley, CA: North Atlantic Books, 1997.

Lozowick, Lee. *The Alchemy of Transformation.* Prescott, AZ: Hohm Press, 1996.

————. *Feast or Famine: Teachings on Mind and Emotions.* Prescott, AZ: Hohm Press, 2008.

Martin, Sita. *The Hunger of Love: Versions of the Ramayana.* Prescott, AZ: Hohm Press, 1995.

Matt, Daniel. *The Essential Kabbalah: The Heart of Jewish Mysticism.* Edison, NJ: Castle Books, 1997.

Merton, Thomas. *Entering the Silence.* San Francisco: HarperSanFrancisco, 1997.

Mitchell, Stephen. *The Enlightened Mind.* New York: HarperCollins, 1993.

Mother Teresa. *Mother Teresa: Come Be My Light: The Private Writings of the Saint of Calcutta.* New York: Doubleday, 2007.

Osho. *The Book of Secrets.* New York: St. Martin's Griffin, 1974.

Prendergast, John, and Kenneth Bradford, eds. *Listening from the Heart of Silence*. St. Paul, MN: Paragon House, 2007.

Prendergast, John, Peter Fenner and Sheila Krystal, eds. *The Sacred Mirror*. New York: Omega Book, 2003.

Rawlinson, Andrew. *The Book of Enlightened Masters*. Chicago: La Salle, 1997.

Ray, Reginald. *Indestructible Truth: The Living Spirituality of Tibetan Buddhism*. Boston: Shambhala, 2000.

———. *Touching Enlightenment*. Boulder, CO: Sounds True, 2008.

Rilke, Rainer Maria. *Letters to a Young Poet*. Revised paperback. New York: W. W. Norton & Company, 1993.

———. *Uncollected Poems*. New York: North Point Press, 1996.

Ryan, Regina Sara. *Only God: A Biography of Yogi Ramsuratkumar*. Prescott, AZ: Hohm Press, 2004.

———. *Praying Dangerously*. Prescott, AZ: Hohm Press, 2001.

Saint John of the Cross. *Dark Night of the Soul*. 3rd ed. Edited by E. Allison Peers. New York: Image Books, 1959.

Saint John of the Cross. *Dark Night of the Soul*. Edited by Mirabai Starr. New York: Riverhead Books, 2002.

Saint Teresa of Ávila. *The Interior Castle*. New York: Riverhead Books, 2003.

Seager, Richard Hughs. *Buddhism in America*. New York: Columbia University Press, 1999.

Shaw, Miranda. *Passionate Enlightenment: Women in Tantric Buddhism*. Princeton, NJ: Princeton University Press, 1994.

Simmer-Brown, Judith. *Dakini's Warm Breath: The Feminine Principle in Tibetan Buddhism*. Boston: Shambhala Publications, 2002.

Smith, Huston. *Why Religion Matters: The Fate of Human Spirit in an Age of Disbelief.* San Francisco: HarperSanFrancisco, 2001.

———. *The World's Religions: Our Great Wisdom Traditions.* San Francisco: HarperSanFrancisco, 1991.

Svoboda, Robert. *Aghora.* Albuquerque, NM: Brotherhood of Life Inc., 1986.

———. *Aghora II: Kundalini.* Albuquerque, NM: Brotherhood of Life Inc., 1993.

———. *Aghora III: The Law of Karma.* Albuquerque, NM: Brotherhood of Life, 1997.

———. *The Greatness of Saturn.* Twin Lakes, WI: Lotus Press, 1997.

Trungpa, Chögyam. *Cutting Through Spiritual Materialism.* Boston: Shambhala, 1973.

———. *The Lion's Roar: An Introduction to Tantra.* Boston: Shambhala, 2001.

Tweedie, Irina. *The Chasm of Fire.* Rockport, MD: Element Classics, 1993.

———. *Daughter of Fire.* Nevada City, CA: Blue Dolphin Publishing, 1986.

Vaughan-Lee, Llewellyn. *Before I Was Born: A Spiritual Autobiography.* Inverness, CA: Golden Sufi Center, 1997.

———. *Circle of Love.* Inverness, CA: Golden Sufi Center, 1999.

Waite, Dennis. *Enlightenment: The Path through the Jungle.* Winchester, UK: O Books, 2008.

Walsh, Roger. *Essential Spirituality: The Seven Central Practices to Awaken the Heart and Mind.* New York: John Wiley & Sons, 2002.

————. *The World of Shamanism: New Views on an Ancient Tradition*. Woodbury, MN: Llewellyn Publications, 2007.

Washburn, Michael. *The Ego and the Dynamic Ground*. New York: State University of New York Press (SUNY), 1995.

Welwood, John. *Perfect Love, Imperfect Relationships: Healing the Wound of the Heart*. Boston: Shambhala Publications, 2006.

————. *Toward a Psychology of Awakening*. Boston: Shambhala Publications, 2000.

Wilber, Ken. *The Collected Works of Ken Wilber*, volumes 1–8. Boston: Shambhala, 1999.

————. *Integral Psychology*. Boston: Shambhala, 2001.

Wilson, Colin. *Rogue Messiahs: Tales of Self-Proclaimed Messiahs*. Charlottesville, VA: Hampton Roads Publishing Co., 2000.

Young, M. *As It Is: A Year on the Road with a Tantric Teacher*. Prescott, AZ: Hohm Press, 2000.

About the Author

Mariana Caplan, PhD, received degrees in cultural anthropology, counseling psychology, and contemporary spirituality. She attributes the majority of her education and inspiration to years of research and practice in the world's great mystical traditions and to living in villages in India, Central America, and Europe. She is a professor of yogic and transpersonal psychologies, and the author of seven books in the fields of psychology and spirituality, including *Halfway Up the Mountain: The Error of Premature Claims to Enlightenment* and *Do You Need a Guru? Understanding the Student-Teacher Relationship in an Era of False Prophets*. Mariana resides in the San Francisco Bay area where she has a private practice in counseling and teaches at the California Institute of Integral Studies. Her web address is realspirituality.com.